Essays on American Atheism

Jon Garth Murray

Jon G. Murray

Essays on American Atheism

Volume I

American Atheist Press
Austin, Texas
1986

A reference is made to the above picture on page 58 of this volume. The picture is a line-drawn reproduction of the cover photo for the March 1979 issue of *American Atheist* magazine.

American Atheist Press, P.O. Box 2117, Austin, TX 78768-2117

Published September 1986.
Printed in the United States of America

ISBN 0-910309-28-0

Contents

Introduction

When Jon Murray was sucked fully into the vortex of the American Atheist cause following his graduation from university, he had little or no time for contemplation of Atheist theoretics. Prior to that he had worked part-time at both The American Atheist Center and the American Atheist Library and Archives, Inc., while he was still enrolled at the university, where his interest had been in both writing and American literature. And, both prior to and coextensive with his formal education effort he had been a full-time participant in the melange of the Murray-O'Hair family.

The literary skills which his professors had enthusiastically encouraged were of no benefit to him as he plunged into the logistics of the battle for state/church separation and civil libertarian rights for Atheists. He was almost a year into the fray before his first article, "Take A Stand!" appearing in the March 1976, issue of the *American Atheist*, was directed to the thin ranks he tried to muster to battle. The following month, in April, he presented the historical reason for that stand, in "200 Hundred Years of American Atheism." Then, overwhelmed again with keeping The Center afloat in the Christian sea of hostility which from time to time threatened to swamp the small boat, he did not write again until July. One can see his thoughts developing as he presented then the case "On Confrontation."

In January of the next year, 1977, he was obviously angry as he replied to the question, "What's Wrong with A Little Prayer?" But once again time and work constraints denied him the luxury of putting his thoughts in writing. For the rest of the year Chapter Directors presented "Guest Editorials" in the organization's voice. And then, as it always does at the end of each year, "Christmas" rolled around with its saturation of the American culture — and his protest was in the December issue, "Seize The Symbols!" as he demanded of the Atheists to set themselves free.

In February, 1978, momentarily he posed his challenge, "Do We Dare Question The System?" In April a featured column was begun under the byline of "All Things Considered." He was, apparently, squeezing some time out now to begin his writing, for the column continued for a four-month period, April through July. It was a record of continuity. But, then, once again his organizational activities took him too often from The Center, and the column was not continued. In October, however, he was back, this time in full command of the editorial offering, demanding that Atheists get to the task of "Recognizing Reality." From that time forward, each month his editorials appeared as he got his sealegs and, rolling and pitching in that hostile sea, he took and stood his ground at the helm. First, he fought back, and then he took to the attack, explicating his and American Atheists' contemporary positions as he analyzed current theopolitical events, refuted theistic contentions, chastized political opportunists, and fumed at the general entrenched stupidities in the cultural milieu of the nation.

Jon Murray reveals in his writings what it is to be thoroughly, completely, acculturated to Atheist reasoning, life-style, and battle. He demonstrates continually the phenomenon of a life totally free from theism. There is not a tittle or a jot of it in him. Born free, reared free, maturing free, living free, his intellect knows neither bounds nor bondage. He can explore every avenue of thought. He can challenge every predisposed idea. He can analyze every precedent. So, he does just that, going to the job with a certain intellectual iconoclastic zest that is refreshing.

His enthusiastic university mentors were correct: he can write — because he can think — not the short stories to the production of which they had encouraged him, but intellectual probing and questioning research into our value systems, weighing of the fundamental premises upon which the culture rests, developing new criteria against which accepted basic premises must be tested.

As one sees the expanding range of his interest, follows the developmental path he has pursued during this ten years of writing, it is apparent that he will become, in our nation, one of the leaders that it needs.

September 1986
MEMO'H

About The Author

Born in 1954, Jon Garth Murray represents the new generation of Atheist intellectuals who are dedicated to activism much more than they are dedicated to debating. Being the son of Madalyn O'Hair, he was reared in an environment of Atheist activism. It is quite natural that when he completed his studies and undergraduate degree (B.A.) at the University of Texas in 1975, he took on the demanding position of Director of The American Atheist Center in Austin, Texas.

His creative writing abilities quickly established him as one of the most popular regularly featured columnists in the *American Atheist* magazine. His administrative ability and editorial skill soon singled him as managing editor of the magazine. As a coauthor and rewrite editor, he has collaborated on several of the books issued in the name of Madalyn O'Hair.

As co-sponsor of World Atheist Meets in collaboration with Lavanam, Director of the Indian Atheist Centre of Vijayawada, India, Mr. Murray acted as co-chairman of that event in December 1980 when it was held in Vijayawada, Andhra Pradesh, India and as chairman in June 1983 when it was held in Helsinki, Finland. Beginning in 1976, he had been called upon to make appearances on behalf of American Atheists throughout Europe, Canada, Scandinavia, Japan, and India.

A recognized television personality, veteran of hundreds of radio talk shows, he has appeared as an Atheist spokesperson in the United States on every major program of importance. His forte is lecturing at universities and colleges, where young Americans can identify with this youthful Atheist activist. Dignified but determined, humorous but caustic, prepared on his own position, he routs his religious protagonists with well-placed and well-researched barbs.

Mr. Murray has, with his famous mother, been a co-litigant in lawsuits to remove the phrase "In God We Trust" from the nation's currency and coins; to stop prayers in governmental institutions; to prohibit the display of religious artifacts in government buildings (particularly the créche or nativity scene during the Christmas season); to force the governments of five Southern states to accept Atheists and agnostics for jury service, government offices, or positions of public trust; and to stop the pope from holding a Roman Catholic mass, at taxpayer expense, on the citizen-owned Washington, D. C. mall.

He also was the coordinator for the first picketing of a pope in world history. He was himself at the head of the picket line in Chicago's Loop during the pope's 1979 visit to that city.

Most recently, Mr. Murray has acted as co-host with Dr. O'Hair on the "American Atheist Forum," a television series which analyzes state/church separation news. As of the time of the release of this book, the "Forum" is on ninety cable systems.

On April 19, 1986, Mr. Murray was unanimously elected by the Board of Directors of American Atheists to the position of President of the parent corporation.

Essays on American Atheism is a two volume collection of his 100 "Editorials" which appeared in the *American Atheist* magazine from March 1976 to May 1986. A smaller booklet, *Essays of an Atheist Activist*, issued in 1980, consisted of those editorials which had appeared intermittently from March 1976 to November 1979. The original essays are included in this larger volume. In addition to including a decade of Jon Murray's eidtorials, *Essays on American Atheistsm* contains his three lengthy articles, "WAM III," "Religion Regulates Ratings," and "Why Is An Atheist Organization Needed in the U.S. Today?"

Take A Stand

March 1976

Historically, the Atheist community has had a less-than-sterling representation of itself circulating among the rest of the population here in the United States; most often we have appeared before the unenlightened majority as communists, heathens, or just the guy on the block who is downright unsanitary.

Over the past year, however, this unsolicited black eye given to Atheists everywhere has lessened in its intensity. For the first time in American history, Atheism is being viewed as at least acceptable if not yet thoroughly American. This dramatic reversal is due primarily to the efforts of a few dedicated Atheist spokespersons who have braved the onslaught of words that did hurt as well as did the occasional stick or stone. Their bravery has been in the form of merely speaking up on behalf of Atheists as upstanding members of the human community. "Not hard!" says the armchair agnostic or Atheist from the comfort of his closet. But hard indeed it was for those who were willing to stand alone.

As a result of the efforts of a few, others now casually drop the appellation of "Atheist" at a business meeting here or a cocktail party there, forgetting for a moment the times gone by when such disclosures brought social and economic reprisals by the score. Now, however, Atheists are getting away with identifying themselves and going somewhat farther besides. Once identified as an "unbeliever," the Atheist finds himself somewhat of a celebrity in the community, as never before.

Taking an outstanding example, Dr. Madalyn O'Hair of our staff has been the recipient recently of many heretofore strange requests. Mayors, governors, senators, and even recently the White House, have issued Dr. O'Hair invitations — both social and professional. People of prominence are actually vying for the opportunity to be seen with the village Atheist as somewhat the social event of the year.

Why the sudden acceptance in the face of previous spurning? The answer lies in the nature of Atheism itself. Atheism comprises much more than the disassociation of one from the "god idea." Atheism is a way of life, an entire standard of living centered around trust in oneself and one's own abilities to cope with the pressures of a modern existence. We are inner-directed rather than outer-directed, unlike those of theistic persuasion. This iron-willed ability to grapple with life unassisted by outside sources places the Atheist head-and-shoulders above the rest of the human community. The root of the original hatred of the Atheist stemmed from this ability to face life head-on. The theist has never been able to muster such a healthy attitude towards life, and has therefore reacted with envious hostility toward the Atheist. We have done what others could not find the inner strength to do and have been hated for it for centuries. Now it seems that the theist has turned from envy to appreciation. It is beginning to become evident, in the light of such debacles as Watergate, that the Atheist was right all along. Reason should be one's guide to better living, along with a straightforward approach to the problems that face us all.

Atheism is the life-style of the future. It is now only in the primary stage of recognition, the stage in which Atheists are accepted as those of esteem in the community. It will soon progress to the stage of dominance, as the idea of "representation by the people" did in our nation's early history.

We urge you to join the crowd now while positions of command are still available, for soon being an Atheist will make you just one of the boys. Those of you who are in the closet have waited too long; now is the time to move. We stand for the concerns of health, conservation of resources both material and human, peace, and above all the preservation of human dignity worldwide. Such forgotten concerns can no longer be delegated to minority student groups or those limited few of insight; they must be upheld by all of us, together, as cohabitants of a planet in trouble.

The Atheist *can* be counted upon for the solutions that have eluded mankind for so many years. This fact is only now being recognized, and we deserve every bit of the praise such a recognition brings along.

Those of you who have been fighting, take a bow; you've earned it. If not, take a stand today.

200 Years of American Atheism

April 1976

(Speech delivered at the Sixth Annual National American Atheist Convention at the Sheraton Hotel in New York City on April 10, 1976.)

Our nation is currently involved in the celebration of its bicentennial, and surely, as you have seen the array of its heroes paraded before us in a veritable orgy of national pride, you must have wondered if there was not at least one Atheist among them.

We are reminded almost daily that this is a Christian nation and that it was founded as such. That neither statement is true does not deter the religious community from asserting them.

President Ford has designated a national day of prayer and the Bicentennial Committee a week to observe religion's contribution to our nation. I do not feel it inappropriate, therefore, that we take a quarter hour here today to honor our heroes.

The American Atheists in our history have never been identified as such because these great materialists have been involved with the most intangible of all things — ideas.

Indeed, as we talk of freedoms today, and identify Gay Lib, or Black Lib, or Women's Lib, or even Kids' Lib, we do not hear of the ultimate liberation — "Freedom of the Mind." And it was under the euphemism of "free thinking" — of "free thought" — that these people often tried to make their contributions.

It began early as our founding fathers themselves repudiated Christianity and opted for deism — nature and nature's god — a precursor to the full-blown Atheism of our day.

And the American Atheist has never been a rationalizer — despising philosophy, disdaining it as an "apology for religion"; he has not steeped himself in nor followed Nietzsche or Hobbs, Hegel or Feuerbach. Instead, he has stood where the action was.

What was freedom of speech if not the freedom to say something: and the American Atheist took to his soapbox, or to his pen, or to the speaking podium, to right the wrongs he saw in our culture.

There were no secular schools in the beginning colonies — so Girard financed and founded one, stipulating in his will that no clergyman should ever be permitted to set foot on the grounds of Girard College, in Philadelphia, Pennsylvania.

There was no place to collect and display for study the spectrum of nature, and so Smithson financed and founded the Smithsonian Institution.

There was no way to study the vault of the universe, and so Lick financed and founded the Lick Observatory.

And William Haywood, Joe Hill, and Ralph Chaplin fought for and won in Spokane, Washington, in Fresno and San Diego, California, the right to demand improved working conditions, reduced hours, and better wages.

Eugene V. Debs determined to make insurance available to an average man.

And Clarence Darrow brought us workmen's compensation and unemployment benefits.

Emmanuel Haldeman-Julius decided that any book should be available to anyone cheaply, and he founded the paperback book industry.

And Ernst Haeckel coined the word "ecology" and began the movement for conservation of the world's natural resources.

Florence Nightingale taught us the compassion of nursing care.

And Charles Dunant built up the concept of the Red Cross as a relief agency for people caught in the catastrophe of wars and natural upheavals.

They were Atheists all:

Mark Twain, who introduced laughter into literature;

Thomas Alva Edison, who founded the base of our American technology in his harnessing of electricity in the common light bulb — in his development of recording sound — in the beginning of cinematography;

Henry Ford, who conceived of the production line;

Luther Burbank, America's greatest horticulturist;

And even Honest Abe Lincoln, our most beloved president.

An entire army of American Atheists gave us what freedom from censorship we have — they went to jail in numbers for our right to freedom of speech. Beginning with D. G. M. Bennett, they fought through imprisonments and legal harassments against the notorious Comstock laws, still imposed against us today.

There were no schools to commingle blacks and whites, so Frances Wright founded and financed the first of them, and she hit the lecture circuits over a hundred and fifty years ago to fight for the rights of women to air their views.

We have a proud heritage, for without Moses Harmon there could be no recognition of common law marriages;

Without Margaret Sanger there would have been no birth control clinics;

Without Jane Addams and "Hull House" there would have been no settlement houses, no in-ghetto servicing of the poor — perhaps no social work concepts.

They were Atheists all.

The abolitionists, almost to a man, were American Atheists.

And every first woman involved in the struggle for suffrage (we now call this Women's Lib) was an Atheist. No one today stands as tall as Elizabeth Cady Stanton, foremost in this fight. The movement was set back 100 years when Christian women gained control of it — and even today ERA, the Equal Rights Amendment, is not a reality.

Who can forget our very own Colonel Robert Ingersoll?

Individual Freedom
Individual Rights
Freedom of Speech
Freedom of Conscience

These have been our battlegrounds. This is where we have shown just how much we have cared.

The rights of human sexuality — the right, even now, of the use and control of our own bodies, lately being approached, comes from the basis of the earlier rights won by our own.

They all contributed as individuals — freewheeling, unattached. And we have all of American history upon which to draw, with their places in that panorama.

Now, we need to reach out and grow. We have something new — a good, stable, viable organization with educated and dedicated leadership. We have the examples of prior Atheists and their contributions to all humankind.

We have a place to put our feet, and like Archimedes, now there is no reason we cannot lift the world.

On Confrontation

July 1976

"If you are mean, greedy, selfish, hypocritical, and untrustworthy, go to church next Sunday; birds of a feather flock together."

That's the way it read, in black and white, with lettering you could read across the room. Most of the people who saw our reproduction of it were shocked. How can any Atheist, a person of reason, be so insulting and direct. We must, after all, be tolerant of our fellow men, leaving each man to express his own thoughts. How terrible!

Weeks passed and still the letters of protest came in. All over a reproduction of one small sticker in a past issue of the *American Atheist*. Was the sticker to blame, or is the force of its comment so distasteful? I don't think so. The reaction to these few words of scorn against our Christian cohabitants of this planet is only the beginning of a trend that should have been started long ago by the intellectual community. They, however, preferred to sit about in parlors and rap about this injustice and that injustice in terms often befuddling to those suffering under the oppressions they described. Those nebulous men and women whose thoughts were in the right place restrained their actions on a principle of action long thought to be valid. That is: in any confrontation on any issue, the rational party must give way to the irrational party in order not to demean himself by falling to the level of his opponent.

The only thing that such a position accomplishes is that the irrational position always wins. Such has been the case with organized religion. The intellectual communities of every nation have allowed themselves to be spat upon in the name of "turn the other cheek" dignity. Dignity is one thing, but standing up for a principle regardless of the opposition is quite another.

We have come to the point in the history of the struggle for freedom of the mind that we must stop kidding ourselves that parlor conferences can solve human problems any more than the Bible can. A direct approach is the *only* solution. Atheists must begin to directly inform their fellow humans who are still hooked on the opiate of religion that the latter are sick, mean, greedy, hypocritical, and a score of other adjectives. If someone has cancer, would one expect a physician to look him in the eye and say, "Well now, son, I think you're quite healthy. You just keep right on smoking three packs a day and everything is going to be fine"? Of course not. By bowing to the irrational person, you, as an Atheist, are doing the very same thing that sounds so absurd in a medical setting.

Find a Christian today and tell him he is sick. Convert him, if that term means anything, to a healthy life-style. Christians don't have a monopoly on morality. We too can do "the good work." Ask a Christian today, "Do you really believe that your god talks to you? What does he sound like? Is it a male or female voice? Does he speak in your language or some other?" Make him answer with a rational explanation for his insanity. You will find out quickly that they cannot. What you are doing is evidencing to them that they are quite mad. As soon as they come to a realization that this is the case, they *will* drop their faith like the proverbial hot potato.

Does such an approach sound familiar? It has been used by every religious sect down through the ages to gain converts by the millions. All you need to do is convince some that they are mad and that their only *redemption* lies in following the true words of wisdom, words which you are then free to define.

Sneaky, you say? Of course it is. But does it work? Yes! That is the point — affirmative action rather than parlor semantics. As Gerald Ford would say, "Let's WIN."

Dr. O'Hair of our staff recently appeared on the "Phil Donahue Show." She was attacked verbally, on the air, by a group of Roman Catholic "Stepford wives." So she attacked them back. There was more thought given to the rationality of the beliefs held by those women than ever before. True, they were defensive on the surface. But inside, where it counts, many questions would stir over a period of many weeks to come.

A subscriber on the East Coast felt that he would be crucified if he publicly spoke out for his position as an American Atheist. He did so at a city council meeting, substantively telling them all that they were sick in opening every meeting with a prayer. He still has not been crucified. And the entire city council has a greater respect for him; he has a greater respect for himself, and the community is on its way to a better way of life.

I was invited to a convention of evangelicals who delighted in spreading their emotional disease worldwide. I walked right in among them and told each and every one who confronted me that they were sick and that we would wipe their philosophy out if at all possible in the near future. I am here today to tell about it, and many of them are perhaps a little better off.

To get scientific for a moment, the entire approach I have been using is often termed "rational-emotive psychotherapy." In short, confront the subject with his or her mental problem head-on. Show him that he is wrong and in what ways. In the face of absolute reality, reality will overcome and replace the insanity.

This means must be employed now. This Atheist, and many others, cannot and will not bow to the overwhelming insanity of organized religion any longer. It is time that we press our point and press it hard. For some 2000-odd years we have been punished for having clear heads on our shoulders, for advocating those things that everyone else has been against: like peace and justice, freedom and equality, and liberty. Are these concepts so terrible that we dare not seek to implant them in the minds of men at any cost? No! These are the things that are dear to us and our civilization. Indeed, such values as honesty, integrity, and equality must be reinstated in the minds of all who have forgotten them for our very existence to continue. Next time the bank rips you off on a loan, or your new car falls apart, or a Christian knocks on your door for a contribution, ask yourself if letting the situation ride or the rip-off pass so that you may "let the other man live" is really what you should be doing for yourself and all mankind.

I hope that the answer will be to join with those who are determined to work for a better future, instead of allowing the present to pass by peacefully ("Don't rock the boat!" or "Don't stir things up now!"), and become that horrible future of which poets warn where freedom is a dream and reality is twice as heavy on all as it was before.

What's Wrong with A Little Prayer?

January 1977

Devoting an entire issue of the *American Atheist* to the subject of prayer is not a small accomplishment. I say this because prayer is the most useless ritual that man has ever devised. It accomplishes absolutely nothing and promotes even less.

In order to understand this particular form of insanity, let us first see what prayer is. Prayer is the communication of a supplicant's desires to some form of authority that he *believes* to be greater than his own. Thus, the person asks to have this greater authority do that which he feels he cannot do himself. This may be as simple as a request for keeping his mother-in-law quiet for half an hour or as complicated as the establishment of world peace. Whatever the request, the point remains that the supplicant does not think that he can accomplish it himself, which may or may not be the case in actuality. In most cases the supplicant has many adequate means of arriving at a solution to a particular situation without any help whatsoever. But, *he believes* that he cannot handle things himself. It is this belief that leads him to be seeking help anywhere he thinks he can find it, except within himself.

There are times when all of us have problems that we find, for the moment, insoluble. Our first tendency is to seek the easiest solution possible. The easiest solution usually means finding someone (or something) else onto whom one can pass the proverbial hot potato. The problem usually doesn't end up getting solved very rapidly at all. My inclination is to pass a seemingly insoluble problem off on a friend or associate or at least to obtain his advice. But others find that a lot of situations seem to be common to almost everyone they turn to for assistance. When no one else is left, who is always around to ask or blame, as the case may be, to whom can one turn? Why, god, of course!

With attributes like omnipotence and omnipresence, who else would be privy to every problem one could conjure? The answer again is god. What a perfect *creation* on which the human mind may fall back! He is always there, always listening, and doesn't even charge. For what more could anyone ask? He is a private analyst right between one's own eyes. How convenient. Why drive out in the snow to spend $50 an hour for someone to tell you that you need to face up to your problems yourself, when you can escape them right in your own living room with someone who always tells you what you want to hear?

The one amazing point is that all of those wonderful answers that so magically come from this wonderful being all come from the same place as he did — one's brain. If a worshiper can think up someone on whom to cast his problems, he can just as easily solve his problems himself.

Also, all of the action required to solve a problem must be supplied by the supplicant. If he doesn't do it himself, it will not get done. Why then should he sit around and wait for some omnipotence to step in when time is often of the essence in any problem-solving method? The obvious answer is that he should get on with the solution process.

Turning to that process itself, what must one do in order to begin to solve a problem? One must first define and delimit the problem. In order to explain a problem or situation to another, one must be able to define exactly what the problem is and delimit it. Thus, a prayer said is the first step in the problem-solution process. When a supplicant defines his problem to his god, he invariably finds a solution right in the definition itself. Of course, now I may be asked, "What is wrong with a little prayer, if it helps one solve one's problems by inspecting them more closely in the prayer process?"

My answer is that the human mind needs no such *motivation* to begin running a complete true problem-solving process. Man is capable of initiating that action on his own in response to a problem situation. In fact, the human brain does just that in an automatic fashion with thousands of small problems concerning the maintenance of the body on a daily basis. Concerning the point that prayer adds a bit of comfort to the process, I politely say, "Bunk!" Prayer only delays the inevitable. The problem is still there when the supplicant gets up off his knees.

In view of all of this, millions of people still persist in this useless activity. Government officials are falling in line for prayer meetings and breakfasts in large numbers. While they pray, the nation's problems are still there and growing in intensity.

Prayer is the root of much greater insanity as well. It is the entire basis of *any* religious system. In any such system, its adherents must communicate with their deity or must involve some intermediary. The fact remains, however, that it is a form of communication and a very special kind at that. It is communication between one real party and one un-real party. Communicating with a nonentity is the same as communicating with oneself. One who talks to a bush must answer himself in order to receive a reply. The same applies to communication with a deity. The supplicant speaks and he receives an answer — from himself.

We here at the Atheist Center are embarking on a campaign against prayer's intrusion into public policies as a solution method. The human community has a multiplicity of problems with which it must cope. All of them are soluble by the very people who create them. No power of any kind can replace the most wonderful problem-solving tool around — the human mind.

Our fight is for *Freedom of the Mind* so that our minds may be unencumbered in their struggle to solve the concerns of today and tomorrow.

As the pope would say to an anti-abortion crowd, "Let's show them where we stand; get out there and breed!" We, as American Atheists, say to you, "Get out there and think!"

An elderly gentleman once remarked to me, concerning my wish for the outcome of a certain event the following unforgettable line: "Wish (i.e., pray) in one hand and shit in the other, and see which one fills up first!"

I in turn say to you: "Think and let the others pray, and see who goes further in solving the problems of the day."

Seize The Symbols

December 1977

Witch doctors would agree that a lock of your grandmother's hair or the little finger of a departed uncle would be strong medicine to get you out of the hut and back into the war party. Even primitive cultures knew that attachments to certain objects or words could be a powerful motivational tool to evoke a positive attitude towards recovery or social action.

Our culture has taught us to ignore these superstitions, but we have not yet grown out of the deeply ingrained respect we have for the symbols associated with them. The title "doctor," for instance, is still respected in every human community. Coats of arms are still collected and treasured. Millions follow the daily horoscope related to their birth dates. All "powerful medicine," as the witch doctor would say, but nonetheless surviving in a twentieth-century costume.

Organized religion, too, has found the continuation of symbolism useful. Witness the wine and the wafer, the cross, the prayer cloth. All useless in terms of twentieth-century technology, but highly impressive in the world of the mind and the emotions. The one great force of the human personality that must always be dealt with, stepping in to cloud even the most thinking man's view. Nothing impresses a man so well as that which hits his heart at the same time as it hits his head.

The symbol-emotion link is an immovable opponent to the warrior armed with the sword of reason. A shield of paper plus one's faith can often be more valuable than one of iron. With faith removed, iron stands better in the fray.

Our struggle — that of reason's army — is to remove the faith, that the shield may reveal its true weight to our opponent. Seize the symbol and the battle is almost won.

During this holiday season the battle for control of the symbols of our culture comes to the limelight. The Christian community delights in flaunting the birth of its mythological Jesus. Their greatest ally in this thrust is the symbol — the Christmas tree, for example. The great conifer, symbol of nature's rejuvenation, was long revered and used as strong medicine for evidence that spring will return to relieve the hardships of winter. The wonder of primitive minds at the only tree in the forest that defied winter with its display of green, nature's own symbol of its cycles, is now being used as a symbol of a mythological birth. What better way to enlist the pagan minds than the use of their own symbol to be applied to a new director, god, in place of natural law.

The star, a thing of wonder, conjuring up notions of infinity, life on Mars, games of gods, astrology, is perverted as is the majestic conifer to the symbol of another power. Once the evidence of energy bursting light-years away and now the light leading nomads to the birthplace of a myth. How clever are the clergy to usurp nature's power for their own. Mere light, perhaps a remnant of a now dead source, the everlasting symbol of a fraud.

Earth, all that we know, orbits on its relentless circular journey, a journey that dictates to all, without thought; winter, spring, summer, fall replayed over and over again. We struggle to adjust to its forces that display breathtaking beauty and destructive force. Winter, the hardest of these, majestic yet respected for its might, seems longer than the rest. Men yearn for its close and the buds of spring to appear. The uncomfortable aspects of the season, the expectation of relief, especially in primitive times, often bordered on dismay. The days grew short and the weather progressively worse, but would the sun come back again? Gone for longer and longer periods of time, would it return? Could it be trusted? To the modern mind, a child would not waste his time with so foolish a notion. But to those of little means to protect themselves from winter's bite and those who must rely on the grain for bread, the threat was real. In such a way evolved a great abiding respect for the power of that "great lamp in the sky." The return of the sun king became an event of great joy. Game returned to the hunter, crops to the fields, heat to care for the sickness of body, color and light for the sickness of the spirit.

The sun was symbol of life itself, the great symbol of all. The sun, motionless, waiting for the earth to move closer to its energy, was not the bringer of spring. But to those of little science who knew nothing of the earth's movement, the sun moved for them. It moved their lives, and its return was the subject of much concern.

But it soon became the symbol of another sun, of a different spelling, to whom was also attributed the giving of life. Energy from a man to rival that of our star? How clever of the clergy. The symbol — indeed the source — of all energy, now emanating from their mythological savior, come to redeem the earth as the increased energy of proximity to the star had done year after year. A birth date for this chosen one set on the same day as the earth rounds the bend heading for a closer part of the ellipse it treads around its star. The ultimate deceit. The seizure of a reality as great as life itself to back up the greatest lie in the annals of human history.

How could anyone object? How could they doubt? "He" is born and the sun returns — an association so staggering to modern intelligence that it would be adequate grounds for commitment. Like walking under a ladder or breaking a mirror or the whole concept of luck itself, yet swallowed hook, line, and sinker by the gullible *en masse*. The symbol of it here, in the twentieth century, in church after church after church, still the evidence of the greatest lie. Enhanced by the commercial spirit — Give Uncle Joe a new hat to celebrate his rebirth and the rebirth of the world. Never think, however, O how horrible it is to doubt, that without the savior the cycle would renew itself again unaided by human thoughts.

Reality stands helplessly by as symbols conjure thoughts that block the minds of men once again. Symbolism is a powerful tool for the religious community and must be fought in the only manner in which it can be fought, by seizing the symbols back once again. We must grasp hold of the trees, the star, the earth and hold them for what they are and what they mean, not what they may seem to be.

Do not let the opportunity pass to place the art of symbolic illogic on the pedestal to be recarved by the hand of logic. The smell of a fresh-baked pie is never so rich as its taste. Taste reality and use the symbols to lure others to its grasp, as the odor of the pie might lure a small boy to the kitchen.

Happy Winter Solstice season from all of us on the staff of the *American Atheist*. We have but the seasons of the earth to enjoy as they provide many faces for our lives here on planet earth. Let us not waste life's precious time in pursuit of any greater support than the earth beneath our feet.

Do We Dare Question The System?

February 1978

"O'Hair Raids Bingo Party," said the *Austin American-Statesman* caption, with another untoward photo of our noble leader for which photographers get promotions. The proper citizens were aghast. After all, "Why didn't she just send her attorneys?" said the church officials when confronted by reporters. Doesn't she know the difference between right and wrong?

The answer to that pointed question is a loud **Yes!** Perhaps she understands that difference better than anyone might know. Although it places her in a small minority group, Dr. O'Hair knows all too well the difference of those two small words of much human debate over centuries. At least one other has come to the realization that that which is proper is not axiomatically "right."

I am speaking of Peter. Peter Qoboza, that is, editor — or former editor, I should say — of a very different newspaper out of Johannesburg, South Africa, called *The World*. I say "former" because since October of last year he has been detained by government security police — along with freedom of speech in South Africa. The paper, the only black voice of independence in his area, was guilty, as he was, of the terrible crime of "articulating, without fear or favor, the aspirations of our people," in his own words.

We here at American Atheists articulate and often even holler for "our people" — American Atheists — and, indeed, Atheists of every nationality, on a daily basis. We have been somewhat more fortunate than Peter, due to the more subversive nature of our system of government. Losing one's insurance is a bit less obvious than direct police intervention, but it gets the job done just the same if we allow it to. Yet, we do continue to shout, a course which often brings more heat from our own than from those we challenge. We have made a very important choice between two alternatives known to Peter as well. As he put it to the *Harvard Crimson* in November of 1975, "One has to make a choice whether to be outspoken and go to jail, where you'll be silenced, or take a milder platform, so you can keep working."

The soft approach served us well for some years, until the separation forced by our exodus from social circles and society's grasp to survive gave a perspective to the struggle for freedom that had never broken on the horizon before. One must be forced into a different world than those around oneself, almost a subculture, in order to have the "born-again" (pardon the use of these words) awakening that being fed-up, and that alone, is simply not going to hack it anymore.

In Peter's case, it took a year at Harvard studying journalism in 1975 to give him the inspiration that our extra-social existence gave us. He described it in a letter to some of his American friends upon returning to Africa.

> For the first time in my life, I could distinguish between what is right and what is wrong. The thing that scared me most during my Cambridge year was the fact that I had accepted injustice and discrimination as part and parcel of our "traditional way of life." After my year, the things I had accepted made me angry.

What we had accepted made us angry as well. One of Murphy's Laws says somewhat the same thing: "If you are not worried, you don't fully understand the situation." We are now worried beyond belief. The sudden realization that you are adrift in a sea of discrimination, selfishness, inequality, *etc.*, is wonderful. At that point one can fight by the light of day rather than at night. It will astound you how well you can fight unreason once you have seen the light. (These phrases keep popping up — I write it off as some small bit of undigested indoctrination that still remains as a sign of life inside.) The realization that you are surrounded by injustice serves to bolster your ideals to a fervor that you never before thought possible.

Groups like the ACLU nationwide fight what they believe to be the good fight, never for a moment recognizing that they support the system by accepting and working within its guidelines. They fight for freedom, but only within the bounds that they are allowed. The realization that the basic human right to disagree is limited by the very system they work within never surfaces. Must one "pray" the court for redress on a religious freedom issue? Is this justice or mockery of the puny plaintiff begging a higher power for redress? It's quasi-religious to defer your human dignity to a black-robed pontifical authority on a bench — yet do we dare question the system itself, the whole concept of appeal to a higher authority? Yes, we do. Those golden few of us who understand.

As long as the systemic discrimination ingrained in the present systems of government, jurisprudence, and social power is ignored, we have no hope for the liberation of the human mind for the amelioration of the human condition. We must press for nothing less than changing the whole system, the basis on which it moves in totality. Too large a task, you say? Perhaps not quite so.

The primary vehicle, perhaps also the only one, is the education of masses of people. If the majority — that great silent body that has retarded human progress for generations by resisting change at every turn — could be reached and educated as to the nature of the system, then they alone could be responsible for its fall by the use of one small word, "NO." A general is only as great as the willingness of his army to follow his commands allows him to be. If for one moment the troops say no, the campaign is lost. It is time for the people to say no to their leadership as well. Can we all be jailed or expelled? The sheer numbers would prevent that.

If organized religion could establish a system of ingrained compliance from scratch in several hundred years, the establishment of a system of human dignity can be accomplished in that time (or less) as well. It seems preposterous that dignity and pride in oneself cannot be impressed upon a populace with any amount of force, but servility and denial of one's worth can be disseminated as quickly as the common cold.

Peter sums it up in classic words concerning his own South Africa:

> My fear is that when history catches up with us, there's going to be an awful lot of white people in this country who will repeat those tragic words that were said in Germany at the end of the Second World War, when every German there said, "I did not know it was happening." It's true that for evil to succeed it takes far too many good people to keep quiet and stand by.

This situation is extant in the United States at this time. We, as American Atheists, know that we cannot allow it to go unnoticed. For this reason we seek litigation which is educational first and perhaps rewarded (monetarily, etc.) later. Once the news media exposed Nixon, he was forced to resign. If through litigious education we can show up religion for what it is, just as Watergate showed up Nixon for what he was, the American people may drop religion as they did their president.

So, breaking up a bingo game or being arrested in protest activities at a city council meeting brings about a kind of public demonstration and thus education which is needed to awaken that sleeping giant, the people, to action. We must expose overt discrimination in the system which has remained as covert as that of World War II in Germany.

Peter came to the final conclusion in his own struggle that "the enforced silence of jail was preferable to another kind of silence — the voluntary silence of those who stayed out of jail." Liberty should not be had only at the extraordinary cost of one's human dignity. As an American Atheist, I should rather remain an Atheist in bondage than a hypocrite at large. I shall not practice my life-style on my knees.

I wish to free all of you from necessity of ever having to practice your life-styles on your knees, either. Yet, for this Dr. O'Hair and I are both reprimanded. You cannot have your liberty and serenity at the same time; a choice must be made. On the covers of *American Atheist* issues are persons who have made the choice, and I urge you to do the same. (If I sound like Billy Graham asking you to cross the fifty-yard line to be saved, so be it.)

"Peter Qoboza is in jail," says *The New Yorker* of November 11, 1977, "and has been silenced, just as he had feared in his milder days whenever he contemplated the disadvantages of the outspoken path." My hat is off to a man of dignity.

You may say, "You cannot fight in jail; it is a useless exercise!" Standing up for your rights is never useless. You have then demonstrated your desire to stand free. Whether you lose that right or not is not as important as your willingness to demonstrate it.

The Vernal Equinox

March 1978

Whan that Aprille with his shoures sote
The droughte of Marche has perced to the rote,
And bathed every veyne in swich licour,
Of which vertu engendred is the flour;
Whan Zephirus eek with his swete breeth
Inspired hath in every hold and heeth
The tendre croppes, and the yonge sonne
Hath in the Ram his halfe cours y-ronne,
And smale fowles maken melodye,
That slepen al the night with open ye
So priketh hem nature in hir corages
Than longen folk to goon on pilgrimages.

These immortal words are, of course, from Chaucer's Prologue to *The Canterbury Tales*. They describe the wonders of spring bursting upon the English countryside — the most awaited season of the four, when winter's blight is lifted and the green of life returns to the land. But even this joy must be denied to those who follow the false savior, for as Chaucer puts it, their first duty is "the holy blisful martir for the seke"; death to be honored first before the wonders of birth.

On this, the holiday season for all mankind, transcending all boundaries of nation or race, the Christian gang of bandits rob us of life to salute the death and imagined resurrection of their "lord." The vernal equinox is the first day of spring. Visions of baby bunnies, chicks, and ducklings bounce in children's heads. Eggs, the symbols of life itself, the new chick bursting forth colored brightly for the celebration — all subverted by lilies of death and the carnage of crucifixion.

How dreadful to celebrate the murder of one's only son. A kind creator who kills his only child in cold blood in order to save him? Such a story is not fit for the eyes or ears of a single child. The renewal of life is the most wonderful of all events. A birth of any new entity, be it plant, mammal, insect, or fish, is a moment of happiness — new adventures, things for the fledgling to do and see and learn. Is death and the promise of a dream world more dear? To the uneducated mind, the savage who dwells in the valley of ignorance still, perhaps, but to the twentieth-century mind tales of horror fit only for the films of Vincent Price.

The choice is yours: spend your life preparing to die for the experience of a never-ending dream, or live now in the only world you know. Ingersoll put it best when he said, "Give me the storm and tempest of thought and action rather than the dead calm of ignorance and faith. Banish me from Eden when you will, but first let me eat of the fruit of the tree of knowledge."

In short, life is to be grappled with, and in that struggle enjoy all the victories and defeats as they come, because they are all you'll know. Seek to pass on as you go a bit of kindness to all who cross your path, so that their struggle may be enjoyed all the more.

"Atheism breaks down the barriers of nationalities and, like one touch of nature, makes the whole world kin," said Joseph Lewis. The seasons of life, the four great holidays we seek to save from the Christian cloud of gloom, do just that.

In this season of so much life, let nature be your guide to the best of all things. Like the bluebonnets in a Texas field, bloom so that you and your fellows about you may fulfill your only purpose here, to *live* and to help others to come to live better.

A Time for Living

April 1978

Being somewhat of a sports fan, I recently attended a basketball game that was fairly ordinary on the surface, except for the fact that it was a playoff game. The score was close down to the final seconds of the contest, with the home team winning by a narrow margin. As the crowd slowly started to disperse, I followed the stream of humanity to the exits, absorbed in the faces of victory mingled with those of defeat.

As I rounded a corner I almost ran into a young white male and his date who had just come upon a Black man with his lady friend. The white man, suddenly recognizing the Black, moved rapidly to him, shaking hands with the common "How have you been, long time no see" expression. His female companion hugged her Black counterpart. It was, in all, a warm reunion of small dimensions. The couples involved were, at my best guess, in their late teens.

This scene struck me as so meaningful in the brief moments it encompassed, that I stood startled, blocking traffic until a nudge from behind drew my attention back to the business at hand, that of making my way to the car. On the way home I remarked to the friend accompanying me that the parents of these couples would never have exhibited that kind of friendship in public during their youth — especially in a Southern state.

The history of the Southern part of our nation is no secret with respect to attitudes towards Blacks. Racism dies hard, as does any other prejudice, for as with all biases, the roots lie in the inability of people to communicate. Only through communication can groups separated by any natural or intellectual differences relate to the heritage and founding principles of each. The type of communication demonstrated by the young couples in the crowd is an emotional one, but that type is but the overture to the harmony of intellectual symphonics that should follow.

Communication is easy in those areas which are of common concern. Differences retard the process, almost like trying to talk through a heavy door, aided by emotion, which acts like weather stripping as it seals the little spaces around the edges where words could slip through. Religion is like this, for religion is chiefly emotion. That is its central quality, for emotion overrides thought very effectively. The result is well documented historically. Religious wars of every description have plagued mankind for centuries: conflicts which defy logic but feed on emotion.

I take no exception to emotion. It is part of all of us and has its valid place, for without it one could no more function than a continuously stoked boiler with no outlet for the steam buildup. The mark of a rational person is, however, his ability to check that emotion in the cause of communication and the ensuing understanding of others that minimizes conflict.

I do not suggest that such checks always are either possible or even desirable. In the area of sexual concerns, for example, such checks are usually particularly elusive. This is good in some cases, since struggle produces a healthier generation from an evolutionary standpoint. In most cases of human contact, however, rational checks on emotion are well placed, especially when that contact is nonphysical in nature.

Atheism has always based its life-style on rationality, or, to put it another way, the scientific examination of events and ideas prior to the taking of action with respect to their resolution or to the formulation of opinions concerned with them. Thus, Atheism is a logical opponent to religion, which turns to emotion first, while Atheism turns to unbiased evaluation.

All religions do this without exception. Terms like the "religion of science" or Church of Scientology, as it is called, are misnomers. Religion and science are mutually exclusive. When one considers then that it is science, the very thing that religion cannot allow, that has brought mankind to the level of well-being that it has reached today, it is hard to fathom a reluctance to accept it.

I challenge anyone to demonstrate that religion has been a catalyst to human progress, as science has been. Yet the idea of religion has taken precedence over all else. Our foreign policy has been dictated by religion, our hospitals have been taken over by it, our tax structure has been robbed by it (keeping monies from needed human applications), the liberation of our bodies has been controlled by it, even the minds of our children have been directed against nature itself by it.

Yet small sparks of hope are seen here and there — sparks like the couples in the crowd I mentioned earlier. The sad part is that *generations* have been wasted needlessly in order to generate these sparks. The components of liberty, equality and fraternity have always been around, but the catalyst of communication has been missing. Due to religion's pernicious influences, scenes like that in the crowd are the exception, when they by all rights should be the rule.

Humanity stands on the brink of self-destruction over a lack of communication. We have even gone so far as to cease communicating with nature. We not only don't communicate anymore, we even deny any relationship with nature. Other creatures are referred to as "animals" in a derogatory manner. I have news for everyone; we too are animals.

It is no wonder then that our goal is the elimination of religion. That goal cannot be subverted by anything else, least of all by a lack of communication among ourselves. Once religion is removed, humanity can get down to the business at hand, the business of life. Life is all we have. It has no purpose but to continue as long as possible. The cycle of existence is good. It is not wicked, or "animal" (in a derogatory sense), or pointless. It is merely something of which we are inextricably a part.

The Atheist movement in the United States has been similarly hampered by this lack of communication. This deficiency takes the form of lack of transmittal from one Atheist to another of the understanding that life is here and now and is all we know, and that therefore it must be rich and wonderful and happy. The very problem that religion presses on everyone has become part of the movement against it. The problem has become part of the solution. This cannot be.

I am an Atheist first and a member of any other group second. Being an Atheist means being part of the life cycle in harmony. Being religious means being part of that same life cycle, but fighting it to the bitter end. Fighting the inevitable becomes unbearable.

You may say that an Atheist then lacks communication with a religionist, that he has an unwillingness to understand the religionist's point of view. Consider then that the religionist does not even understand himself, for he is but a part of the life cycle and nothing more, and *that* he denies. Denial of reality is insanity. Atheism is the only position that is consistent with life itself. Atheism communicates with life.

If you don't understand something that you are a part of — like it or not — you can do nothing but fear it and resent it. We simply say "Understand! Don't feel uncomfortable with living."

A famous poem says it all: "Life is so full of a number of things/that we should all be happy as kings." I can't think of anything that expresses the thought better.

So, next time you are in a crowd, look around you closely. What you see is what there is to work with, to enjoy, to communicate with, and to make the best of it all with. To those who accept life and its wonderful things — bad things included — welcome. To those who would run away, remember you cannot play another day; you must live now.

Individual Action

May 1978

We recently received a wave of distressing news: birth control clinics across the country had been firebombed; our president has said that he bases his support of Israel on the "fact" that Israel's existence fulfills biblical prophecy; the Kentucky legislature has a bill before it to make the display of the Ten Commandments mandatory in all public school classrooms; the state of Texas is a functioning theocracy due to a provision in its constitution requiring all elected or appointed officials to have a belief in a "supreme being"; and countless city meetings across the nation open with invocations, as do both houses of Congress.

Each of these is a flagrant violation of the constitutional principle of separation of state and church. The list is almost endless; it could go on for pages. Why? Because the Constitution of the United States has suffered a grave transition in our recent history; it has now become just an advisory document. Our rights to life, liberty, the pursuit of happiness and other freedoms have now been left up to the discretion of powerful political forces.

The only line of defense left is the individual citizen. Think about it: In the years since World War II the U.S. Supreme Court has handed down a number of decisions which served to enhance human rights, but all of which resulted from litigation brought by individuals who felt they had to force their government to deliver freedoms already promised and guaranteed them by the Constitution. All the so-called civil rights decisions of the 1960s were rights that the government had already granted in its founding document, but generations later the descendants of those founders needed to petition the government for those very same rights all over again.

Why? Simply put, the people of the United States have by and large not cared for the protection of their rights for many years now. As long as they had two cars in every garage and a chicken in every pot, all was OK. Meanwhile, in the halls of Congress, legislators were taking away one freedom after another under the guise of caring for the people.

The great silent majority slept through the conversion of our national symbolism and ideals from "freedom for all" to those of "love it as it is or get out." The idea that to love your country is to fight to make it better is but a recent notion. If you loved it before, you simply kept your mouth closed tight and went along so as not to rock the boat, thereby qualifying as a "good citizen."

All those "good citizens" have now almost cost us the very right to exist as Atheists in the United States. While they remained "in line," the administration of President Eisenhower began to convert our nation into a Christian democracy, and none knew what was going on. Now organizations such as American Atheists are being urged to do something about it. Well, it's too late now for ordinary effort. It is only with extraordinary effort and boldness that we can hope to have a chance at reacquiring our constitutional liberties. The fighting should have been done during the 1950s to save those symbols and ideals our forefathers held so dear.

In three short years — 1954, 1955, and 1956 — out nation was symbolically delivered over the Christian scheme of salvation. Actions that guaranteed our descent into a new Dark Age went unopposed. In 1954, the words "under God" were inserted into the Pledge of Allegiance. From that moment on no Atheist could swear allegiance to this nation. In 1955, the words "In God We Trust" were made mandatory for the currency of this nation. From that point on, no Atheist could exist without being forced to acknowledge a supreme being with every monetary transaction. In 1956, our national motto was changed to "In God We Trust." From that time on, no Atheist could consider the United States a safe home.

As early as 1908, the Congress of the United States made clear what its position was with respect to a destiny for our nation. In a committee report on the restoration of the slogan "In God We Trust" to certain coins under consideration at that time, they said

> Your subcommittee is unanimous in the belief that as a Christian nation we should restore this motto to the coinage of the United States upon which it was formerly inscribed . . . as an outward and visible form of the inward and spiritual grace, which should possess and inspire American citizenship, and as an evidence to all the nations of the world that the best and only reliance for the perpetuation of the republican institution is upon a Christian patriotism, which, recognizing the universal fatherhood of God, appeals to the universal brotherhood of man as the source of the authority and power of all government.

The power of government was thus given over to a fable. No viable organization existed at the time, nor was to exist for many years to come, to counteract that kind of sickness in leadership. For that reason we are now caught up within a flow of history that we cannot reverse short of tremendous social upheaval.

Where were the lovers of freedom when our nation was given over to the god idea and sold out to the most disreputable of all existing systems of thought — organized theism?

On November 13th, 1861, a minister from Ridleyville, Pennsylvania, wrote a letter to the Hon. S.P. Chase, then Secretary of the Treasury. It said in part:

> One fact touching our currency has hitherto been seriously overlooked. I mean that recognition of the Almighty God in some form on our coins. . . . This would make a beautiful coin, to which no possible citizen could object. This would relieve us from the ignominy of heathenism. This would place us openly under the divine protection we have personally claimed.

That letter initiated the placement of "In God We Trust" on certain coins, an initial defeat for the free mind, a signal of many more to come.

We now have a "born again" president and the pledge of "god's word" has made its way into every nook and crany of our life-styles. It is almost too late now to eliminate a concept so entrenched in the inner fabric of our culture. It should have been stopped 100 years ago. We are now faced with a cancerous growth, a growth which will perhaps die out — but only by killing its host. All we can do is to slow its progress and relieve the pain because the opportunity for cure through early diagnosis has passed. We will do the best we can, as any good physician might.

Due to the silence of the many, the few have suffered. Now the few who knew that suffering perhaps cannot save the many. If only those who cried wolf had been heard.

Only the hope of individual action remains, action against the government asking it to restore the United States to the noble experiment of our founding, a complete separation of state and church. No other nation had ever thought of such a separation, but a few brave men dared. Let us not forsake them now. Each of us owes it to ourselves to strike out in whatever way we can for the restoration of collective reason as a guide for our nation and its affairs. Americans must get back a guide for our nation and its affairs. Americans must get back to thinking together — not praying together. The solution is only as far away as the space between our ears.

The harm one minister can set in motion seeking a return to serfdom surely many organized Atheists can remedy for a return to liberty.

Atheist Pseudonyms

June 1978

On a recent trip to our beautiful state of Hawaii, I had occasion to meet with a group of persons who had been or were at that time members of our national American Atheist organization. Those attending could all be classed as business or professional persons. All were fairly well educated, and by that I mean each had achieved some level of university education.

Dr. O'Hair and I met in an intimate hotel room setting with this small yet representative group of persons. I say "representative" for I feel that they typified the mainstream of middle-class America, the same sort of persons one would find in any city the size of Honolulu anywhere in the United States.

What I had expected to be a rather ordinary conversation among individuals who admired Dr. O'Hair for her accomplishments and who seemed generally open-minded turned out to be most unexpected and enlightening. All of those assembled classified themselves by one of the less definitive titles which Atheists all over the United States unfortunately use to shield themselves from the social pressures of outright identification with their true felings. Terms such as humanist, agnostic, ethical culturist, deist, freethinker, rationalist, secularist, realist, and objectivist all serve a purpose for their users, but often are not a true expression of their thoughts.

The use of such terms is common, and the initial argument we had over the question of "Why lie to yourself and others by not coming out and saying what you really are?" went as expected. When we began to probe the subject a little deeper, however, a position statement on the part of those gathered began to emerge. This position has deep implications affecting the struggle for civil rights for Atheists and indeed the freedoms that we all attempt to secure for our own enjoyment.

Perhaps that is the key word — "enjoyment" — for these typical representatives of our nation expressed a desire to enjoy their freedoms without going quite so far as to covet them. The personal ramifications of the Constitution as it applied to them directly was their primary concern. "What can I get out of the Bill of Rights as far as personal leeway for me to conduct my everyday life?" That was their question.

Every Man For Himself

My reply was, "What can you do to ensure that not alone you retain those freedoms but that they are retained and strengthened for future generations?" Their reply was, "Why bother?" Why should they have any obligation to look out for anything but their own backside? "We must protect ourselves and not rock the boat," they said in summary.

Their feeling was that the proper concern of an individual should be for himself first. Any objection raised in favor of additional rights or for initial rights for others was unthinkable, since it would entail generating waves in their social pool. Their position must be protected at all costs, even to the detriment of the continuance of those freedoms for posterity.

The question then immediately comes to mind: "Don't we owe anything to those who withstood the storm of social ostracism and even sacrificed their very lives for the benefit of the whole?" Is it not incumbent upon everyone benefiting from what the handful have laid on the line to continue to nurture those benefits and indeed even expand upon them?

Their answer was a resounding "NO! We have no obligation to uphold those measures defended by the few for the many. We need only maintain our own tranquility at all costs."

I find such a position staggering in this day and age. Educated individuals, products of our social and educational system, cannot find it within themselves to realize that all future freedoms rely on the maintenance of those won in the past and the building of new ones on that well-laid structure. Sad as this may seem, it is a continuing phenomenon I find all across the country in the numerous public gatherings in which I am involved.

The forty-hour week which was long in the coming and was won even by the blood of workers is now taken for granted. Guaranteed freedom of the press, a landmark in world affairs for which our forefathers were willing to die, is now being used as a weapon against those who dare to speak out against the erosion of such rights. After all, under journalistic freedom should not the press be obligated to sell advertising to Atheists who can meet all lawful requirements? Shouldn't they be required to report our victories as well as lauding our defeats?

The supreme tragedy is that the United States, as the first nation in the history of the world to include separation of state and church in its founding documents, now turns its back on that principle. The very thing that separated our nation from all others which had gone before — a desire to separate the forces of religion from those of government — has now been allowed to lapse. They ask, "What do I get out of it if I stand up for such a separation? It's not worth my time. I may lose my job or my mother-in-law may get upset."

Because no one cared enough to resist, we now have a growing religious symbolism suffocating our nation in a kind of civil religion which gives god and Uncle Sam blood-brother status. Patriotism is god and god is patriotism. Slogans on our money, slogans in our pledge, indeed, even the national motto has fallen because no one cared enough to speak up.

We cannot in less time repair what took generations to build and which was allowed to fall. Therefore, it is essential that we stand up now for the preservation of those freedoms that we already enjoy and strive for their expansion into other areas. As an American Atheist, I accept this as a primary task and ask that others who consider themselves to be Atheists take a similar stand.

Each and every precious bit of progress gained by man must be maintained so that we do not lapse into a continual cycle of having to redo that which has been done at great cost before. Let us move on to other areas of human development which are never tended to because we remain stuck in the treadmill of having to resecure basic human rights. Once the first winning is recognized, it must only be acknowledged by each succeeding generation. Therein lies the problem.

Instead of striving to duplicate rights already guaranteed to all, we should acknowledge the freedoms we now hold and make them stronger. The Equal Rights Amendment is a good example. Though endowed by the Constitution with the basic freedoms laid down for all, we are of necessity now striving for a redefinition of those same rights to include women — hence we must forsake the needed fight for many other freedoms yet to be won but once. Those basic freedoms are even endangered by that redefinition process. Let the women of America stand up and speak out for themselves, and they will have the rights they are willing to demand.

The essential point remains that any person or group has only as many freedoms as they are willing to fight for. Silence only buys repression. I agree with anyone who asks us to stand up and proclaim our Atheism joyously.

The Enemy among Us

July 1978

When one reviews the histories of Europe and the United States seeking an overview of the slow but steady movement to free the human mind from religious bondage, one finds a litany of defunct groups and dead heroes scattered among the many and varied battlefields of this relentless campaign.

Each of these heroes, during his glory days (brief in terms of history's records, but long and often agonizing at the moment) led those he could persuade in grand skirmishes against oppressive regimes of every shape and form. The battle won or the retreat sounded, he went again and again to war, determined to reach that ultimate goal that still awaits tantalizingly down the road like Jason's golden fleece. But as in the case of those ancient Greeks who sought the fleece, sleeping dragons lay awaiting the column on their march.

These reptilian foes are of many different shapes, sizes, and colors, yet are mostly recognizable. But some are sly and hide themselves, as if surrounded by a fog, so that they may appear to be marching within the ranks of the liberators. They are misunderstood (or rather they breed misunderstanding) in the ranks of the freedom fighters who trustingly direct their attention to other surroundings — ever cautious for ambushes from without, but unaware of treachery from within their own ranks.

Such misunderstandings within the ranks come in strange shapes. Some confuse motives, making the stragglers of the column drop off unbeknown to those ahead. Some confuse the meaning of the goal which the struggle seeks to gain. Some ignore the rhythm of the drummer so that the column loses step and gives ground to the enemy. Some confuse the goal with others. The most dangerous of all these serpents, though, is the one who confuses the identity of the army as a whole.

The crowds of liberated minds along the way see the troops less clearly and become discouraging to troops in need of support. The bearers of sustenance for the weary troops are unable to locate the column to deliver their burdens where they are needed.

What was once an army of liberation is now only a scattering of individuals chanting the battle cry alone, their heads peeking out of the fog here and there like blades of grass in fields of snow. The battle anthem has been silenced for the lookers-on, for the emphasis is now on one head here or there and not on the union of all.

Times have not changed that much in these many years, for as we fight today for that freedom of the mind, hanging on the tree of liberty as the fleece of Jason's day hung on a lonely branch far from reach, the dragon of misunderstanding weaves its path among us. We are seen as personalities rather than as the army we are. Mercenary soldiers whose thoughts are strengthened by the memories of those of brave heart who went before them are now stranded, awaiting the supplies needed on the front. Only with adequate support can the war continue. If the lines of supply are cut, the army will perish.

Mercenaries

We are your mercenaries, hired by those who care to be liberated but who have not the taste for the battle required to gain the victory. We are willing to taste the bitterness of the front day after day, but only as long as we know that the lines of supply will be kept open with more than just minimal rations for many battles yet to come.

A comforting word is always welcome, but in the face of any foe another round of ammunition is always more fortifying. Keep the supply lines open. Dig deeper into the raw materials where they can be found, but keep the forge producing those bullets.

Those who desire others to sow for them that they may reap must provide the seed. This is all we ask of Atheists month after month after month. This we will continue to ask, hoping that you will not permit the dragon of misunderstanding to screen our efforts and our needs with its foul breath.

Feel free to keep your cards and letters coming, but don't be offended when we use them for fuel for our campfires.

Atheists and other Americans as well have but two roads. Sit behind the walls and load the guns for those in front, or join them on the line. Hopefully, you will choose to join us out front rather than to reload in the dark; but as long as you will back us, we welcome you just the same.

The third option should hardly be given comment at all, but, sad as it may seem, there are some who prefer neither to load or to fight. In the face of history's challenge they mouth the infamous evasion of *Bartleby the Scrivener,* "I would prefer not to." For them, freedom must slip from their grasp forever.

From those of us still in the march, we miss you. Come along.

Recognizing Reality

October 1978

It was my distinct pleasure to attend the opening of the American Atheist Museum in Indiana recently, and at that affair I was asked the same questions over and over again by persons in attendance: "Why an *Atheist* museum?" and "How is this different from any other museum?"

These questions are very important ones and ones which require some understanding of fundamental Atheist thought for an appreciation of their answers.

Think for a moment about the techniques of human problem-solving. An essential part of mankind's existence and growth is the requirement laid on him to use this process. Two views are extant. One is the theistic view which states that an illusionary "god" is the origin of all solutions to human problems, an imaginary solution after the fact. A god entity is given the ultimate credit for the causation of the solution as a benevolent influence over all things.

However, it must be observed that the process of asking for a solution from a god for any problem involves the first step of the other view to solving problems, the Atheistic view; that is, the identification, delimitation, or proper definition of the problem itself — the first step in any human problem-solving method.

In solving problems without the aid of a proxy (god) — the method utilized by Atheists — one must rely on one or all of three factors to determine a solution to the problem.

The first is reason, or, as like to call it, "common sense." Reason can also be referred to as "the scientific method," but all the scientific method really amounts to is category analysis, or the process of breaking things down to their lowest common denominators so that their simplest parts may be categorized and dealt with one at a time, instead of all at once when they are more confusing.

Any complex issue is merely a combination of sub-problems, each individually solvable by data collection and examination. A reassembly of the sub-problems nets a solution to the problem in totality.

To submit a problem to a deity requires a delineation of that problem so that the deity (actually, the mind of the individual) can understand what is being asked. The Atheist contends that one should simply continue the problem-solving process oneself to its logical end: a final solution to the entire problem.

A second factor requiring due consideration is human history, which is actually the accumulation of the results of the application of reason/scientific methodology (or lack thereof) by previous generations to their problems. This accumulation enables the present generation to compare our contemporary problems to those of our predecessors to determine if our particular situations have been confronted before, thus perhaps relieving us of the burden of endless attempts to overcome difficulties which have previously been dealt with.

As a result, the accumulated pool of solutions makes it possible for each generation to tackle more complex problems, which break down into sub-problems now less complex than they were for the generation before. This can readily be seen by the fact that our technology has progressed further in the past twenty years than in the previous century. So, this second tool, when combined with reason, can be used as a catalyst to further advance humanity's problem-solving capabilities.

A third factor to be considered is natural history, which is essentially the study of evolution, or the continuing process of change within the boundaries established by natural processes. These natural forces or physical laws define the limits within which we must work during the application of our problem-solving methods. These cycles, which are oblivious to humanity's wishes, set the stage upon which we must act to work out life's needed solutions. We can only work with and within the boundaries these demonstrable realities provide in the natural surroundings in which we find ourselves.

We cannot reach into an illusionary world for problem-solving tools which do not exist. Thus, you cannot stir batter with an imaginary spoon, nor forecast tomorrow's weather with no input regarding atmospheric conditions, emerging patterns, *etc.* We must work with what we have — with what we know to be real and actual.

If we are to maintain the standard thus far attained in humanity's evolutionary journey upward (much less attempt to better that standard), then we are limited to our reason, our knowledge of our own history and that of our natural environment to work with.

The American Atheist Museum differs then from other museums in that it demonstrates not only our reliance on these sources for problem-solving, but also our recognition of the fact that they are all with which we have to work. The "god idea" is simply not admissible as a fourth alternative.

The museum also seeks to demonstrate that the god idea itself has evolved from the concept that a god is an ultimate source of problem-solving which overshadows all others, to a semi-modern one which finds god as a partial problem-solving alternative in combination with one or more of the other genuine, existing tools. The American Atheist Museum demonstrates, however, that we should go beyond that stage and discard the god concept altogether and simply accept the limitations of that with which we have to work. Those limitations have, after all, brought us to a position of mind-boggling development in a comparatively short period of time.

Other museums merely acknowledge the existence of the limitations with which man must work by displaying them. The American Atheist Museum goes beyond that by insisting that they must be honored as we have no other choice, or else we must escape into the soothing fantasies of religion. That alternative is not acceptable to us. Our minds stand ready to accept the task of playing by the only rules we have. We cannot make our own rules, which would require that we play off the board of reality. We choose to stay on the board.

A Change in Perspective

November 1978

We hear a lot about the population explosion these days. Posters and fliers remind us that the geometric increase in medical technologies will soon make it possible for a greater and greater number of generations of any family to be alive at the same time. We are confronted with the soon-to-be reality of having our great-great grandparents alive when we are adults.

Imagine then the same thought applied to religion. What if the older religions never died but lingered on to co-exist with the newer ones? Generation upon generation in the continued evolution of humanity's insanity would all be surviving together side by side.

Thor, Jesus, Zeus, and Krishna, all plaguing the minds of men simultaneously with still more mythical deities on the way: a dim prognois that will never be realized? No, not quite. This very stituation exists today in exotic India.

Descending into India on a modern jet, one could just as well be landing in Florida for a vacation on the beach — until one emerges from the airplane. One then enters the world of a Disney-like "Religion Land." Nothing seems quite real from that moment until the plane thankfully lifts one out again.

In India, poverty and ignorance are the order of the day, with that civilization's countless theologies feeding off both as if such human miseries were manna from heaven. Each passerby has his own god(s) from origins as old as the Ganges, yet each deity is uniquely different from those of his neighbors. Temples and mosques litter every corner with gods so numerous that their sequence requires the lifetimes of the pious just to memorize. Primitive sacramentals and offerings rot in the blazing Indian sun. Phallic totems stand proudly as they did generations before.

All of the exotica one can read about the "primitive" peoples of our own heritage stand before one's startled eyes in modern-day India. Sacrifices, holy baths in a befouled river, potions to ward off countless devils, sacred marks superstitiously painted on the body and around doors and windows, ornaments and symbols to curry favor from above for their wearer — all these grotesque insanities fester side by side and all are oblivious one to the other.

In the midst of this sea of insanity stand a few proud individuals who say "bunk" to all the surrounding madness. These are the freethinkers who go by different nomenclature. They call themselves rationalists for the most part, with a smattering of humanists, agnostics, realists, and ethical culturists evident. Each group struggles against the generic concept of god existent in their particular area. The individual sects and subsects of the different cults are too numerous to address individually. The primary foe of these local freethinkers is the village prevaricator. These "god men,' as they call them, subsist by tricking the ignorant with magical cures and potions.

India has a near eighty percent rate of illiteracy. Hence it is that religion has in that statistic a natural breeding ground, a warm, moist place where its mind sicknesses can grow like a voracious fungus. Even the most rudimentary of sciences is unknown to the masses.

The ugliness of past failings of the mind remain and are venerated. India is a picture of what science prevented in the Western world. It is a window into the past to remind us what can become of us as well should we slip into the path of a return to the ways of the church.

The wall of separation of state and church established by our founding fathers separates us from and lifts us above the same conditions of ignorance which abound on the Indian subcontinent.

The continuance of massive individual salvation schemes depends solely on their practitioners being kept ignorant. This entails not only a disregard for the lessons of the past, but an unwillingness to experiment to determine the lessons of the future. No one religious practitioner knows what the other believes or does concerning the other's belief. Each has their own road to bliss already mapped out with its own rules and penalties. Is this so very different from the Baptist who has no idea what a Methodist believes, or a Catholic who knows nothing about the evangelicals' salvation scheme, or that of the Jews who could care less about any of the others?

All theological systems call for a paddling of one's own canoe to everlasting destinations filled with whatever one considers the finest of luxuries. Whether this striving to remain ignorant is done with poise or with vulgarity matters little. The vulgar is more shocking and evident, as in India, but the genteel is just as pernicious.

I learned a great deal from my Indian experience. To see religion with its mask of social graces removed is a shocking experience. Bared to the objective eye, all god ideas are ugly, and the people who adhere to them are ugly as well. I urge anyone who can to visit a "backward" or educationally deprived nation and to observe the religion(s) of its people. Such an experience will lead to a reevaluation of one's neighbors who still believe in infant damnation, in the superstitions of baptism and virgin birth, or in the value of a crucifix.

What is required is a change of perspective so that the theistic system can be viewed by the theist as the non-theist sees it. My journey into another culture magnified the perspective I had previously enjoyed while adding a final shading to the overall picture of religious blight. I am now, more than ever, determined to see all religion become a vestigial part of the human experience.

Witness the enemy as it really is. Don't be fooled by ignorance and superstition shielded with the mask of individual liberty. "They have the right to their own beliefs." "This is a free country." "If I can be an Atheist, he has the right to his church as well." All of these are excuses we have heard over and over again. Is the "right" to submit oneself to a system of institutionalized ignorance designed to subjugate one's mind really a right, a privilege?

There is no such thing as freedom of religion when religion itself is anti-freedom by its nature: the freedom to be a slave. Choose which brand of slavery, but have no option not to be a slave at all.

We here at The American Atheist Center feel that the time to speak up is now. Ignorance is not a right. It must be outlawed with its partner — religion. If we can vaccinate against polio, we can likewise immunize our citizens against an infection of god ideas. I want to wipe out religion in my lifetime.

A Celebration of Life

December 1978

The young generation in America has popularized the phrase "Mother Earth," a concept which identifies our planet as the beginning, as the provider, as the nurturer of mankind. The Earth is all we have and all we know. It is home. We require no special equipment to thrive in its atmosphere. We belong here. We are adapted for life on this sphere spinning through yet-indefinable space.

The terminology of the young is appropriate, for in a sense the Earth is mother to the realities which surround us. Everything we see is a product of the resources contained within its mass. We are confined, like it or not, to life on this planet and the joys and problems which flow from that life.

We are free to investigate and speculate and even hallucinate about things outside the boundaries of our planet as we may. Such speculation doesn't, however, free us from the necessity of coping with the realities of life on Earth on a daily basis.

The physical realities of planet Earth form an environment which cannot be ignored. The weather, the air pressure, the terrain, even the night and the day shape our behavior and our attitudes. Our physical environment surrounds us, and we cannot escape or ignore it.

Theism requires that one do just that. All religions tell their adherents to ignore the environment which embraces us at all times, so as to replace it with a fantasy world — a phantom environment of mythical characters and ephermeral laws which affect nothing but the minds of their believers.

Such is nonsense.

Can you ignore that you are a man or a woman? Can one be oblivious to the rain or to the cold or to the day or the night? No, we must all learn to cope with the conditions in which we find ourselves.

Can you ignore hunger? Theism asks you to do so. It asks you to focus blearily only on those myths it projects on an otherworldly screen to hide the ever-present realities of life from view. In this impartial universe, realities can be and often are as unpleasant as they are delightful. They are always there — theism or no theism.

How do the fantasy environments created in the tales of Hans Christian Andersen relate to reality? The answer is that they don't. In the same manner of reasoning, how do the fantasies about Jesus Christ or David Copperfield or Peter Pan relate to the actuality of our daily existence? Like all fairy tales, not at all.

Those things which we can feel, imagine, hear, and see are celebrated as fact. Those things which we can imagine, we are asked to celebrate as fact in disregard of what we can feel and hear and see. Does this make any sense?

Here in Austin, Texas, each year the University of Texas students celebrate an event called "Eeyore's Birthday Party." Eeyore is a donkey taken from Winnie the Pooh. The frivolous celebration is fun. Those who participate do so for enjoyment only.

Christmas, likewise, is frivolous fun based on utter fiction. Yet one cannot say so to a Christian, for(s)he would insist that the event is quite serious and not to be taken lightly. For the Christian, make-believe has become reality.

Well, reality for Atheists comes not out of the pages of a fairy tale. I can *observe* the leaves fall and can *feel* the wind grow cold. Eventually I can *see* the spring blossoms return again as I bask in the sun. I am part of a cycle, a *physical* and ever-moving cycle, a cycle in which I must participate as must all others of all species.

I cannot remove myself from what and where I am in disregard of the physical boundaries in which I find myself. Only in one's dreams can one fly. Only in a dreamworld can a theist return from death.

Life is a series of wonderful experiences to be enjoyed. Even in defeat, it is possible to laugh. I shall not in this or any other year celebrate an illusionary escape from that sweet reality of life which is so dear.

With winter's arrival I want to see and feel the snow and the cold and sit by a warm fire. I do not wish to celebrate the birth of a character from a book of myths. I would rather enjoy my life.

In the spring I want to see the flowers and inhale their fragrance. I choose to run with my friends or picnic in the park. I care not about the death of a storybook character. I am concerned with life.

In summer I would swim and travel and enjoy the life-giving sun. I need not kneel in a dark hall and be told that I am damned because it is so written. I am not concerned with that which is outside life.

In the autumn I want to see the crimson leaves and feel the cooled autumn wind on my neck. I care not about giving thanks to a myth for my food. I will instead thank the farmer and the trucker and the grocer — and I would wish them a pleasant day.

In essence, I live. I celebrate my life and savor every minute of it. If ever I should lose myself in the pursuit of non-life, I will have lost my opportunity to participate fully and honestly in life itself. I shall have joined the ranks of the "living dead" of theism.

During this and every season, many wonderful opportunities and experiences present themselves in a continuing panorama. These are the very best reasons for celebrating of which I know.

I urge all to celebrate as often as the experiences of life so move them. Leave death and its monuments to the theist community. They don't know what they are missing.

From all of us here at The American Atheist Center, we would like to wish you and yours a happy Solstice Season. In all seasons, may you enjoy the reality of that of which we are a part — the wonder of life.

Atheist Children

January 1979

American history has been characterized by persistent efforts toward securing individual liberties on behalf of a number of groups. At first those of differing religious faiths labored for the free expression of their beliefs. Later followed the issue of slavery, with Black Americans straining at the yoke of misfortune to which they had been unjustly chained. Still later, this nation's workers joined the struggle for freedom with their demands for better working conditions and an end to sweatshop conditions. Currently the women of America are exercising their right to dissent in their struggle for recognition as an equal part of the human community.

One group of citizens, however, still remains in the background of these struggles for equality. These citizens, perhaps the most important of all, have been more or less ignored as far as rights are concerned. This group is composed of our most valuable national resource: our children.

Considered for many years to be but adults in miniature, children had been relegated to the role of replacement field hands in our earlier agricultural society. The Industrial Revolution likewise subjugated children to intolerable factory conditions. In fact, it is only recently in our historical panorama that any concern for the welfare or education of the child has been noticeably evident, beyond those biological concerns of the mother's love. Mandatory public education came late in our nation's two centuries of existence.

America's children have been — and in the majority currently still are — victims of the adage which would have them be "seen but not heard."

Is it any wonder that in our age they are eager to begin their initial flight from the nest so as to secure their full share of human rights and dignity?

Along the way, however, we have had and still do have a number of institutional organizations which seek control of the child's mind in order that his or her growth to maturity (or lack thereof) might be in a direction which these institutions deem no threat to their continued dominance. Paramount among those seeking control of our children is organized religion.

Through control of the parents, organized relgion today guarantees perpetuation of its power by implanting the god idea in young minds which are yet incapable of recognizing the detrimental effects of such unfounded beliefs. Churches assume a position of exploitation no different from the exploiters of children in former times, in that they have no concern whatsoever for the overall welfare of the child, so long as he or she remains loyal and unquestioning and, in turn, so long as that child's offspring are likewise taught to have "faith" in the irrational.

As Atheists we are essentially anti-authoritarian, especially in regard to authority that is thrust upon us without rational explanation as to the merit of its acceptance. We prefer to accept only those authorities which we can see are reasonably concerned with our welfare and the welfare of others. Why, then, should we surrender our children to the Grim Reaper of Religion, which uses blind acceptance of parental authority as a palliative to smooth the process of enslaving the minds of our young? Should we allow ourselves to be used as the means to enslave our children? Never!

Yet those within the confines of the religious community chastise Atheists for not allowing our offspring the "freedom" to know their unknowable god. Is it proper for us to allow our children to be exposed to the detrimental effects of religion under the auspices of providing them with a well-rounded education? I don't think so. Such is comparable to my allowing my child to leap off a precipice so as to give him or her the chance to experience the sensation of falling, never taking into account that it may well be his or her last sensation. I think it far wiser to stand close while holding Junior from behind as he peers over the edge — safely.

Our children are our assets, true; but not in the sense of their being used as fodder for the machinations of religion and its attendant wars. Our children have the unique ability to carry on our social concerns, tempered by their individuality in a way that mere writings cannot. They are a living legacy. All that has been achieved is only as valuable as its ongoing contribution to what will be achieved, lest it be forgotten. The bedrock of mankind's future happiness and welfare depends upon the continuing maintenance of the foundation upon which it began. The blueprints for that maintenance will always be there, but the individual touch of the contractor will determine future quality and stability.

Those future "contractors" are our children, and we can see to it that they are not handicapped with an inability to read that all-important blueprint: the U.S. Constitution.

Our children are the basis for a better tomorrow. The lawful removal of compulsory religious ceremonies from public schools in 1963 was only the first step toward the assured maintenance of our and our descendants' liberties. All of you as parents, potential parents, or assistants to parents are next in line, for it is your ultimate responsibility to provide for the liberty of future generations by seeing to it that reason is not extinguished by religion.

Just as the all-new *American Atheist* magazine is off to a new start for a new year in 1979, we urge you to start your children on the road to a new world through reason.

Easter Charade

March 1979

Nature's season of rejuvenation is upon us once again. Spring, that welcomed harbinger of more pleasant times, warmth, color, and an orgy of sensory delights, arrives on Wednesday, March 21st. This is not to say that we shouldn't partake equally of the pleasures of all seasons, but this chapter of our year — the one of rejuvenation — holds all the promise and joy of a bright-eyed child.

Yet amid the abundance of new sights, sounds, and fragrances of burgeoning life, the religious community celebrates its morbid dogmas of death. At the very apex of life's rejuvenation cycle, we are told to believe that nature's wonders are eclipsed by the barbarous execution of a religious myth. The closing of the senses forever is proposed as a response to beauty and new beginnings.

Christ dies annually, bleeding on the criminal's cross in a reenactment of one of the most primitive tortures: a crucifixion — slow, brutal, agonizing death supposedly followed by life-after-life, entirely outside the laws of nature. Religion promises an ascension into something ephemeral as a replacement for life's realities.

Life and death are mutually exclusive. We know everything about living and nothing at all about death. How, then, can death be a gateway to a better life?

As Atheists we prefer to deal with reality, the sensory abundance in which we find ourselves. We explore, we question what we see, we gather data of all types, and we bequeath the benefit of our experiences to those who replace us. We know better than to turn the seasonal cycle of life into a grotesque worship of death.

Religion's attempt to pervert this loveliest of seasons serves as a reminder to us that the adoption of a healthy — and sane — life-style is the most important choice we will ever make. We owe it to ourselves and to our children to give full examination to that life-style before becoming locked into the mind-deadening delusions of religion.

The *gestalt* of Christianity (or any religion, for that matter) is one not conducive to the continued well-being of the individual. Religions project patterns of unreal experiences as guidelines for us to follow, in disregard of the realities we face day after day. The most blatant example of this jaded, life-denying theological bent is Christianity's annual ritual of promising "life through death" as a replacement for our natural, healthy responses to the rejuvenation accompanying spring's arrival.

We as Atheists must see to it that such grotesque religious "holidays" feasting death and torture are discarded and replaced with the enjoyment and challenge which are part and parcel of an existence which is both pleasant and harsh.

We should not, however, lose sight of the fact that we as individuals will terminate at some stage. But that termination need only be accepted, not feared. It may even be useful as a constant reminder that we must provide for the continuation of a positive life-style through the coming generations. We have but one chance, like our little frog on the cover of March's *American Atheist* magazine, to snatch the fly of life and pass on to our young the technique of accomplishing that feat.

It is its basic inquisitiveness concerning all things that makes Atheism uniquely applicable to the world of tomorrow. In this season of the beginning of that search for data by the young, the notion of a torturous death has no place.

Life has been too long time-tested. It defies the mind to come up with anything better. Many have tried and failed. The successors of those who have failed to "transcend" life are still, much as they may wish it or pray otherwise, a part of all that life is — in and of itself.

Isn't such other worldliness rather silly? It's like a frog trying to imagine itself outside the pond with which it interrelates and in which it was spawned. Theism makes such a demand on its adherents. But we Atheists know a good thing when we are in the midst of one. We bask in the spring sun warming the pond of life, with no delusions of there being any treasure "transcending" the here and now.

From the staff of The American Atheist Center, I would like to wish you all a "Joyous Vernal Equinox."

Religion and The Media

April 1979

"Freedom of speech" is a concept taught early in life to almost every American. We hear about it in school, listen of struggles to retain it on radio and television, and our parents tell us that it is good. In fact, I think it would be easily said that the general consensus of Americans would say that "freedom of speech" is a good thing, something that everyone should have for his or her own. Going further, most would say that it was one of the cornerstones of the founding of our nation, a part of the basic philosophy of our founding fathers.

This valuable commodity is often spoken of in another way. That is with the familiar phrase, "Everyone has a right to his/her own opinion" or "This is a free country."

To this notion I give a hearty round of applause. I quite agree that this should be the case in our country and that our founders intended it to be that way. I am also aware, however, that there is a concerted effort abroad in the land to limit the scope of influence that one's "opinion" has, unless it remains within the confines of a preestablished spectrum. What is acceptable is governed by the boundaries of the spectrum, which are defined by common consent among those who govern the means of dissemination of opinion. Your "opinion" on any subject is your own, and rightly so, as long as you do not attempt to broadcast it to others in an effort to establish some solidarity among those who share that opinion.

On your own your are limited to an insignificant number of persons with whom you cohabit or co-work or with whom you interact as social or business acquaintances. With the aid of the media (radio, television, newspapers or magazines), on the other hand, you can reach very impressive sections of the population. It is at the point at which you desire to reach these significant numbers of persons with your opinion that the restrictions of that preestablished spectrum of allowable expression steps in.

Who establishes this spectrum and of what does it consist? The establishment part is easy. You establish the spectrum yourself by your compliance. That's right. You accept the definitions of what is right and what is wrong which are placed before you by those in political, legal, social, and other leadership roles without question. For example, you would not hesitate for a moment to say that murder is wrong, but when the state does it (capital punishment), it's okay. In the same way, you accept that certain four-letter words for body functions should not be used in public. When someone uses the unacceptable word, you admonish him. If he uses the accepted word, you say nothing at all.

What the spectrum consists of is a set of subjects that may not be dealt with openly or, in some cases, not even at all. Some of those are: sexual conduct, minority political views, speaking favorably of activities which are against the law, and religion. The latter is the most important one. If any of the untouchable topics appears, you must either very carefully talk about it by using acceptable topics to move it about like a scientist may handle uranium with mechanical arms, or avoid it altogether. Religion is like that to a far greater degree than the rest. Religion is considered sacred, and can therefore not be spoken of like football or auto mechanics.

Compounding the problem of dealing with the topic of religion is that those who control the media, from the standpoint of administration and ownership, are almost solidly of the Judeo-Christian camp; that is, those persons who fully accept the Christian scheme of salvation and the authenticity of the mythical characters attendant to that scheme.

How, then, can an Atheist partake of the "freedom of speech" concept in this country above the level of personal interaction? She or he can't. Not unless she or he is willing to use the media within the media's rules. That is what the leadership of this organization has been attempting to do for years: speak about the unspeakable — religion — within the rules laid down by the media and still be effective in broadcasting the viable alternative of Atheism.

The public is largely unaware of this censorship for two reasons: one, most people never have an occasion to participate in the mass media; two, the only thing that is ever seen or heard or read by the public is that which has already been censored. If you are given only censored material, you cannot tell it apart from that which is uncensored. There are some things, however, that are obvious enough to provide some clues to what is going on in the media today. These take the form of various techniques of censorship which are made to appear as though they are "fair."

The most widely used is the technique of presenting an unacceptable opinion as a novelty item. An opinion is aired simply to show that it does not fit. Example: Everyone loves the clown at a circus. Why? Because he is doing what is not acceptable under normal circumstances. He is doing things that are not necessarily wrong, but things that you would never think of doing outside of that context. In the same manner, guests with minority opinions are placed on talk shows as novelty items. They are "funny" because they do and say things that those in the majority of the audience would not do or say. They are exhibited as a curiosity, something out of place. The audience or the master of ceremonies often tries to find out what makes them that way; that is, not like the bulk of the audience. This is too often conducted in a cruel atmosphere, like children taunting a classmate who is unusually tall or fat. In short, their opinion is taken far less seriously.

A variation of this technique is to focus on the personality of the individual who maintains a certain opinion rather than on the opinion itself. What the person's background, education, lifestyle, habits, *etc.*, are becomes more important than the opinion he holds, which is his real distinguishing mark.

Another technique is the watering-down of a person's opinion by the addition of many others of conflicting nature. Opinions that are expressed over and over again in various settings are brought in on the occasion when a much less heard opinion is aired. Example: An Atheist spokesperson comes to a particular location with the dissemination of the alternative of Atheism in mind. Opponents of that view, who happen to be in the majority, show up demanding equal time. They have a constant forum for their opinion year-round, unopposed. Still they feel they must take up the allotted time of the Atheist in a one-time-in-a-year opportunity at airing an alternative. What starts out as a one-hour program for the presentation of Atheism turns into a quarter-hour for Atheism and three-quarters of an hour for religion.

Fairness in broadcasting should consist of an *equal* opportunity for all opinions. It seems, however, that some are more equal than others. In place of permitting each opinion to be expressed with the audience viewing each, the opinions are mixed so that neither gets a proper airing.

The most widely used technique of all is the presentation of what is average, in terms of public participation, as novelty or comedy, with the treating of that which is below average seriously. Example: "All in the Family" is a far more accurate description of an average American household than "The Waltons." Or the "Peanuts" cartoon strip depicts how children behave to a far closer degree than "Dear Abby" deals with questions about behavior.

The important thing about this technique is that what is below average is projected as the desirable by the mere fact that it is taken seriously. The media projects an image, like a slide on a screen, of the "perfect" American; that is, one who does not deal with those subjects that are taboo. "The Waltons" never talk about abortion, but "Maude" does. The comedy goes into those things that the average American talks of and thinks of and argues about. The non-comedy does not. The non-comedy portrays the image of what the "perfect" American should be, rather than is.

This same technique is also used widely in another setting: the Bible. In the Bible, an image of the "perfect Christian" is presented. Only that image is taken seriously. The image that is the personification of natural tendency is not taken seriously. It is treated as evil. This projection of the perfect Christian in the Bible has nothing to do with what the average person is actually like. It is that to which it is hoped the average person will conform in the future.

Just like in the Bible, the media projects an image of what is hoped for, rather than what is. I like "what is" better, don't you?

What happens, then, when someone spills the beans and announces to everyone that what they are laughing at is what they are? The system of constant projection of a false ideal fails to produce the desired emulation of that ideal and the desire to reach it. That which is emulated is unreal, and that which is laughed at is real. The media system is backward, just like the Bible.

If you see something over and over again, you feel that you are not normal unless you are like what you see, when in actuality you are doing well if you don't fit the image. The image is what is *not* normal.

As Atheists, our point is that the projection of what others desire that you should be or could be is not important. It is what you are and what you should or could do within the boundaries of what you are.

We urge you to investigate all opinions, but especially those that are laughed at. From these opinions form your own, tempered by your own common sense. In order to do that, you need a full menu of images, each presented equally. This brings us right back to freedom of speech or the freedom to enlarge that menu.

In order for those enlargements to be treated seriously, we must break the projected image of what is desired and present what is, so that we can pick what we desire on an individual basis. An open forum of ideas and opinions is the basis for a rational society. There is no place for religion as special in such a forum.

We are capable of picking what is good for ourselves. We need only have a wide-open selection from which to choose.

A Few Who Understand

May 1979

Once upon a time, a group of old and wise men who belonged to a very special class thought that they would change the order of things in a way no one ever thought of before. They were members of a planters and landowners class and were well-educated and had plenty of free time to pursue ideas. They knew that until their time, people had always been separated into the rulers and the ruled. There was no in-between. So they thought of what it would be like to split up the rulers into a wider group. And then give some of the non-rulers a say in what they would have the rulers do. With this notion, a new system called democracy was born.

These men also knew that the church had always held an honorary place in the ruler's circle. This new scheme would upset this honorary position of the church, giving them more rulers to try to influence. They knew that the clergy would not fit in their new system. Their only function had been to support whatever the rulers wanted by getting the people to obey. If the people were to be free to submit suggestions to the rulers, the church must not be allowed to put them in their place of only being permitted to follow. That would not fit in the new system.

Thus, the wise men excluded the church from their new system. Oneness of mind could not be solicited in a system that depended on a variety of input, from which input the rulers could rule.

Now, this system was not the best, but it did give the people the first voice they ever had in the doings of the rulers. It was better than no voice.

It worked fine at first.

But as the years passed, the church began to feel uncomfortable in its new position. It was not needed anymore. The church knew then that it had to make things the way they were before the new system began.

So, for many years now the church has tried to regain its place as keeper of the people, even though the rulers intended not to have the people kept any longer. If the church regained its position, the people would no longer be free to speak to the rulers and the system would not work.

But still the church tried, and as it tried, some of the people realized what it was doing: that it was trying to convince the rulers to go back to the old system. And the rulers were beginning to listen.

So these people knew that if the church was not stopped, all the people would lose their input to the rulers.

These few people who understood had to ask the rulers to keep their promise and stick to the new system as they had set it up.

Unfortunately for them, the church could whisper in the ears of the rulers all the time, but they could not reach the rulers except as they were allowed.

Since the church had more time and more direct access to the rulers, the rulers listened to them first.

If you can only talk to someone once a year and your opponent can talk to him every day, your opponent can get his idea over first to the person you both wish to influence.

In order to have a fighting chance, you must have the same chance to present your ideas.

The few are making a very simple request. It is complicated, however, by the fact that only a very small number of people are making it. The majority of the people want to go back to the old way before the system changed. They do not want a say anymore. The few people must convince all the rest that it is important to have a say to the rulers and that they must help get the church out of the way of their having that say.

We hope that you, like us few people, want a say, too. That is why we appeal to you each month to help us to convince other people and to help enlist the aid of one group of rulers to talk to the others.

We must keep the best system that we have ever had. People must continue to be heard by the rulers. This is very hard to do. It is much easier to fix one system than to build a whole new one.

We are trying to fix our system of government, because we feel that it is worth fixing.

The People Need to Be Told

June 1979

Our Constitution has weathered many a battle over the past 200 years over issues such as slavery, women's rights, alcoholic beverages, business conglomerates, and the right to vote. But none has been so fierce as that with the forces of organized religion. Since the inception of our nation, when the founding fathers saw fit to set a world precedent by kicking the church out of state affairs, organized religion has tried to oil its way back into its favored position reminiscent of monarchies gone by.

The latest barrage unveiled in Washington this month may be the turning point in the war.

We now have a newly-registered Washington lobby. It's called "Christian Voice," and if the mean name is not enough to send Jefferson reeling in his grave, it states a purpose of promoting "Christian morality" in government by dedicating itself to "turning the nation toward Christian principles." The group plans to promote legislation and candidates who advocate "Christian morality" through "television and thousands of pulpits."

The group eventually plans to give money to candidates deemed worthy on the basis of their Christianity. They also plan to issue a monthly "legislative alert" to their network of clergymen, along with congressional voting records on "moral issues."

The governing board of "Christian Voice" is composed of four U.S. senators and eleven representatives. Their names are: Sens. Orrin Hatch (R-Utah), Gordon Humphrey (R-New Hampshire), Roger Jepsen (R-Iowa), and James McClure (R-Idaho); Reps. Dan Crane (R-Illinois), William Dannemeyer (R-California), Bob Dornan (R-California), George Hansen (R-Idaho), James Jeffries (R-Kansas), Tom Kindness (R-Ohio), Marvin Leath (D-Texas), Trent Lott (R-Mississippi), Larry McDonald (D-Georgia), Warren Paul (R-Texas), and Floyd Spence (R-South Carolina).

Their religious spokesman is the Rev. Robert G. Grant, and their legislative director is Gary Jarmin, former legislative director for the American Conservative Union.

The group says it plans to spend $3 million initially ($1 million on television alone) to organize. It has opened up its assault by attacking television sex and violence, the abortion movement, pornography, the Supreme Court ban on prayer in public schools, and the lack of administration support for the white minority in Zimbabwe-Rhodesia.

It estimates that fifty to seventy-five million Americans are fundamentalist Christians.

The most stunning aspect of the emergence of such a lobby group is that part of their stated purpose is in direct violation of Department of Internal Revenue code. Section 501 (c) (3) of that code prohibits "political or legislative activity" on the part of tax-exempt organizations. Yet, "Christian Voice" is asking thousands of clergymen to use their pulpits for such prohibited activity and is even providing them with the information to do so. In short, they are urging clergymen all across the country to violate the law. Every church group participating in such activities should by all means be stripped of that which keeps them in business — their tax-exempt status.

Let's look for a moment at some of the things they are against.

The abortion movement. We can't feed or find adequate fuel for the population we now have, but as long as they are Christian and someday will vote, bring on the babies. The mother's health or wishes need not enter into the picture. After all, all she has to do is go along with the pregnancy. Without Christian lobby groups, where would all of those loyal abortion clinic torchers go for the opportunity to be let off the hook by a loyal public official?

Television sex and violence. If you can't learn about sex on television or in the schools, where do you go for information? To the streets where venereal disease is nearly epidemic and unwanted pregnancy is a continuing tragedy? Or to the church, with their absurd morals that were unfit for human use 2,000 years ago, and today only serve to promote sexual maladjustment. We must save our children from television violence — then indoctrinate them in the religion that has caused more bloodshed than any other!

Pornography. If you think dirty pictures are fun, try reading the story of Lot. The Bible would make Anita Bryant's hair turn white if she ever read all of it. Whatever happened to freedom of speech? Does that only apply to that which is spoken from the pulpit?

Banned prayer in the public schools. The Supreme Court thought it had settled this issue in 1963. Ever since the ruling, though, the religious community has tried to worm its way back in. Meditation, released time, distribution of Bibles, required "brotherhood week" assemblies, required assemblies for speeches by converted convicts, and a series of other backdoor approaches have plagued the nation's school system, most recently in the Helms Amendment in the Senate and the Walker Amendment in the House. The church realizes how important snaring the children is. The Jesuits say it best: "Give me a child until he is six and I've got him."

Last, but not least, **against majority rule in Rhodesia**. This gives our conservatives a chance to speak out on events in another country when, in reality, they are opposing the very basis of our own government. I don't know what they call denial of self-government rights to persons on the basis of their color, but I call it racism.

It's hard to believe that our nation has come to this from a foundation on the principle of separation of state and church. Faced with such a new and massive attack on our Constitution, we must remember one important fact: the "people" do not want a "Christian" nation, *they are being told they want a "Christian" nation*! Those are two very different things.

Each month we at The American Atheist Center try to emphasize this. The "people" need to be told — if indeed they must be told at all — to want something else besides mental slavery. We try to do that each month with each issue of the magazine. The continuation and broadening of that effort becomes ever more imperative with this newest advance by the forces against freedom of the mind.

A Challenge

July 1979

The position of Atheism as a viable lifestyle alternative is unique among *causes celebres* in America. Unique because it is rooted in a freedom that is the prerequisite of those around which other causes have grown. That is: freedom of the mind.

Unique as this aspect of Atheism may be, however, the cause surrounding it holds certain similarities in store in terms of pitfalls for those who espouse it. These pitfalls rest historically upon the shoulders of the cause leadership. Their duty is to place before society a new concept for expansion of the allowable limits of activity or expression. These notions are opposed (as all change is opposed) initially. The cause leader must bear the indignity of being for that which the majority is against, and must stick that position out to the end result of its acceptance by the whole. This tenacity must be uncompromising.

If the cause leaders allow any majority dissatisfaction, in whatever form it may take, to sway them from their position, they have lost it at that point. Should they give any credence to the opposition, it would evidence their weakness. Should they compromise their technique, it would evidence weakness. Should they agree on collateral issues with the opposition, ignoring even for a moment their faulty premise, the cause is disserviced. Should personal discomfort force the leader into lessening the pursuit of the ideal, the ideal is lost.

Few have the determination necessary for such a career. Those who do act alone act partially out of the lack of dedication in others, but mostly out of a desire not to form a tie that could hold future interference with the cause as a trump card. This solitude of purpose is often labeled as dogmatism or elitism or as undemocratic.

Worst of all is the fact that a great deal of the labeling, negativism, and pessimism thrown in the path of the leader is thrown by those they lead. This unfortunate fact is caused by the failure of followers to understand that any cause leader is pleading a case of first impression to the world. He stands for what has not been stood for before. He champions the unchampionable.

Nature itself evidences a system of evolution where the mutation is the catalyst for the required change to perpetuate the species. Causes provide that mutation for the evolution of thought. Cause leaders are the first to evidence the change that all will come to embrace. Their precocity breeds their opposition. What others fail to understand or find strange they resist, not realizing the benefit of ideas strange at present, but common in the future.

Given, then, the experimental nature of the beast, cause leaders fail as experiments fail. Each failure brings another experiment to determine the cause of that failure and to continue until success is realized. In nature, many mutations must die before the most sturdy remains. Thus successions of leaders are needed to perpetuate the experiment to fruition.

Every cause shares the failing of not recognizing this chain. A single, fearless, uncompromising leader is a necessity. But an irreplaceable one is dangerous. The chain of experimenters must remain unbroken until the goal is realized. The chain is only as good, however, as its weakest link.

We encourage Atheists to come out of the closet. That mere act is only the beginning. For those who come out of the closet today are the potential leaders of tomorrow — leaders needed to maintain the chain, with each link growing fainter until the end disappears into the commonplace.

I am asked many times by religionists what the purpose of life without god is. I know that purpose now: *to strive to meet the qualifications to become a link in the chain of freedom.*

Ida Husted Harper, in her biography of Susan B. Anthony, lays those qualifications out as follows:

> During the fifty years which have wrought a revolution, just one woman in all the world has given every day of her time, every dollar of her money, every power of her being, to secure this result. She was impelled to this work by no personal grievance, but solely through a deep sense of the injustice which, on every side, she saw perpetrated against her sex, and which she determined to combat. Never for one short hour has the cause of woman been forgotten or put aside for any other object. Never a single tie has been formed, either of affection or business, which would interfere with this supreme purpose. Never a speech has been given, a trip taken, a visit made, a letter written, in all this half-century, that has not been done directly in the interest of this one object.

> In those years of constant aggression, when every step was an experiment, there must have been mistakes. . . . Future generations will read [her history] through tears, and will wonder what manner of people those were who not only permitted this woman to labor for humanity fifty years, almost unaided, but also compelled her to beg or earn the money with which to carry on her work. . . . Let it be remembered that . . . Miss Anthony was in advance of public sentiment . . . and that the radicalism which we reject today may be conservatism at which we will wonder tomorrow.

I challenge you to meet those qualifications. Your freedom depends on it.

The Cancer of Religion

August 1979

The American people have always, in the melting pot environment of our nation, been imbued with patriotism. To some extent, this has been so more than any other nation in the recent historical past. It is that melting pot nature of our country that has led to the individual need for a common bond beyond that of ancestral pride. Religion in America has also faced the unification challenge among a diverse people. Unlike the rallying point of the flag, a pledge, a slogan, a motto, or a uniform, the church has gathered its flock around common icons and sacred words.

A Marine dress uniform symbolizes pride in the United States. The flag symbolizes a unification of states under a common governmental principle. The pledge to that flag speaks of unification for the common good. The national motto (prior to 1954), *E Pluribus Unum* (out of many, one), spoke of the unification of diverse peoples. Our currency carried that Latin banner of unification into every home and business.

A cross, however, symbolizes personal salvation, the route to escape personal torment. A statue of Jesus Christ points your way to personal happiness through a personal relationship. The Christian doctrine of imputation is a selfish one. The savior imputes his personal goodness to you, not to your neighbor. You must have a deep personal faith in this transfer of goodness, as in the transubstantiation of wafer into flesh and wine to blood. Or, as in the effect of the voodoo artist's pin, personal faith is of the utmost importance. God is responsive to your individual needs. He (or she) is omnipotent, able to respond to all personal situations at the same time. The Bible is your personal guide through life. It is open to your interpretation, generating denominationalism.

What have we, then, with the union of a philosophy of self-preservation with a government based on unification and cooperation? We have two inimical systems struggling for control. Democracy speaks to the whole; theocracy speaks to the salvation of the individual. How, then, can the churches survive within a host nation of mutually exclusive goals? They can capture unification symbolism to weaken the catalyzing of democracy, implanting their self-centered salvation symbols wherever they can.

Our national motto is now "In God We Trust." No longer is it "out of many, one." A solution to human problems out of many minds working together has now become one omnipotent solution — take it or leave it. We pledge not to "one nation, indivisible," but to "one nation, under God." The combined strength of the people has been replaced by the false security of faith in a single power. Our currency proclaims a devotion to subjugation for personal salvation. The collective power of many minds is no longer good enough. We must be "one nation" trusting in one "God." Trusting one "God," we can survive.

Our children were led each day, captive, in salute to their personal salvation in public schools. The challenge to that was successful, but now Congress is encouraging that practice to be renewed.

All along this road, while democracy stood weakened day by day, the Atheist stood by and said: "That can't hurt"; "Who cares about a phrase on our money?"; "A little prayer can't hurt"; "The pledge doesn't bother me; I never say it anymore anyway"; "Christian symbols are *insignificant*." I hear these statements every day, while the cancer of religion eats away at its host democracy. I don't hear them from the religious community. It knows the value of symbols. The churches capture them while we sleep. When we finally awaken, the damage has been done.

We are always too little, too late, reacting to what we perceive in hindsight as the *inevitable* initiative of religion. After the blow has been struck we act in defense or not at all. Religion implants its symbols into prominence first and then defends them from objection. If you value the sword with which you maintain your liberty, don't give it over to be implanted in the stone. We have fought for reversal of precedent, when we should be establishing our own.

As an Atheist, I refuse to be responsible for the consequences of losing a principle to the egotistical hand of religion. I prefer to maintain already sound principles and to move, through offensive action, toward the establishment of new ones. Former President John F. Kennedy summed it up in a very famous phrase, "Ask not what your country can do for you, but what you can do for your country." Even from a Roman Catholic, the theme of unification rings true. Hang in there, for the here and now, for all of us. The nation needs every head it can get, and the more independent the better. Through its preservation of independence of mind, Atheism is the keeper of liberty in each of us. If you've got it, flaunt it. The melting pot has runneth over for the Christians alone for too long.

Atheist Paranoia vs. Empty Pews

September 1979

As a spokesperson for American Atheism on a national level, I have occasion to travel extensively. I have been involved with the media in almost every major city in the United States. As I meet groups of Atheists in each of these cities, I meet with a recurring theme which says something about the position of Atheism in America. That theme usually comes out in a statement like, "You had better watch what you say in this town; this is the Bible Belt," or, "You are in the buckle of the Bible Belt; we have a lot of fanatics here."

These quotes just don't happen where stereotype dictates. You would expect such a reaction in the "Deep South" land of Alabama, Mississippi, Georgia, or Louisiana. This area has been characterized over and over again as backward, uneducated, and a breeding ground for prejudice. The "sophisticated" East of New York, Washington, Newark, Boston, Philadelphia, and the like have been billed as above discrimination.

Where am I told I am in the Bible Belt? In "sophisticated" New York, "liberal" Los Angeles, "flowerchild-anything-goes" San Francisco, "bed-rock-middle-America" St. Louis and Kansas City, "corporations-only-count" Dallas. . . . The Deep South and the mountains of Virginia, Kentucky and Tennessee never enter into the picture.

What this points out is that Atheists everywhere feel that they, wherever they are, are in the middle of the worst organized religion has to offer. They see the church surrounding them in every direction like some blob out of a late night horror rerun. They are terrorized by every new church that goes up in town, driven further and further into the closet until they may never again see life not framed by a coathanger.

Although I feel that a great deal of the closet nature of Atheists is needless paranoia, they do have a point. Organized religion is on the move with an unprecedented fury, or so it seems. What fearful Atheists don't realize is that what they see as a move by all the churches to swallow them up is only a move by a very few. The evangelicals make noise to fit twice their size. With the help of slick ad agencies and religious radio and TV station owners, they can blow up god much bigger than he has ever been blown up before.

While the evangelicals howl, the mainline churches sit in dismay at empty pews and schisms. They are split over such issues as women in the clergy, homosexuality, abortion, relations with Israel, and interpretation of doctrine. They have much more to worry about internally than just spreading the word. Remember, only one out of every four Americans attends church regularly. There are over 91 million persons in our population who have never even entered a church. In that total population of some 105 million churchgoers (that is, assuming church figures only after deducting the 18 percent puffing they do according to the U.S. Census Bureau), average attendance is three to five times a year — usually on major religious holidays.

What the Atheists must realize is that the church is just as scared of them as they are of the church. Organized churches in America know the statistics as well as we do. They know how many persons no longer believe or have become disenchanted with particular doctrines and no longer attend. They know how many closet Atheists and agnostics exist across the country. They are scared of the horrible fact that some day those Atheists are going to come out of their hibernation and realize they are not alone and put an end to religion once and for all. They also know that if they can keep them in their closet and make sure they don't let others know that they are similarly negative toward religion, the churches are safe.

As long as Atheists continue to feel that they are alone and fail to come out even enough to let their family and close personal acquaintances know of their distaste for religion, the church will continue its course unimpeded. If Atheists will identify themselves, they will find that others will identify as well. This is what the church is afraid of.

Identification and organization are the key concepts for Atheists toward the downfall of organized religion. If you identify yourself as an Atheist and then organize with others who have done the same, you can easily keep religious dictates and moral patterns out of your life. If you don't identify, you can't.

Religion has always taught the following:

[1] Your worthlessness as an individual — you must be part of the whole, one of god's children.

[2] The futility of individual effort — you must have god as your copilot in life.

[3] The necessity of giving up those things that you enjoy as a human being for an opportunity at life after death — you give up a list of every human and pleasurable endeavor as "sins" as the purchase price for life after death in a never-never land.

[4] Apathy for the world of here and now — concern only for the ephemeral.

[5] Predestination — you cannot change the present to make the future better because the future is already made.

The opposition, *in an organized manner*, to these ideas has been seriously deficient. Countless *individuals* have come to the conclusion that these are not good concepts for human behavior, but they have failed to gain the needed support to do something about them. We must all realize that we are not alone in our distaste for these concepts. Others, too, are of like mind. We must speak out, so that they can find us, ally with us, and generate an organized resistance movement.

American Atheists has initiated that step. It is now up to all of you out there to cast aside your coathanger manacles and join in the fight. You have nothing to fear. Religion has more to fear from a freed mind actively engaged in resistance than it does from all the empty pews in the world.

Goals

October 1979

Looking at the American Atheist movement today, one would think that American Atheists was but one organization in a succession of groups, each building upon the victories of the former. That is, however, not the case. The history of "freethought" movements in the United States has been one of disorganization; a group here and a group there, often with mediocre leadership and always rent with internal schisms over "policy" matters. Each little enclave of free-thinkers (or whatever nomenclature they cared to apply to themselves) worked independently for some small redress for a particular grievance. The majority of these grievances were violations of the Constitutional doctrine of separation of state and church. The entire notion of coming out directly against god or religious teaching was a bit too much for early groups.

We have now, with American Atheists, become more outspoken in identifying ourselves as Atheists, but have we gained ground on the separation issues that these diverse groups have labored on for so long? The answer is no. If anything, we are worse off today. Though better organized, we have still failed to accomplish some of the fundamental repairs required to keep the wall of separation of state and church from crumbling.

Back in 1874, one of the early freethought groups known as the Free Religious Association sprang out of efforts to amend the Constitution to include religious phrases, as well as efforts to place the words "In God We Trust" on the coins. These sound like current issues, don't they? But the roots of controversies such as these have run deep in American politics for years. This group had as its objective to propound a religion of humanity, guided by reason, and to provide an organization for those who did not wish to remain with diverse sectarian Christian groups. In January of 1874, the group published a list of demands designed to restore the Constitutional doctrine of separation of state and church to working order. Those demands were:

[1] We demand that churches and other ecclesiastical property shall no longer be exempt from taxation.

[2] We demand that the employment of chaplains in Congress, in state legislatures, in the navy and militia, and in prisons, asylums, and all other institutions supported by public money shall be discontinued.

[3] We demand that all public appropriations for sectarian educational and charitable institutions shall cease.

[4] We demand that all religious services now sustained by government shall be abolished; and especially that the use of the Bible in the public schools, whether ostensibly as a textbook or avowedly as a book of religious worship, shall be prohibited.

[5] We demand that the appointment by the President of the United States or by the governors of the various states of all religious festivals and fasts shall wholly cease.

[6] We demand that the judicial oath in the courts and all other departments of the government shall be abolished, and that simple affirmation under the pains and penalties of perjury shall be established in its stead.

[7] We demand that all laws directly or indirectly enforcing the observance of Sunday as the Sabbath shall be repealed.

[8] We demand that all laws looking to the enforcement of "Christian" morality shall be abrogated, and that all laws shall be conformed to the requirements of natural morality, equal rights and impartial liberty.

[9] We demand that, not only in the constitutions of the United States and of the several states but also in practical administration of the same, no privilege or advantage shall be conceded to Christianity or any other special religion; that our entire political system shall be founded and administered on a purely secular basis; and that whatever changes shall prove necessary to this end shall be consistently, unflinchingly, and promptly made.

Each of these demands is still of concern today. Each is a must for the eventual restitution of separation of state and church to the United States. Let's take a look at each of them.

[1] *Tax Exempt Status of Churches*

After 109 years of struggle, churches in America are still exempt on their personal incomes, incomes from non-related business, interest on stock, bonds, and investments, sales tax, personal property, and even license fees for their vehicles.

In 1977, the Internal Revenue Service estimated their total cash donations at some 16.4 billion dollars a year. That was 46 percent of all charitable giving in 1977, all tax-free. Are we better off than in 1874? Hardly.

Not only does organized religion still hold its exempt status, but it has refused to disclose to anyone — even the government itself — the extent of its holdings. A battle is currently raging in Michigan over the issue of church disclosure of nontaxable holdings. The state is losing the battle there. The Internal Revenue Service itself demanded that churches begin to report as of January 1978. They refused, as a bloc, to do so — and the IRS could do nothing about it.

[2] *Chaplains in Congress and Other Institutions*

They are still there. In the Senate and the House both, the chaplains have just received a salary increase to $33,000 and $50,000 respectively. This is your taxpayer money going into direct aid to religion. Chaplains not only remain in the U.S. Congress, but they open the sessions of most state legislatures as well — all on taxpayer money.

[3] *Appropriations to Sectarian Institutions*

Parochial schools in many states are currently receiving tax funds for books, tuition, transportation, and teachers' salaries. Parochial hospitals receive federal funds from the Hill-Burton Act. Church child care centers receive governmental assistance. Year after year the churches receive more than the Pentagon. All from your tax monies, whether you care to support their work or not.

[4] *Government Supported Religious Services*

Religious services still take place in the White House and all over the nation's capital during religious holidays and patriotic events. Prayer breakfasts are a common occurrence now in most governmental offices on federal, state, and local levels.

Bible reading and prayer recitation in the public schools were ended by the *Murray v. Curlett* decision of 1963. But still the schools continue with a series of church-inspired noncompliance measures concerned with that decision.

[5] *Government Appointed Religious Festivals and Fasts*

Both presidents Nixon and Ford and now President Carter call for national days of fasting and prayer. Governors cry out to their god for salvation from natural disasters in their states. Official governmental policy in the Middle East rests on the proposition that Israel exists to fulfill Bible prophecy. The overall piousness of our national leadership has increased dramatically. We now have an official Washington lobby called Christian Voice, dedicated to the election of evangelical candidates to high public office.

[6] *Oaths in the Courts and Departments of Government*

In every court in the nation thousands of persons each day still are sworn in under the phrase "So help me God." Only in the case of the leadership of American Atheists has this pattern been broken. Many Atheists still take such an oath, preferring not to rock the boat or prejudice a judge or jury. Elected officials are sworn in on the Bible on a daily basis.

[7] *Sabbath Laws*

Sunday closing laws still are in force in every state of the Union. In Texas, for example, one cannot buy any of a particular list of items on a Sunday, while other items remain on sale. Differentiation is made between good and bad inanimate objects that can or cannot be purchased on Sunday. Sound like a dream out of the Middle Ages? It is as real as your corner store on any Sunday. We still practice taboos, today, in the twentieth century.

[8] *Christian Morality Laws*

Karen Quinlan, who was little more than a vegetable, was kept attached to machines designed for the artificial prolongation of life because "Christian morality" dictated that she could not be allowed to die. A *doctor* performing an abortion, even to save a mother's life, is *charged with murder*. Magazines with nude photography are banned and their owners are faced with prison terms.

[9] *The Secular Founding and Administration of Government*

The constitutions of the states of Texas, North Carolina, Arkansas, Mississippi, and South Carolina contain provisions prohibiting the holding of public office by any person who denies the existence of god. Many state constitutions have religious mottoes or preambles, or contain no mention of guaranteed religious liberty.

In summary, we stand in the same position as that of 109 years ago. Why? Because we have been divided against ourselves. Each group fights from a different angle for the same objective: freedom *from* religion. Freedom from religion and government neutrality with respect to religion redounds to the benefit of everyone.

Women face the church as their primary enemy. They must be free from the system of thought that inspires their lack of equality, yet they fight for their liberty within the church, that institution which has led in its denial. Blacks have been kept on their knees by the church which condoned their servitude, yet their leadership leads them to freedom through the church. The Mexican-American community that has suffered at the hand of Mother Rome for generations works for freedom through church leadership. All these groups can benefit from Freedom from Religion as well. Do they help?

It's like the old fable of the little red hen. No one would help her in each process leading up to the finished product, a loaf of bread, but all were ready to help her eat it after it was made.

Freedoms are important, but some are more important than others. You must free the mind first, before it can work to free the body. Freedom from religion is freedom for the mind. Whatever particular thing you're for, be for that which makes all of them come true — an uninhibited mind. Atheism can set you free to involve yourself in a number of freedom struggles, but the battle of the mind must be won first. Let's cooperate for that.

The Right of Reason

November 1979

Whenever you hear a news media event coming out of the American Atheist Center, it is usually associated with our founder, Dr. Madalyn O'Hair. The most common phrase associated with her is: "The most hated woman in America." The news media delights in zeroing in on those who hate her as the symbol of Atheism in America.

Americans have been winners, for the most part, since our victory against King George in the American Revolution. Americans work to win, play to win, love to win, and hate to lose (or even come in second place). Most events are clear-cut in their minds. You either win or you lose. If you win, you are right; if you lose, you are wrong. Circumstances around winning or losing mean little to the general public. The medias know this and they cater to it daily.

Other students may hate the person who gets the A, but they learn to respect him with time. Such is the case also with Atheism. The religious community hates us now, but they will respect us in the future.

At present, however, that hate is played upon in the press. They focus on it to the exclusion of the circumstances we face as Atheists. They focus on it as our number one problem. Hate is the problem of the person who holds that emotion, not the object of the emotion. Hating takes energy, lots of energy. You must actively participate in hating someone or something. That emotion must take the place of other emotions and other thoughts. In fact, the thought process works at a disadvantage with emotion in general and hate in particular. Taking into account that thought has little or nothing to do with religion, one can see why hate comes easily to the religious. History can testify to the hate of religion, by the religious, for other religions. The Crusades are but one small example. From combat between nations to individual pugilism, religion has fostered hate in all of its many forms.

Do we, as Atheists, in turn make hate such a large part of our day? I don't think so. First, we have no denominationalism to generate hate. You are either an Atheist or a theist. Second, we operate on an intellectual basis. Therefore, we have intellectual contempt for things that we feel do not make sense, but we do not hate them. A computer does not hate an insoluble equation; it merely does not compute. As an Atheist, theists do not compute for me. They present something that does not yield to logic, so I have an intellectual contempt for them as an insoluble problem. I would like to solve their problem, but as of now I cannot. Perhaps you could call this frustration, but surely not hate.

I am not a follower of cycle theories, such as the assassination of a U.S. president every so many years. I do, however, recognize patterns of events that have led to behavior that was detrimental in the past. The behavior of those who are religious forms a pattern, as do relations between state and church. Both church and state always have a way of getting around to violence as a means of settling disputes. Intellectual settlements are aimed for, worked for, sought after, over long periods of time. When they fail, the same old solution is always at hand — violence.

When intellectual disputes turn into emotional disputes, emotion must be able to realize itself. It does so in the form of violence. If someone will not listen to you over a period of time, you feel that the only recourse left is to make him listen to physical violence. You have all experienced this as a child or parent. Since one's physical stamina is enhanced by one's emotion, the emotional person usually wins these conflicts. As emotion wins more and more conflicts with rationalism, people begin to see the value (if they like to win) of turning to emotion first. Instead of using violence brought on by emotion to win, after rationality fails, just skip the rationality and go straight for the emotion.

Religious thinking has followed these lines very well: abandon rationality, rely on emotionalism, and get to violence via a shortcut. In the end, the number of disputes settled by violence so far outnumbers the number settled by reason that violence becomes the in-vogue way to win. And remember, Americans love to win.

The increasing incidence of violence is alarming. Abortion clinics are firebombed. Hundreds are slaughtered in the Middle East. Blacks and Ku Klux Klan members are at each other's throats. Each group involved thinks it has won, and has won more quickly because it took the direct route. No negotiations, just violence.

Where does it all stop? It stops with the realization that you can win through reason. Human problems can be solved through applied intelligence. That is not to say that emotion does not have its place. It does, and it is a necessity. As a problem-solver, however, it has no place. Time-tested logical methods of arriving at solutions are the answer.

We, as Atheists, must lead the way in showing everyone that one can win with reason. Once you assume an emotional basis to your life, you will always be prone to violence on an unpredictable level. Reason must come first. If we cannot show people how to win with reason, the continuation of emotion and the violence it generates will bring us down. Emotion — hate, if you will — will find Atheism as its first target, since Atheism, as life through reason, is the death of the undesirable side of emotion.

Make it a point to demonstrate to all around you that you can win against the problems of life through reason. The more of us they can see doing it, the sooner they will be convinced that their emotional dogma is letting them win the easy way now, but the hard way in the future. Demonstrate how easy it is for them to use their heads first and spare their broken hearts.

And Not to Entertain

December 1979

As my media involvement on behalf of American Atheism expands I find within myself a growing resentment toward the way media celebrities handle not alone Atheists, but the proponents of many "causes."

Entertainment has its place on the screen and on the airways, but it is now rapidly overstepping the dictates of balanced programming by moving into the educational sector. A pretty face is now far more valuable than a sharp, inquiring, and — above all — an impartial, objective, mind. Talk shows change hosts as often as producers change underwear. Why?

There are three answers to that question. First, a movement exists in our country today dedicated to the making of "fun" out of education as a primary goal of education itself. The most dramatic example of this is the controversy over "math-trauma." This is the notion that a supposedly complicated or "hard" subject such as mathematics can traumatize a child if it is forced on him in a learning situation. It is, therefore, argued that math must be presented "gently" and "pastorally" so as not to induce a reaction on the part of the student — a drawing back from it.

There is nothing either gentle or harsh about the multiplication table. It must be memorized as one of the essential factual conventions of mathematics. Structure is neither gentle nor harsh *per se*, so neither is any structured system of data analysis such as math or the scientific method. Gravity, after all, is "structured." It is also "dogmatic," as is often said of math. But there is nothing emotionally frightening about facts or systems of analyzing facts.

Facts are facts, regardless of any emotion that man engenders in respect to how they are presented. The emotion does nothing to change the facts. Presentation of factual materials must be made — let the emotional chips fall where they may. This is particularly true in journalism of any kind.

There is, unfortunately, a changing standard. The media now takes into account the reaction to a statement, with more weight on that reaction than on the statement itself. To the proponent of a cause this makes a presentation particularly hard. Virtually any minority viewpoint, as all cause viewpoints axiomatically are, stirs up emotion.

The medias are currently experiencing pickets and boycotts on this very issue. Why boycott advertising over an emotional response to the presentation of an ongoing factual situation?

Must we be entertained by serious life situations in lieu of facing them? If the Christian community has its way, we will. It intends to prevent the airing of anything that upsets the "emotions" of the Christians. Emotion is, of course, the foundation of faith. I, for one, am not willing to be entertained by human problems, to wait for some after-life solutions. Escaping from real situations is no solution. They must be recognized, defined, and dealt with. The media are primary vehicles for this. We need to keep media personalities who confront major issues, instead of bringing them down to entertainment levels.

Secondly, the media tries to appeal to mediocrity. Why? Because the American people are mediocre. They identify with mediocrity. A good example is the following repeated scenario. A talk show host invites an expert in some field or with some point of view onto his (usually the host is a male) show. The host then makes the guest lower himself (or herself) to the level of the most ignorant, badgering member of the audience, all under the baner of "freedom of speech." The underlying premise is that "Everyone is entitled to their *[sic]* own opinion." or "My opinion is as good as your opinion."

This is just not the case. When a guest has been involved in the research, delineation, and promulgation of a particular point of view, he has superior knowledge in that area — beyond one who has a spur-of-the-moment opinion in a talk show audience. The opinion of anyone in the audience, however, is given priority by the host over that of the guest. One's right to say something, however, does not lend any validity to the statement.

Yet, the right is used as an excuse to downgrade the opinion of the expert. The emphasis is placed on an emotional and momentary interest in the subject, not a lasting understanding or appreciation of it. In the specific case of Atheism, we have been viewed as an oddity — something momentarily unique, or someone expressing something concerning which the audience may exercise its curiosity. The educational value of the position of Atheism is never allowed to surface — only the entertainment value of it.

Why must everything have an entertainment value? Because entertainment, as religion, puts off the facing of essential issues. If one does not face life because one is waiting for death, why face problems when one can be entertained by them?

The two aspects of the media go hand in hand. Escape from reality is promoted. If one can make an oddity out of something substantial, one can pass judgment on it casually, like one passes on reality to opt for god ideas.

If a show appeals to the mediocre, it stays; if it confronts real issues, it goes.

There is a third attitude of the media which is the personalization of issues, again to avoid dealing with them.

When the Pope came to the United States he was heralded by the news media as a "humanitarian." All coverage focused on his *media-invented* "personality." No one looked at the doctrines he presented or what he actually represented. His call was a call to a dying church to regroup and circle the wagons. It was a call to return to the most conservative of Roman Catholic Church doctrines, a reliance on the fundamental principles of Catholicism to withstand the continued onslaught of progress, the enemy of the church.

What the Pope may or may not be as a person has absolutely nothing to do with his role of perpetuator of the traditional Roman Catholic doctrine. However, I prefer to refer to him as the Pimp of Peace, for he has the same function as any ordinary pimp. He gathers together and sells momentary relief through his agents, with no concern for the long-term effects of coping with human sexuality — as in the case of any pimp. Overtly, as the pimp, he is a kindness merchant doling out pleasure. Covertly, he undermines the position of women, human sexuality and equality, as well as self-worth.

It makes a great deal of difference whether one looks at the personality or the issue. Some of the most outgoing, dynamic personalities in the world have espoused some of the most repressive doctrines.

Sister Teresa, an underserving Nobel Prize winner, trades the goodness of her compassion for the poor for their unconditional surrender of their minds to Roman Catholicism as a prerequisite for receipt of aid. Consistently, I maintain — as an Atheist — that goodness can be offered without the religion. Let us look, with the media, at Sister Teresa as a person.

The same logic is applied in reverse to a sane, non-repressive ideology such as Atheism. Concentrate on the personalities who espouse Atheism, and one can skirt its value. My personal feeling or reaction to Atheism has no bearing on its superiority as an intellectual position.

In summary, the duty of the news media in the United States should be that of delineating the facts and giving a neutral presentation. An interviewer should not argue with a guest, but simply solicit the basic facts of the guest's position.

In view of this, it is imperative that Atheism gain control of its own portion of the airways (as has the Christian community) to put forth its ideas completely to be judged on their own merits rather than on the basis of collateral considerations, such as entertainment value, appeal to the established order, mediocrity, or the personality of the exponents.

The *American Atheist* magazine in itself is a part of the outreach of American Atheism to exert control over the contents of its presentments. It is obvious that this outreach must be enlarged by our acquiring time blocks on the electronic media to bring to all our nation's citizens an unbiased, structured, intelligible message concerned with the fundamental tenets of Atheism.

You're "Out," Mrs. Johnson

January 1980

One of the most common areas of conflict in the arena of separation of state and church is that of civil rights vs. religion. A graphic example of this was played out in Utah last month. There, a good Mormon woman, Sonia Johnson, was excommunicated from her church for supporting the ERA and associating and working with those who favor its passage as an amendment to our Constitution.

Mrs. Johnson was tried by a Bishops' court of the Mormon church, according to internal church policy, and excommunicated. The outcry in Utah was that Mrs. Johnson's civil rights had been violated in that her church trial lacked any of the Constitutional guarantees of the right to face one's accusers, the right to counsel, *etc.* Critics failed to realize, however, that Mrs. Johnson gave up her rights under the Constitution when she entered into a church setting. Civil rights in a courtroom extend only to proceedings in courts operating under the control of some governmental branch of the city, county, state, or national jurisdiction. They do not extend into a Mormon Bishops' court.

Internal procedure within the confines of the doctrinal disciplining of any church is its own business. If one chooses to belong to a particular church one comes under the jurisdiction of the rules and regulations of that church. The Mormon church did nothing "illegal" when it tried Mrs. Johnson (it being "immoral" would be another matter). It merely exercised its internal policy on the subject of women's rights. If Mrs. Johnson wished to remain within the church, she had the option of coming to terms with those internal policies.

The same would apply to the American Atheist organization. American Atheists is perfectly within its rights as a private membership organization (like the Mormon church) to expel anyone who comes into contradiction with its stated corporate aims and purposes. If, for example, Atheists expelled a born-again Christian from membership for practicing religious evangelism under the name of an Atheist organization, it would be perfectly within its rights.

Every religion, and for that matter, every church has a set of rules which are open for the inspection of anyone seeking admission to that religion or church. If one is not willing to remain within the spectrum of allowable activity set up by those rules, one does not join the religion (or the particular denomination thereof). Each world religion, historically, derives the boundaries of this spectrum of allowable activity within the church from its "holy" book, or whatever it deems to be the inspired word of its particular deity. Those activities, both mental and physical, that are allowable are then considered to be virtues. Those that are unallowable are sins.

It is essential to a church for human activities to be grouped into the allowable and nonallowable, or those things inside and outside of the spectrum of church dogma. Unless the spectrum is not only finite, but also a subset of allowable human activity in nature — then — sinning cannot be accomplished. Sin must exist in order for redemption to be possible. If everything one can do as a human being in one's natural environment is permissible, then there is no sin. Without sin, there is nothing from which to be redeemed or saved. The religion would then be useless. Rules for the game of religious life are set up to be broken so that a penalty can be levied and that penalty, in turn, can be absolved by a higher authority.

The ultimate penalty, of course, as in any game, is to be thrown out of the game, or excommunicated. The Mormon church had, in effect, two choices with Mrs. Johnson. It could penalize her so many yards in her rush for the goal of heaven or throw her out of the game altogether. It chose the latter.

Mrs. Johnson does not know how lucky she is for the choice. She is now officially a spectator at the Mormon game instead of a player. She is now one step closer to the position of an Atheist. An Atheist is a spectator to all religion, not just a particular team. Mrs. Johnson is likely to find a new church with a spectrum of allowable activity or rules that is wider, wide enough to encompass her position on the ERA.

Her excommunication, or being kicked out of the game, was an effective punishment of her only because she believed in the intrinsic value of staying in the game. As a player, the team effort for all the players to reach the goal of heaven was paramount. To a spectator, who sees the game as entertainment or "only a game," a player being thrown out is only a temporary lull in the action.

To an Atheist, religion has but an entertainment value. It is something at which to laugh. I can only hope that out of the church, Mrs. Johnson will learn to laugh also.

Within the game she was laboring under the illusion that civil rights had a place within the game structure. Just as any sporting event is irrelevant to human life, so is the game of religion. Real human concerns have no place within the rules of a game; there, the rules themselves are the only relevant elements.

What can we learn from all this? We learn just one more lesson on the point that one must examine any system of controls of human behavior before one subscribes to it. The most important decision one can make in life is the setting up of a system of rules to guide one's self along the way. The choice is between a self-made system which one tailors to one's own needs (tempered by the trial and error guidelines of all human, as well as one's personal, history) and a so-called "inspired" system that one accepts on faith. For my money, I choose the self-made one.

If one chooses a system ready-made, one must be prepared to be let down by it, for ready-made life-styles cannot grow with one; one must instead grow to fit the system. If one makes one's own system, modifying it as one grows, one never has to fear a situation outside of its bounds, for it has none. Don't box yourself in like Mrs. Johnson. Leave plenty of growing room; your mind needs it.

I don't know of any life-style with anymore growing room and self-control built into it than has Atheism. It's like the difference between living in a box or in an ever-expanding balloon.

Think about it.

What Do The Christers Want?
Born Again Insanity

February 1980

I see Iran as a mirror image of what the United States will look like in the year 2000 if the Christers have their way.

For what is it that the Swaggerts, the Bakkers, the Falwells, the Armstrongs, the Roberts, the Humbards, the Brights, the Helms-type U.S. senators want? Looking in that mirror, they all see a full-blown theocracy, a nation of born-againers, mentally stultified automatons, doing the will of "he who speaks for Christ" even as the Ayatollah now speaks for Allah.

They are, all of them, stumping for nothing else. Their time, efforts, and billions of dollars which they collect go for the single-minded goal of a "Christian nation, under god."

They want more than that, for the nation must respond not alone to god, but to god's word, as published by his spokesmen in authorized versions of the Holy Bible.

It is a horrible fate for the nation, that which is contemplated. For proof of this fact, I give you Iran. There, the Holy Book of the Muslim religion is the basis of all law, culture, religion, politics, and customs. Muhammad (A.D. 570-632), receiving communication (some believe actual dictation) through the angel Gabriel, an agent of the god, Allah, wrote the Koran, a compilation of a series of these revelations (114 suras). Just as we, in the United States, turn to the authority of the statutory laws, our constitution, encyclopedias, dictionaries, for statistics, guides, or authoritarian answers, the adherents of Islam (those whom we call Muslims) turn to their Holy Book, the Koran, as supreme universal authority for everything.

At one time in our history the Christers tried for a "Christian Amendment" to the Constitution. The attempt was to change the Preamble to the Constitution of the United States from:

We, the People of the United States, in order to form a more perfect union, establish justice, insure domestic tranquility. . . .

to:

We, the People of the United States, in order to acknowledge

Almighty God as the source of all authority and power in civil government, the Lord Jesus Christ as the ruler among the nations, and His will, revealed in the Holy Scriptures, as the Supreme Authority, in order to constitute a Christian government, form a more perfect union, establish justice, insure domestic tranquility. . . .

Currently, the Christers are urging politicians to give the Bible, specifically the New Testament word of Jesus Christ (Protestant version, please), equal value with other sources brought to the decision-making processes of our country, on international, state, county, even city level — to public schools (equal time for the creation theory), to the smallest governmental bodies (prayers in city councils). The "equal" weight, the Christers hope, will one day yield to the "superior" weight of the Bible.

In the President's Cabinet, there will be a new member: the Bible.

Let us look at a current problem.

The Ayatollah, from the viewpoint of the Muslims, their religion and its authority, the Koran, is acting rationally, consistently, and in accord with the desires of Allah. The Christers would have Carter weigh expert opinion on the rescue of the hostages — such as political expedience, our nation's stated principles, risks with military intervention, and the effect of economic sanctions — and after taking in all that data, go to the Bible and prayer "for the real guide," perhaps to the words of Jesus Christ, Luke 19:27:

But those mine enemies, which would not that I should reign over them, bring hither and slay them before me.

That kind of nonsense could lead to a nuclear war, the use of insanity against insanity, with each side convinced of its righteousness, each hoping its particular god will triumph.

Both governments would then follow a hallucination — divergent fables — yet give these systems of madness greater weight than logic, science, history, economics, world concerns.

What the Christers want will affect our people, all nations, the world — ultimately, all humanity.

The Christer is equivalent to one who is high on a hallucinogen. He sees a fire and believes it to be a brilliant red flower, touches it and burns his hand, then rejoices in the suffering as god's will. If only the Christer himself was hurt, this could possibly be excusable, but when a leader suffers from the bizarre hallucination of born-againism, we can expect, on a small scale, Jim Jones; on a large scale, the Ayatollah.

Particularly, we Atheists must all speak out. We must say to these self-appointed spokespersons for god — "You must be put in strait jacket." We cannot permit them to harm our democratic institutions for which we fought so long.

Danger flags are out. Several months ago, in a national speech, Carter warned of the "Atheist menace" in the world. On January 4th, speaking of Afghanistan, he said: "It is a deliberate effort of a powerful Atheist government to subjugate a Muslim people."

One would have thought that the Soviet bear had moved only for reasons of desiring to convert Afghanistan to Atheism.

If the Christers have their way, by the year 2000, the United States will be another Iran, the president will be similar to Khomeini, and the Bible will be the ultimate authority.

Atheism, in the face of this rising menace, pleads only one point: *religion is not relevant to human life*. It, its holy book, or any of its alleged prophets or leaders, cannot be considered in decision making. It is unhealthy for even a single person, alone affected by it, to turn to religion for solutions.

The only authorities we can trust are from reasonable human sources: a review of history, natural law, and laws of probability.

All their caterwauling to the contrary, the Christers must be at least ignored — at best, isolated — so that they cannot infect the populace with born-again insanity.

Comments on Losing The Ball Game

March 1980

Religion is moving to take over America. It is moving *now* and in great strength. With that movement will come the loss of virtually every freedom you now enjoy. There is nothing you can do about it but watch it happen — and you are to blame. If you, *as an Atheist,* had said something thirty years ago (or twenty, or ten, or five, or last year, or yesterday), religious forces could not do what they are doing today. You did not move. You sat and watched. You were cowards. Now, you must pay the price. You will pay now, and your children will pay later and will pay much, much more.

Religion is winning in several vital areas. Let's take a look at the four most important ones, one at a time.

(1) Prayer: The Congress, state legislatures, city councils and public schools all across the nation are opening with prayers. Federal and state employees are being forced to begin their workdays with prayer. Federal and state lands are being used for prayer sessions. All of these activities are unconstitutional according to the United States Supreme Court.

In *Murray v. Curlett* the Supreme Court held that "religious ceremonies" in public schools were unconstitutional since they violated the Establishment Clause of the First Amendment to the Constitution. There were two factors in this case. First was the compulsory nature of school attendance. Since penalties were provided in every state for non-attendance in the schools, the student could not fail to attend in order to escape an undesirable activity in the schools. The second was the nature of the activity in the schools, namely a "religious ceremony" in which all students were required to participate. This second was the nature of the activity in the schools, namely a "religious ceremony" in which all students were required to participate. This second factor however, depended upon the definition of a "religious ceremony." The Court held, eight to one, that a prayer was a "religious ceremony." It stated that there could not be a "religious ceremony" without prayer and that prayer does constitute a religious ceremony.

As soon as the Supreme Court decision on prayer/religious ceremonies came down in June of 1963, the religious community felt a need to search for a method of circumventing it. It was obvious what they had to do. First, they had to get around the compulsory nature of the ceremony. So they said, O.K., let's say that any student who does not wish to participate may leave the room; or let's say that any student may initiate the ceremony voluntarily; or let's give free time to the students during which period they may do as they please. Let's call that "a moment of silent meditation." That should take care of relieving the student of any compulsion. Second, they had to get around the term *prayer*. If the activity could be defined as prayer, then it would be a "religious ceremony" and would fall under the Court ban. How about "meditation" or "a moment of silence," or even better, let's deny that prayer has anything at all to do with religion. Let's say that it is used to bring the classroom into a proper mood for the day's activities. It is used as a gavel, if you will, to call the room to order. In fact, let's even say that it is secular and that being a gavel is its secular purpose. There, now, said the religious community, that was easy. We have prayer back in public schools like it was. The Supreme Court is happy, we are happy, and the children are happy because we told them to be happy.

Suddenly it all became a matter of definition. The religious community defined its way out of compliance with the law of the land. What did the Atheists do? Nothing. Meanwhile, those of us at the American Atheist Center were screaming help! succor! support! we are alone and outnumbered! Did we receive the help? No.

SCORE: CHRISTIANS — 1; ATHEISTS — 0

(2) Human Sexuality: Religion is fighting very hard to ban the right of women to obtain abortions. Even more, it is fighting the distribution of birth control information and it opposes sex education as a whole — thus forcing women to use abortion as a birth control technique instead of the medical emergency for which it should be used.

Religion has a problem. That problem is two-fold. The first part is education. More people than ever can now read and write. The second part is science. It has advanced. These problems have created a third problem for religion: doubt. People are beginning to doubt its doctrines. When the pope came to the U.S. and said that birth control was a sin for Roman Catholics, many said they felt it was not. Roman Catholic women did not want to keep having and caring for large families. They liked the freedom to enjoy sexual activity and limit their family at the same time.

The Roman Catholic Church could not control its own members' families on the issue of birth control or abortion. So it said, O.K., let's control all families and that will keep the Roman Catholics pure. So, it set out to ban or seriously restrict birth control information availability for all persons. The "Right to Life" Amendment is a part of this outreach. It is moving toward ratification nicely.

What have the Atheists done? Nothing. They don't want to rock the boat. They don't want to lose their jobs — their only freedom. Meanwhile, the American Atheist Center screams help! succor! stop them! The Atheists do nothing.

SCORE: CHRISTIANS — 2; ATHEISTS — 0

(3) Censorship: Your children read many books in the course of their education. The first step in any schooling process is to teach the student to read, then to write. The question is, however, to read what? Religion has an answer for that. Read only what falls within the boundaries of the ethical or moral system laid down by Christianity and the Bible. If you are a Christian, you are urged to teach your children not to read anything outside of what Bible morality allows. Can you always be sure that they will abide by that rule? No, of course not. So religion says, let's censor all reading material so that only that which falls within Bible morality is available for children and then we do not have to worry about our teaching being obeyed. Let's ban things like "secular humanism" from books. If someone in a book is humane without god, then our children may get the idea that they can be humane without god. They may even begin to think that they can do other things without god or even do without god himself. If it worked with sex education, why not try it with books.

Sometimes, however, it is hard to ban or censor a book if what is being censored out of it has become popular. Then what to do? Religion simply demands equal time for it. Evolution is a good example. Science has presented strong facts to make evolution the best explanation of how things got from where they were to where they are now. So evolution is popularly accepted. Creationism leaves many questions with bizarre explanations. It is now not so popular. Creationism will be placed on equal ground with evolution not because it belongs there, but because its mere visibility will help to popularize it. After all, what is popular is best. We all know that. It is like smoking. It is popular, so it must be good for all of us. It remains popular because it has been given equal time with government reports and doctors' warnings.

Where were the Atheists when the school texts were being censored? They were not there. They did not show up at the textbook hearings to select books for the public schools. They did not show up at legislative committee hearings on giving equal time to creationism. They were at home — scared! The American Atheist Center, meanwhile, was again busy shouting help! succor! beware! The Atheists did nothing.

SCORE: CHRISTIANS — 3: ATHEISTS — 0

(4) Financing Religion: Parochial schools are now receiving books, educational supplies and busing of their pupils from government. They have now been granted exemptions from compliance with integration laws. This has made it possible for them to double their enrollment with "white flight" students. Parents will soon be able to divert tax monies directly to parochial schools by the use of vouchers.

The I.R.S. has been unable to enforce a directive that all churches divest themselves of "unrelated businesses" by a certain date. The churches have simply said "No."

The church has said that its interest is in the child, not the money. Busing of parochial school children helps the children get an education. It does not help the church at all. The courts have upheld this "child benefit theory." Is it not obvious, however, that parochial schools charge tuition? The more students they have, the more tuition they get. The easier it is for parents to send their children, the more likely they are to pay the tuition. What could be easier than having the same old friendly neighborhood school bus driver drop the kids off at the church school just like he did at the public school? Nothing, if you attend parochial school. Something, if you are a taxpayer.

The church says that the I.R.S. cannot tax their businesses since in order to do that it would have to define what is and is not church-related. To define what is church-related, they must define what a church is. If they define what a church is, however, that is a violation of church and state. Only the church can define what a church is. "Okay," says the I.R.S. "Fine," says the church. A railroad is a church because you can get to heaven on a train. Holiday Inns are churches. There are Bibles in every room.

What did the Atheists say when all this defining was going on? Nothing. Did the Atheists care about how parochiaid affected their children's schools? No. They were too busy teaching their children how to hide their Atheism from the other children.

FINAL SCORE: CHRISTIANS — 4; ATHEISTS — 0

In a way, I like to see religion put in the position of needing to enforce its doctrines with the arm of the state. This shows that it cannot convince its followers as to the correctness or desirability of following its doctrines intellectually. On the other hand, that makes it bad for us as Atheists. We suffer because religion cannot convince its own flock to follow along.

I hope all of you Atheists out there are happy with the score as it now stands. You did it all by yourselves. In any era of history, the Atheists have never stood up as a group to oppose anything. Only a few Atheist leaders have come forth. There has been no army, just a general here or there.

When the score gets lopsided enough, when you are tired of losing, you will come around. Until then, enjoy the agony of defeat — you earned it. And if you learn a lesson from all this, learn that the church is a survival institution. They will do anything to continue in a style to which they should never have been allowed to become accustomed.

Atheism is a survival institution, too, only it survives in individuals. I am one of those individuals in which it will not die out. Wouldn't it be nice if there were a movement to survive with me?

Have Your Atheist Lifestyle — But Pass It On

May 1980

Every month in the *American Atheist* we try to report the highlights of activity in both the Atheist and religious communities. We report what Atheists are doing around the country so that you can see things that you may want to do in your community. We show you what the religious forces are doing to make you concerned enough to want to do some of what those other Atheists (who are active) are doing. In short, we try to get you to transfer your Atheist life-style into action. That action should be aimed at those who do not share that life-style, but who would be better off with an Atheist life-style than with the one they have.

We know that Atheism is an unpopular position in America. We know that it is a minority position in America. As a result, most of you are apprehensive about identifying yourself with such a position. You continue to hold that position privately, sometimes not even revealing it to a spouse or family members. Atheism makes sense to you, but you are a little apprehensive about whether or not you can make it make sense to others.

Most Atheists never pass this stage. They come upon the Atheist life-style as one valid for themselves on their own, privately. They hold Atheism all their lives inside themselves and then they die. Sometimes they may exhibit it in very select company. But most of the time they are still unsure that they can say anything in Atheism's defense, but they know that it makes sense to them.

Religionists, on the other hand, have been taught for generations that holding a religion is not enough. Whatever the denomination, they are taught that they must pass it on to others. Why must they pass their religion on? Because it is the one true word of god. How many times have you heard that line? Religionists are indoctrinated with a specific closed dogmatic system. Since they know no other, they are happy with it. Therefore, they seek to talk others into the system to be happy as well.

You, as an Atheist, have come to Atheism from a reasoning process. You *figured out* for yourself what was best for you. You were not *told* what was the best.

Now, if a religionist can pass his belief system on to others as "the best" just because he knows nothing better, why can't you pass your Atheist life-style on to others because you know that it works, because you figured it out for yourself, because you tested it yourself? Don't you think it is better to let others know of a tested recipe for life that to let them go on with the same old diet only because they know no other?

If a religionist can push something given to him/her to push, you can push something that you figured out for yourself.

Time and time again, however, as I go from place to place around the country, I hear Atheists saying over and over again that they do not want to speak out. They prefer to keep to themselves the Atheist life-style to which they have come. They do not want to be organized. They do not want an Atheist group. When I ask why, I find out that it is because they feel that they can have their life-style and the religionist can have his and they can coexist side by side with no problems.

You know something, they're right!

But they are right only if one very important condition appertains to the situation. That is that they not be allowed to openly identify as Atheists or make the positive aspects of their life-style known. Only the religionists may do this. As long as the Atheist gives up his freedom of expression in the area of life-style determination, all is fine. The Atheist and the religionist can live side by side.

Another way of putting it is this: in most situations the sane, rational person usually gives way to the insane, irrational, screaming person. The rational one feels that if he/she lets the irrational one have his/her own way, the situation will stabilize. That is correct. It will stabilize. It will stabilize as an irrational situation. The nut is always allowed to win in America because the stable person feels that it is below his/her dignity to take command of the situation or to "lower" him/herself to the level of the nut to argue with him/her. So the nuts take over — inch by inch, mile by mile.

There are a few of us in the nation who do not want the nuts to take over — the religious nuts, that is. We want the non-nuts (that is, *us*) to stand up and take command instead. This can only be done through action.

When Mormons come to the door to tell you the word of god, don't be polite to them. Tell them off and throw them out. If the teacher in your child's school starts class with a prayer, don't tell your child to ignore it. Go over to the school and tell the teacher what he/she can do with the prayer. If you go to a public event and it opens with a prayer, stand up *against* it. When you are asked to swear on the Bible, hand it back and say “No!” If you find a Bible in your hotel room, take it to the desk and tell the manager to keep it out of your room.

Some of the persons on whom we report each month at one time thought like most of you do. They were content to keep quiet and keep their Atheism to themselves, until something happened to them, personally, that changed their minds. What happened to them? They spoke out once in a very polite, dignified, or even apologetic manner about their Atheism and they got burned for it. The religious persons in their town or city found out that they had an Atheist amongst them. Once this was known, the religionists would stop at nothing to either turn that Atheist into a religionist or make sure that he/she never said anything about Atheism again.

At this point, each one of these persons learned that democracy and freedom of speech and fair play only apply to those who join the majority, right or wrong, in their life-styles. If you speak out, you will lose your job, your house, your family, your friends, and whatever else you have to lose. But you will gain your freedom and your self-respect. That you cannot replace — homes and cars and friends you can.

Until such time as all of you are willing to pass your Atheism on, those of us who are willing will be placed in a position of needing to do it and then standing back and taking our licks from society. Every one of us has survived those licks and are still here to tell about it. Everyone in the future who speaks out will survive as well. Perhaps after enough of us do it and survive, you will get the message.

Nothing is for nothing. We at American Atheists will continue to tell the Atheist community this as long as we remain in business. We will speak out, and one by one you will speak out, and the job will get done. Then we will speak as the voice of sanity and the insane will listen for a change.

Join us when you can or when you will. With or without you, those of us who are already out front will continue out there.

Scientific Cretinism

June 1980

Recently the Georgia General Assembly was asked to pass a bill "to assure academic freedom by requiring the teaching and presentation of scientific creationism in public schools if the theory of evolution is taught." Two versions of that bill were passed in the two houses of that Assembly and failed to emerge from committee before the end of the term. We have not, however, heard the end of the outcry from the creationist buffs.

Starting back as early as 1926 in Mississippi, where the nation's first law banning the teaching of evolution was passed, through the famous "Monkey Trial" in Tennessee, to a pending lawsuit in San Diego this summer, the anti-science corps are on the march. A variety of groups led by the so-called "creation scientists," most of whom are from the physical sciences and thus should know better, are campaigning vigorously for what they call "equal time" for the creationist view in both the classroom and textbooks.

Most of their argument hinges on "academic freedom" — that is, that both sides of any issue must be heard. But their definition of this concept is as one-sided as their definition of the FCC fairness doctrine. If you put an Atheist on the air, religion must have the chance to rebut. But put a religionist on the air, and the Atheist is given no chance to rebut because Atheism does not represent a "significant community interest." In a similar manner "academic freedom" does not extend to Bible criticism classes in public schools or comparative religion courses from an objective viewpoint, but only to combating the peril of "secular humanism" somehow generated by any course of study unlaced with moralistic overtones. Science has turned a lot of heads away from the Bible in its initial days and is doing so at an ever-increasing rate. The cry for "academic freedom" comes from the religionists' realization that it is becoming of increasingly more difficult to beat science in explanations of things that once awed the savage, and increasingly more difficult to accept the tales of the clergy. The old Uncle Remus-type solution to how the leopard got his spots does not even hold water with a second-grader anymore. The religious community knows this and must react with the tactic that has worked for it over and over again — that of attacking the more credible explanation on morality or other collateral grounds. Part of "academic freedom" in my book is the freedom to expose irrational or illogical ideas for what they are. If exposing fallacy make *me* immoral, I would like to know what closed the deal on morality for the religionist who covers up contradictions and pursues the path of hypocrisy?

Our children should be guaranteed the right to "academic freedom," starting with exposés on the Inquisition for openers. I don't think our creationist counterparts are willing to dig that deeply into freedom, however.

The creationism push has given a little as time has gone on, and the scientists' score in the skeet shoot against myth has gotten a little out of hand. Back in the 1920s when it all began (in the United States that is), the creationist view was that a conflict existed between the true word of god and the Darwinistic *theory*. That is, that evolution was only a theory postualted by a mere mortal and that it could never compete with the word of god. As the proof came in for evolution, from the fossil record, from botany, from biology and related sciences, evolution began to emerge for what it really is, not a *theory* at all.

Evolution is nothing but an ongoing cycle of adaptation to environment. Darwin merely was among the first to notice the overall system that had been at work for many years. It is like being a single link and one day realizing that there is a whole chain. Evolution *is*. It is an ongoing process in both nature and man-made worlds. Animals evolve or change with respect to the environmental demands upon them. Automobiles have been forced to change by the environment of our changing society and their change has changed society in turn; so has evolution. It is a continuing cycle from which we cannot escape any more than we can escape from the fact that we are animals. Evolution is and has always been. It just took humankind a little while to notice it.

Now that overwhelming evidence is in, the creationist position has softened to saying that *neither* creationism nor evolution are absolutes. They are *both* theories that must be given equal consideration. That is quite a departure from the "perfect word of god." It is interesting to note that, when the going gets rough, god can suddenly have "theories" like the can be "patriotic" on the coins — anything to keep a foot in the door.

The next step is for the theists to go on to say that although both are theories, the theory of god has more "scientific" evidence on its side. How did science get into this? I thought science was the enemy of theism. I guess since the pope pardoned Galileo, science and religion have kissed and made up. (Except for the pill, of course. But that gets into sex, which is too personal to make up over just yet.) Well, from my point of view, religion has a long way to go to catch up to science — and it never can. Science and religion are quite mutually exclusive. Logic and fairy tales don't mix.

The "scientific" evidence these theistic scientists give for creationism is even better than the pope giving the last waltz to Galileo. It boils down to one of three things: *First*, that modern historical events are fulfillments of ancient biblical prophecies. Any book that can foretell future events with such accuracy would surely have known about evolution. Since it does not mention it, evolution must not exist. This argument fails to take into account, however, the general nature of the biblical prognostications. They fall into the same category as your horoscope. Virtually anything you do can be interpreted as falling within the prediction of your astrological horoscope for the day. Interpretation then becomes the word of the day. Since biblical interpretations are for the most part subjective, not objective, how do they qualify as science? They don't.

On to number two. The *second* argument is that one "cannot have a watch without a watchmaker," or complexity and organization cannot come out of randomness. There must be *intelligent* design to turn randomness into order, they argue. When faced with this argument, all the scientist must do is to evidence the "intelligent" design of cancer. A disease, the purpose of which is the destruction of its own host and therefore its own destruction, is quite logical, isn't it? Or, another way of looking at it is that the random combination of genes makes some pretty well ordered and complicated organisms.

On to number three. The *third* argument is the entropy argument. Entropy is a measure of the tendency toward randomness; that is, that everything tends to be random, not ordered. The religionist says, "See, that means that something outside nature (god) must come in and provide the order if everything naturally tends to disorder." But, entropy, alas for the theist, is definable only in a closed system. Is nature or the universe a closed system? Who knows? One can't apply the entropy theory to the nature of the universe because it is not a closed system, as far as we know. That would be an assumption, but a damned convenient one for the religionist.

The creationists are not only on the warpath on the legislative level with all this very "scientific" thinking, but they are trying on the school board and state board of education level as well. In 1970, they succeeded in getting the California State Board of Education to modify is "scientific framework for public schools" to include the notion that "several theories" need to be viewed on the topic of evolution. The science teachers in that state were primarily responsible for the elimination of that notion, but something called the "Creation Research Society," operating out of the Institute for Scientific Creationism in San Diego, has taken the issue to court. As a result, we now have another "Monkey Trial" in the making. Especially since the California state courts have now consented to allow cameras in the courtrooms.

This same Institute for Scientific Creationism has also been circulating, nationwide, a form bill for legislators in every state to introduce into state congresses demanding "equal time" for "scientific creationism." The bills introduced in many states are all patterned after the one circulated by the Institute. The Institute also recommends a textbook, *Biology: A Search for Order in Complexity*, for use in the schools to implement this "equal time." It just so happens that the textbook is published by Creation Life Publishers, which is the textbook arm of Zondervan Corp., the second largest distributor of Christian books in the world. Zondervan has such titles as *The Late, Great Planet Earth* by Hal Lindsey and Harold Lindsell's news magazine, *Christianity Today*, as two of its most famous productions.

What is heartening, however, is that the biology teachers in the United States are beginning to see the error of their ways with the "unwritten policy of total aloofness" to the problem of creationism as science that "professors" at San Diego State have uncovered. These same professors are teaching a course in "Evolutionism *v.* Creationism" in an attempt to confront the problem head-on. We, as Atheists, knew it was there all along. The scientific community has always thought of itself as too respectable to get down to answering the Bible thumpers they must fight for their very lives. If science is not to be replaced by the likes of alchemy and metaphysics, scientists and science educators have got to wake up. I am happy to note in the March issue of *Bio Science* and in the June issue of *Scientific American* that the National American Association of Biology Teachers is ready to do something about it. American Atheists has already offered them our full support and we welcome them to the battle.

I hope this is the signal that the pope had better take back his pardon and put up his dukes. It looks like science has its second wind in the final rounds. You don't need to guess on whom we at American Atheists will put our money.

Is Victory So Certain They Only Need Their Second-String?

July 1980

Back in the winter of '79, Gerald Tholen, National Chapter Coordinator, and I undertook an organizing tour of the Eastern U.S. At that time, we had the occasion to participate in a radio talk show in Virginia. The opening phone-in question on that show initiated discussion of whether clergymen should be in governmental positions. Was this a violation of state/church separation? Our answer was yes.

Clergymen and women, in general, owe their allegiance to their theology above all else. We maintained that such an allegiance seriously hampers their ability to consider and vote upon a number of secular issues. Their religious "values" cloud their better judgment. Also, in the case of Roman Catholic nuns or priests, they are of the lower strata of a system of ranks accountable to a foreign head of state, the pope. As minions of a foreign leader, they must reflect his desires on many issues that should be considered internal U.S. policy. What right does a foreign dictator have to influence government policy in the U.S. through his agents, especially under the cover of religion, in a nation founded on the principle of separation of state and church?

It is absurd to expect a government to uphold separation of state and church when some of the state officials are concurrently church officials.

Our position, of course, was poorly received. The response was a torrent of angry calls, the thrust of them being that it would be a violation of the constitutional rights of the clergy to exclude them from holding public office. "The people can elect any person they please to any office," was the cry. The callers would not accept the notion that the allegiance of an elected representative to a foreign power or to an authority outside of reality would do anything to hinder their impartiality on any issue.

The realization that the essence of clericalism, namely unquestioned obedience to authority, makes for an ineffective representative for anyone, could not be tolerated by the listeners. Any representative who goes into a collective bargaining position as a member of a government body when that representative has obedience training is going to sit quietly by and let the tide roll in. In doing so, he fractures the democratic idea of competition of spokesmen for differing positions reaching a compromise acceptable to all parties. Instead, the outspoken parties win out, as long as they are speaking out for conservative trends with which a stagnated mind can identify.

Clergy in public office, then, only serve to strengthen conservative opinion by their lack of participation or originality. Solutions to often-complex problems do not come out of a group of persons taking the path of least resistance, which is to remain with programs that are stagnant and provide no new alternatives for solutions.

Any scientist will tell you that the way to arrive at the correct formula to do something is to try many combinations until you find the one that works. If you try to do this with a group of people reluctant to try anything new, you don't get very far.

This is exactly what religious intrusion does in government. It retards the trial and error system that generates solutions.

Religious representatives feel comfortable with a position of condoning acceptance of directives without discussion or trial and error processes. Even a basically authoritarian nation such as the United States offers the opportunity to question authority and express dissatisfaction, even though one most often ultimately ends up accepting what is handed out. Totalitarian nations, however, go for straight hand-to-hand spoon-feeding of the population. Even smelling the food first is prohibited, or asking for it, content unchanged, in a different flavor. Such totalitarian systems fit the ideals of any religious system. Thus, increased participation of religiously oriented individuals in influential positions in government moves us towards totalitarianism. The pope is a totalitarian figure, not a merely authoritarian one.

Then, in May of '80, Father Robert F. Drinan responded to the papal directive that priests and nuns resign from public office. The callers on that show back in November said that clergy in government would not necessarily respond to god or religious leaders first. Well, who was right? The pope's minions responded to his orders like a dog on a leash. The Constitution, their duties to the general public, and their duty to their contituency went out the window.

Make no mistake, however. This was *not* a move on the part of the pope to come into compliance with the constitutional principle of state and church separation. No pope has ever felt any compulsion in that direction. Instead, it is a recognition on the pope's part that he can, and in fact does, control elected officials anyway. He does not need his people in power positions directly anymore. This is as important as the I.R.S. anouncement of recent years that church income in general has reached a level where it no longer needs donations from the flocks. I.R.S. reported that church income would double every twenty years just from the earnings of the churches' holdings on prior investments.

This means that the power of the Roman Catholic Church is much greater than one may have expected. As an Atheist I am glad to see Rep. Drinian and his cohorts out of office. At the same time, I realize the implications of the pull-out order given to them. It only tells me that, as an Atheist, I must double my effort to see that true separation of state and church is achieved before it is too late.

A theocracy is unthinkable in the U.S. for me, but I realize that slavery in a land across the Atlantic was unthinkable to the African Negro until it happened. I plan to be prepared. As Atheists, we can begin to look more carefully before we pull that voting lever for those who exhibit a compulsion to align themselves with religionists, regardless of our stance on other issues. If separation breaks down, other issues will become unimportant. Remember, the most effective population control device yet used has been and still is organized religion. Its alignment with any secular control system (*i.e.*, government in general) makes an unbeatable team.

Respectability Be Damned

August 1980

In reading over the "Roots of Atheism" series for this month, I was particularly taken by a statement of Frances Wright to this effect:

> *Alas, my friends! we have tampered with imaginary demons through all the ages of human ignorance up to the present hour — we have quailed the human heart with fear — we have shaken reason from her throne with the agues of superstition — we have broken down the self-respecting spirit of man with nursery tales and priestly threats, and we* ***dare*** to assert, that in proportion as we have prostrated our understanding and degraded our nature, we have exhibited virtue, wisdom, and happiness, in our words, our actions and our lives!

And, this — of course — is the bane of the Atheist. He or she will sacrifice anything for respectability, and unfortunately that respectability goes with the prostration of understanding and the degrading of human nature.

During the last two years I have been "on the road" attempting to encourage Atheists out of the closet and into an organization which will restore human dignity and personal integrity to them. Yet, often I loathe to face the Atheist more than I loathe to face the irrational religious fanatic. For everywhere I am met with the arguments that "humanism" is a more *respectable* "term of identification," that it would be more *respectable* if we "assumed the Agnostic position," that more *respectability* would redound to our position if we "coordinated our position with the Unitarian Church," that we must "seek the cover of the Libertarian party," to be *respectable*.

Like hell we do. My position has always been to put a big verbal check mark in the block which says "none of the above."

From the time of Frances Wright to the present day, the Atheist has been ashamed of his position, except for the few frontline stalwarts screaming "Damn the torpedoes, full steam ahead." Why is this?

In part, the answer is simple and I will speak to that. For over eight millennia of human civilization, only the religious were permitted to speak. With the psychologically crippling features of religion assisting the political despots of all ages to remain in power, subjugating mankind's mental powers to the harness of fear, every challenge to the combined power of state and church was anathema. The "good" or the "*respectable*" mental attitude was one of compliance and acceptance. It was "dishonorable" or "disrespectful" to question.

The only education permitted was indoctrination into accepted positions of faith within each parameter of human grouping. The scope of human understanding was contained in "philosophy," which educational discipline came to be simply an apology for religion, manifesting itself in different schools of thought, but vying to best support and sustain the religion in power. The philosopher's quest was for the *summum bonum* and that supreme good was always god. The cultural lag which primarily speaks to this phantasmagoria is the continuing granting of "Doctor of Philosophy" degrees as those still the highest obtainable and the most prestigious in the land.

Deriving the word philosophy from the Greek *philo* — love, and *sophia* — wisdom, the ancients corrupted the idea by using the discipline for the abnegation of human intelligence.

For countless ages, everyone who disagreed with those in power were simply killed. As the dissidents fought on, they won the right to be merely tortured and imprisoned. Soon, they were merely imprisoned. At each stage, always, they were stripped of all their property, all possessions, even their children. Systematically, their names were defamed. Often, years after they were dead, their bones were dug up and scattered or burned.

But the dissidents always appeared. They were brave beyond our ability to understand. They were isolated. They were overwhelmed, but they were always there.

I am stunned when there is no indication in an assemblage of Atheists that they understand that freedom of speech took 8,000 years to obtain — and that we really do not have it fully yet. And what is freedom of the press, but an extrapolation into print of that freedom to speak?

Yet, the Atheists are there at a meeting and the first question, the first discussion, is "How can we most effectively hide?" I often stand aghast when I hear, "Why can't you send the magazine in a plain brown wrapper?" The words flagellate me in the oft-repeated question, "Why can't we change the name of the organization?" The organization's symbol is often attacked by the anti-nuke proponents, when all of matter is nothing but a collection of atomic nuclear whirls.

Implicit — behind it all — is fear. Inherent in each question is the basic principle that there is a lack of respectability in the Atheist position. But what is respectability? Would you please consult your dictionary? The root of the word "respect" is the Latin *respectus* — literally, the act of looking back. How aptly that definition coincides with that of the word "religion" from the Latin *religio* — to tie back.

The world of Atheism is not in the backward glance, or the adherence to the old and discredited. Our view is to the now and the future.

It is from this viewpoint that we, here at the American Atheist Center, formulate our fundamental principles. We have decided that we will not buy into the "respectability" of an insane position. Nor will we treat the proponents of those positions with any kind of respect. They deserve none. They will get none from us.

Adherence to a religious faith is the manifestation, by one person or a group (or groups) of persons, of psychotic behavior. We intend to scoff at them, malign them and verbally abuse them at will. Under no circumstances will we traffic with them. We do not desire the "respectability" of the blood of hundreds of millions of victims of state and church. We do not desire to look back with approval.

But more, we also cannot accept the yearning of our contemporaries for the acceptance of that "respectability," be they humanists, agnostics, unitarians — or even Atheists. We eschew their company.

We are clean. No human blood has been spilt by American Atheists. We stand in dignity. No human mind has been bespoiled by American Atheism. We walk with pride. The human community has not suffered at the hands of American Atheism.

The irrationality of religion can only be met head-on, in the open marketplace of ideas. There we must slug it out — with no quarter given. I have no hesitation about the outcome . . . if only the Atheist can overcome the need for the security blanket of a false respectability, which — as pointed out so well by Frances Wright — has "prostrated our understanding and degraded our nature." We are not alone; we are not isolated; we cannot be overwhelmed *as were our cohorts in history* who, at such great price, bought for us those freedoms which we now should hold dear. And I demand that Atheists stand with me, not against me, as we turn our backs on the "respectability" of mental subservience and opt instead for sanity.

Time for A Change

September 1980

Over the period of time that I have been actively involved with the Atheist movement, I have had occasion to be at many a media event and to talk to many individual Atheists. Out of all those discussions, with Atheists and non-Atheists alike, I have come to the conclusion that both groups are "hung-up" (to use an expression) on a number of philosophical arguments. All of these are concerned with the central issue of "causation," which is to say in venacular, "How did everything get here?" The central issue can be broken down into a number of sub-issues, such as "How did I get here?" (*i.e.*, whence was life derived?); "What was the origin of the universe?" (*i.e.*, presuming that there is a knowledge-based definition of "universe"); or "Why does there seem to be an order to everything?" (*i.e.*, imposing upon the material world, we see the criterion of order which we allege to be in our culture).

For thousands of years, philosophers have divided into camps and argued back and forth over various causation theories. None of them have prevailed either one way or the other. Some theories are no longer used because scientific data is now available which rules them out completely, but others remain — as yet, irrefutable. All of these philosophical theories are based, however, on speculation. They are all subjective interpretations of what little we know of the "universe" — an indefinable term. They are attempts to solve an equation that still has too many missing variables.

The discipline of philosophy has concerned itself with rationalizing the yet-unrationalizable. I like to call a philosopher's work "mental masturbation." That is because it accomplishes nothing and impedes progress toward any real solutions by endless circular argumentation on subject matter that is not relevant to human life. I know that my "hate mail" basket will overflow now from all of you philosophy Ph.D.'s out there but I couldn't care less about the origin, if any, of the universe. When all the parts of the equation are in from science, *not from philosophy*, it can be solved and we can all swell up together with pride in that knowledge. Until that time, the human community needs many concrete answers to many pressing concerns in health, education, and welfare areas, to name a few.

You say, "Alright already. You don't like philosophers. So what?" Well, the fact that so many Atheists are hung up on philosophy has been reflecting itself in the pages of this publication for too long. I think we seem to be beating a dead horse. Month after month we tell you what you already know. You know that there is no god. You know that god theories are psychologically harmful. You know that evolution is not theory but fact. We don't need to keep hammering away at these things over and over again.

Therefore, I am proposing a change in the entire format of the *American Atheist* magazine, a change that will emphasize the pragmatic nature of Atheism. I am, literally, "fed up" with the causation question. Whether or not I — or you — can prove the existence or non-existence of a god is immaterial.

A major format change in the magazine will take time, however. It cannot be done in one issue, but must be approached in steps.

You will notice in this issue the first such step. We have divided the news into two parts. The first section will try to give an overview of what is going on in the "separation of state and church" area of all across the United States. Most of you see state/church news with blinders on — the blinders of your individual geographical area's newspapers and electronic media and what they care to air or will permit to be aired. A very important state/church battle could be going on in the courts of the state next door and your newspapers may not have a word of it. This first news section is designed to change that and to keep you informed. The second news section is designed to report on what individual Atheists and chapters of your American Atheist organization are doing. Instead of filling the whole news section every month with American Atheist organizational events, you can see both spectra — national impactful news, regional news — and what we are trying to do to combat religion's pernicious influence. In addition, the "Chapter Chatter" page will inform you what the Chapters are doing each month.

Over the next several I hope to begin phasing out more and more philosophy and moving toward articles explaining aspects of state/church case law, church lease-back gimmicks, new scientific findings that have a bearing on religious claims or science outreaches of concern to Atheists (such as research on aging), exposes of religion in politics so that you can be informed as a voter and a citizen, and information on how the churches reach into foreign affairs to cause changes in your life-style (such as oil and Jerusalem).

We will have one new column, which is "Atheist Masters," in which pragmatic essays of the old master Atheists will be printed. The first is in this issue.

I would like to hear from ALL of you in respect to this change. If you are as fed up with the same old philosophical garbage as am I and you want some real information on which to chew, I want to know it.

To make this a successful transition, however, we need your help too. If you are knowledgeable in any area of the continuing separation of state and church controversy, or if you have information which should be made known, please get it to me.

If we all pitch in together, we can make the *American Atheist* the most valuable reference tool in the United States, not alone for you, but for everyone.

The research we propose will need hands, minds, and research time. Therefore, we need money to do this. Make certain that you send your share to the Magazine Sustaining Fund. I have never mentioned money before in an editorial but — you know where to write: Jon Murray, Director, American Atheist Center, P.O. Box 2117, Austin, TX 78768, for both your letter of comment and your check. The magazine and I need your issue-oriented feedback, and what we have here is an issue.

Wishing Won't Make It So

October 1980

In the pages of the *American Atheist* one often reads article after article primarily concerning the inadequacy of Christianity as a lifestyle guide. It has many illogical aspects. It is not, however, unique in its illogic. All religions are based on fundamental "faiths." These faiths are speculative and consist mostly of wishful thinking. They are based upon what one would like to be the case, rather than what is. Therefore, there has always been a separation between those who live by a system of wishful thinking and those who live according to a realization of what is. As an Atheist, I realize what *is*, what is demonstrable. I acknowledge facts and I base my actions upon them. I do not live in a world of wishes.

Essential to all god theories is "wish fulfillment," the "coming true of a dream." Adherents of all religions strive toward their "wish" coming true, but they strive hypnotically. They do not work toward a reasonable goal. They cogitate in endless circles about their "wish," hoping that tangible results will be forthcoming. This circular cogitation is like an S.O.S. being given out by a buoy in the sea in hopes that someone will hear and provide aid. In the same way, the religionist runs over and over the same "wish" in his or her mind hoping that something "out there," someplace, will hear and fulfill.

This whole scheme is very egotistical. It places the individual in a position of centrality to all things around him or her. He and his "wish" are of utmost importance. Sending out the endless signals for fulfillment of the "wish" comes first. So, essential also to all god theories is a *personal* centrality, a feeling that each religious man is the central figure and all that goes on around him is separate and secondary to his wish fulfillment. So, man has always been billed as the center of the "universe." Man is then supposed to be the "special creation" made only to float in the sea of reality and to be intent only in putting out the constant signal to be saved. Saved from what? Why, reality, of course.

Reality and scientific interpretation of the facts of reality which we have amassed to date dictate that we are merely part of a system, a very large system. The nearest fixed star is Proxima Centauri, which is four and one-half light years away. That is approximately twenty-six trillion one hundred miles. We cannot think in terms of such distances. If I say one hundred miles, one can think of two hours in one's car on a short trip. That kind of figure has some meaning to man. Four and one-half light years does not.

A better way to put it is this: Think of the earth as one grain of sand on a beach that runs as far as one can see in both directions. That is about the relative "significance" of the earth in what we know as the "universe." Actually, we know very little about what we call the "universe," since we can only measure (with any accuracy at all) what would amount to perhaps a circle with a radius of an inch in all directions from our grain of sand on the beach. We can only measure (and inaccurately, at that) the light which is given off from any grain outside of that inch radius. In fact, in most cases, that light from the birth of a distant star only reaches us after the star has gone full cycle and died. What then do we have? But even that is speculation. That makes the earth overall rather insignificant, wouldn't one say?

It is very ego-deflating to think of ourselves in terms of being occupants on one grain of sand on a beach. In fact, however, that is the case. The earth is very insignificant and we, as organisms on it, are even more insignificant. Insignificance bothers most people. It bothers them very much. That is why they hang on to their god ideas so tenaciously. The god idea tells them that they are very significant, that they are central, and that all the other grains of sand on the beach revolve around their grain.

As an Atheist, my "insignificance" does not bother me in that I can acknowledge the fact. Part of that "insignificance" is that I will terminate and possibly be forgotten for all time. This I acknowledge. I acknowledge that I am on a planet in what is chaos so far as we now know. It has no design. We, as individuals, have formed a certain set of rules for the behavior of objects we can measure based upon the use of the scientific method. We cannot, however, extrapolate those rules to things that we cannot yet measure or observe.

The basis of the scientific method is this: A scientist collects data by observation of things. After he has compiled a list of everything he can observe or extrapolate from his observations, he can be said to have "described" something using all the tools available to him. He sits back and says, "What can I conclude from this descriptive list of observations (*i.e.*, data)?" That first conclusion is called an hypothesis. He then takes his hypothesis (theory) and asks other scientists to observe the same thing and describe it also to see if their conclusions match his. If no other scientist can come up with a significantly different conclusion, then the hypothesis turns into what is called a "law." Even a "law," however, is something that is relative. It is relative to the available data at the time. When the data base increases over time, the chance increases that someone will find a flaw in the hypothesis on the basis of of conclusions drawn from new data.

The current new wave of "creation scientists," however, do not follow this procedure. They lay down a "law" first that "god created the earth" and then try to go over the existing data base for bits of data that may tend to support the hypothesis. Their tendency is to overlook data that leads toward invalidation of their "law." Thus, working in contravention to the scientific method, they cannot be considered "scientists" at all, in respect to "religious creationism." They simply use the title of "scientist" to give themselves credibility.

At the present time, the data base to determine such questions as "What is the universe?" "Is the universe finite or infinite?" "Does life (another undefinable term) exist anywhere else but on earth?" simply does not exist. Much more information is required. We all simply need to have the intellectual integrity to say that the data is not there as yet and wait (and work) until it is. As an Atheist, I can do this. My ego is secure. A religionist is not secure. He requires the security blanket of a god theory that tells him that he is central and that his "S.O.S." signals are being received.

Chaos does not bother me in the least. Insignificance does not bother me. If the "universe" (whatever that means) does turn out to have some order, so what? Both of these determinations are irrelevant to my life as well as to yours. I am a pragmatist. Concerns here and now that affect us all are of interest to me. One might say that I am content in my ignorance, but not in the self-imposed ignorance of the religionist, for my ignorance is a result of the limitations in the available data base. Astrophysics and space exploration will enlarge that data base; another day, my sphere of ignorance will be reduced and my knowledge enlarged.

If someone wants to posit chaos and then posit an external all knowing, all-powerful agent acting on the chaos *in response to individual S.O.S.'s uttered,* let them play the game. Even the recent "big bang" theory merely internalizes into the primeval stuff that an external agent (god) caused the "big bang." It is a thinly disguised religious solution.

The job we have to do now as Atheists is to restructure our culture from the ground up on the basis of sound concepts rather than on the basis of "wishful thinking." This striving for the "wish" has permeated our language so thoroughly that one cannot even discuss such ideas as origin topics without using non-sense words such as "universe" or "infinite," *etc.* We even are trapped into using terms like "philosophy" to refer to our thought system as Atheists. The needed change is so fundamental that we must invent a new vocabulary to describe it.

What you — and I — need to do as Atheists is to help to change the social system we have to ameliorate the condition of mankind. To do this, we need not fight our way into the system. We must restructure it from the ground up and have the system understand that it must be built on our base — the rational base — not upon religion, the irrational.

Reverse Evolution

November 1980

Recently I was in attendance at an Atheist party and a woman accosted me with the following questions, "Why must your entire approach be so warlike? Why must you always talk in terms of a battle, or a fight? Why do you have a fighting stance all of the time? Why can't you have your ideas, and *they* have their ideas and live together?" I have given that some thought since the day of the party and find that the answer is in the theory of evolution.

If one goes all the way back to the beginning of ideas, both Atheism and theism had the same source. There was an ignorant savage, a primitive man, out in the bushes. He knew nothing. He was tremor-filled at lightning. He did not understand storms. He had no answers. He was awed by the moon, the sun, the earthquakes, tornadoes.

One day, one of these primitives had a personal subjective opinion — and came up with the idea that "someone up there" was throwing the lightning he feared, making the thunderbolts which terrorized him. It was his personal opinion, dawning in a brute and beginning brain.

He went back to his hut or cave to communicate this. But, his fellow dumb, hairy, half-ape brethren, who had no more education or sense than he, his co-ignorant, sitting there hunting fleas, came to a dim understanding through their grunt-like exchange and replied "No. No thing make. *Not so.*"

But this opinion was based on ignorance — which is to say, lack of knowledge. They had conflicting opinions. They may have picked up clubs and "gone to" over the difference. But, the idea was subjective, not based on data or material evidence of any kind. The scientific method was not used to arrive at these "opinions" unfounded on fact. But in essence, one of the primitives was an Atheist, the other a theist.

Over the centuries, as more understanding came with more obtained data, the Atheists changed their opinions or had evolving opinions, while the majority stuck to the old ideas. The persons who were intellectually curious enough to accept the altered or new ideas, based on accumulating observable phenomenological data, were usually in the minority.

The mass remained with the old, the accepted, the traditional. Those who understood that their opinions must be altered as information accumulated from studying their environment, enlarging their data base, could be described as mutants of the tribe. They strayed from the old established ideation formats, adjusting, adapting, altering their intellectual life-styles to include such activities as would give them the ability to better adapt to their increased information base.

The larger group — that is, the non-changing, the static group — became the "**idea**ists," basing what they came to call their religion on the first unsubstantiated "idea" which someone subjectively had had. They stuck with it: *In the beginning god. . . .* The few, seeing some answers in their environment, slowly understanding how it came to be, enlarging their knowledge of the material world, demanded that there be an intellectual accommodation to the enlarged information base. They changed their opinion in a continuing unending evolutionary way with the input of more data, until now, after many thousands of years of human civilization, they stand in a direct 180° opposing position to the mental Neanderthals. They are in a confrontation with the opinions remaining with those who persist in being fixated in an intellectual lag which holds them to a primitive time. Why is there a battleline drawn? Why not ask me why we do not accept the striking of flints together to light the kitchen stove!

Somewhere down the line, however, the accumulated pressures of an increased body of knowledge became so great on **idea**ists that they had to accommodate to some mechanical (technological) new ideas (such as the plow and the automobile) — but the accommodation was external. The original opinion then became internalized (much like a recessive gene which they carried with them and passed from generation to generation by implantation in the mind of each babe), a rigid, static, unaltered, unchanging ideology: *The lightning thrower is god.* They abandon the peripheral ideas once associated with the lightning god, but the core, the root idea of god and associated insane ideas are still there — and so they kill a Galileo who is a threat to their belief system. All of these primitive ideas are alive even today. The fascination with the idea of werewolves is quite real. Mothers murder their children to rid them of demons today in our nation. Magazines, newspapers, and books on exorcism sell by the millions. Possession films garner profits in the hundreds of millions. The most primitive ideas of afterlife, creation, prayer are abroad in the land, hallowed, honored, respected.

The theists are internally terrorized, holding fiercely to the god idea out of fear, anxiety, guilt inadequacy. The Atheist is hesitant to arouse the primitive rage trapped in the theist.

The first two ideas are still alive today, so that now in our modern times there are two stances. One has followed a natural evolutionary intellectual progression, from one uninformed subjective brute mind idea to multifaceted idea systems based on observed phenomena and analysis of material nature; the other has remained intact, fixated in pre-civilization.

The evolution of mankind then is exactly backwards to the evolution of the rest of the entire animal kingdom. For, in the animal kingdom, that species which evolved by adaptation and change became dominant. With the human species the exact opposite is true. Those who did not change intellectually remain dominant. Those who evolved, those who accommodated to the increase of data, were deliberately killed off by those of meek mind who would inherit the earth.

The dumb, slow, lame deer is eaten by the wild mountain lion. In the human community, the dumb, the slow, the intellectually lame killed off those who would have advanced the human community. Their solution was death to the innovator, the curious, the intelligent.

In every other species natural progression took its course, but in the human species the process has been exactly the opposite. The scoff is at the egghead, the intellectual. **It is reverse evolution**. We have been held back socially, culturally, intellectually by the dominance of the unchanged Neanderthal mind. Out culture exalts war, racism, chauvinism, stupidity, irrationality. By all natural progression, in ten thousand years of human civilization the materialist should have been on the top of the heap, attempting to ameliorate the condition of mankind by the application of reason to his problems. Instead, we drag with us the insane ideas of 8,000 or 10,000 years ago.

But, I must get back to the original question which was asked of me. Why do we have the fighting stance? The reason we have the fighting stance should be clear in that it is not natural that the strongest should have succumbed. Reverse evolution is outside of the laws of nature. By every right, there should have been the survival of the fittest in the human community as in the other animal communities.

I do not know why this reversal of the natural order exists. However, we can no longer permit the reversal.

Why are we militant? We must capture our rightful dominance. We cannot coexist with pre-civilization relics who threaten to use the eschatalogical Christian concepts as an ideological base for a nuclear holocaust to destroy our world.

We must turn our existing culture completely inside out. We must live naturally — *i.e.* by the use of intelligence. We cannot give our world to the idiot.

I am uncomfortable in a society which tells me not to think. I cannot accept the solution of human problems to be in a book written by illiterate primitives. Prayer gains naught.

Why are we militant? The woman may as well have asked me, as a lion, why I would track for food the gazelle which cannot get away from my attack. I fight because it is the right of the person with brains to be dominant in the human community, and that right is mine. I cannot permit solutions to humankind's problems to be bypassed because there are those who want to coexist with ignominy.

We understand that what sets us apart from the ape is our capacity for creative thought. If this is what distinguishes man from the other primates, then why has certain of the human community been punished for exercising that ability, the ability which gives us the prowess to organize a civilization?

But our civilizations are highly irrational. The wrong value systems are almost everywhere in ascendance. Everything is at variance with reality. The cultures are backwards. It is the Atheist who must set them straight. The scientists, the thinkers, the educators do not cause pain and human suffering, but the popes have caused more human misery than any other class. The physician heals, the educator teaches, but the preacher causes anxiety, a sense of sinning, and feelings of personal inadequacy. What impacts against humankind is an affront to me. The bell tolls for me.

Why should we fight? That is not the question. The question is why has not the Atheist fought more vigorously until now? It sounds like a battlefield because it is one. We cannot opt for insanity as a solution to human problems. The future is ahead and I am in it. I cannot yield it without a fight.

My question to the woman then had to be, "Should we enter tomorrow with the Stone Age for a lavaliere?" No. We must confront the Neanderthals.

Intolerance and Dogmatism

December 1980

The recent election of Ronald Reagan to the presidency of the United States through a conservative backlash has been written off by some as reaction only to the failures of Jimmy Carter. This argument has its merits, but the roots from which the conservative takeover springs run far deeper than Jimmy's term in office. What we see now when we look in dismay at Moral Majority, right-to-life amendments, resurgence of the school prayer issue, Gay rights, pro-war, and many more issues is the ripening of a boil that has been building in our country for over one hundred years.

Like it or not, our nation was founded by a group of well-educated aristocrats, by elitists — not by the people or the "will of the people." This group of elite men came to the conclusion that separation of state and church was a necessary prerequisite to keeping our nation from becoming fascist over the long term. *They* started the nation, not the "people." The "people" could have cared less what kind of government they had at the time. The nation was started by revolution of thought. Yet, when we had our revolution, we had it in the fields and the streets. After it was over, however, the "people" still had not had the revolution that counts — the one between the ears, the one which had been the inspiration for the elite group of men who had spurred the people on. It is that very failure of those great men, a failure to educate the people, that will now, over two hundred years later, bring their dream to an end.

The mechanics of state geared up and ran and ran and ran. It has been running fairly well for these 200-plus years. The minds of the people for whom it is run, however, have not changed. The same ugly values that made it possible for witches to be hung in Salem, or Negroes whipped and hung in the South, or brother to kill brother in a civil war, have remained inviolate. Intolerance, ignorance and incompetence are still the names of the game in America. All of these "qualities" are awarded. Why? Because they are the building blocks of Christianity. They are what you "go to heaven" for accomplishing.

Although our technology has progressed, no substantive attempt has ever been made to change our thinking. Intolerance, ignorance, and incompetence are the same if spread by modern jet plane or horse and buggy. Only one group has tried to pick away at the *minds* of America. That group has been the Atheists. The Atheists have had their troubles, though, as well. They have been essentially ineffective. Why? Because the same kind of thinking they seek to "cure" has been at epidemic levels in their own ranks.

Every Atheist or pseudo-Atheist group that has ever existed has based its activities on the proposition of "live and let live" or "tolerance." Almost every Atheist I have met in America, with the exception of a very few, has always had the attitude that "I don't believe in god; I don't go to church; that is my right and I can do as I please. I don't bother my religious neighbors and they don't bother me. After all, science and technology will kill religion in time."

You cannot face a concept based on intolerance, based on denying your rights, based on annoying you day in and day out until you can't stand it anymore and give in and join them, with tolerance. Intolerance will always win out over tolerance. This is natural. It can also be very just if the intolerant stance is the one of the person who is correct. What we have had in America, however, is the intolerant position, being the one held by the person who operates on that which cannot be substantiated in fact. That is very basically wrong. The person with the position based on fact, on logic, on science is tolerant — and loses out.

There is no god. That is fact. Yet every Atheist I have ever met has inside them some doubt. "Well, maybe there is something out there and we can't condemn the person who finds solace in that thought. We cannot be dogmatic. We must give everyone the right to think what they please."

The hell we can't be dogmatic. Facts are dogmatic. While we are being undogmatic, the dogmatic position of Christianity is being systematically shoved down our collective gullets.

One hundred years ago, a single crazed minister in Pennsylvania got to the then-Secretary of the Treasury with the idea of putting "In God We Trust" on our money. He planted the seed and it grew; now that phrase cannot be removed. Meanwhile, the Atheists were tolerant. There are thousands of such stories that could be related here. The point is, however, that *because* of our tolerance, we have earned the "right" to have our freedoms to operate as Atheists taken away from us one by one.

The legislature of the United States is now closed to Atheists. The court system of the United States, including the Supreme Court, is now closed to Atheists. The executive branch of government, on city, county, state and federal levels, has now closed its ears to Atheists. Atheists have earned it; I hope they like it. They have earned it with their "tolerance."

If something were to have been done about religion, it should have been done starting two hundred years ago. *It is too late now.*

It is the hope of this author that Atheist children are forced to pray in school every day, several times a day; that Atheist children are beaten in school out of parental control with no appeal allowed; that Atheists are forced to pray at their place of employment every day or be fired with no hope of getting any job anyplace; that Atheists must pray in court or any public meeting to be heard as citizens; that Atheists be made to vote in a church and in a church only and that they be made to sit through a prayer service before being given the ballot; that Atheist women have to buy a casket for a bloody spot on their sanitary napkins and pay for a funeral or be jailed for murder of a living "soul"; that gay Atheists never can work or have a place to live again unless a gay employer or landlord will take them in.

In the last analysis, I speak to you. You and your parents before you and their parents before them have earned your right to be dominated by the Christian ethic. I would not for anything in the world stand in the way of your reaping what you have sown. You paid for it; now wrap it up and take it home.

The American Atheist Center will continue to do what it can, how it can, to the end — with the few who value their freedom. When there is no Center anymore or no magazine or no outreach, as individuals we will continue to resist. Those in the great "silent majority" have earned a place in slavery. Relax, no one will take it away from you; it is all yours.

When you have lived under a fascist Christian state for awhile, you may value the "intolerant" style we at The American Atheist Center used — that which you all say you hate so much and about which you grumble in such overwhelming and continuing ways.

Don't look to the scientific community. It won't help you. The most important thing to scientists in America today is the same thing that has been important to them, above all, for two hundred years: keeping their tenure, maintaining their salaries, having their ideas accepted by the *non*-scientific community, and keeping their grants. The scientists of Alexandria permitted Hypatia to be killed, didn't they? They handed the Ionian culture to the Christians. The same surrender is imminent today.

You can soon "live and let live" with a whole new meaning. Militant evangelical Christianity lives *its* way and lets you live *its* way too.

No Middle Ground

January 1981

One of the most frequently asked questions of me by the news media in general is "Do you grant others the right to believe in a god if they wish to do so?" I choke on the answer to this over and over again. I know what the reporter is attempting to get me to say. He wants me to say that I do object to someone having a god-belief system and thereby pin the label of intolerance on me. Knowing that the media will distort an honest reply and not give the reasoning upon which it is based, my answer is always a stock one. I say, "I realize from a legal standpoint that all persons in our society should have freedom of thought, and therefore I can see that each person has a civil right to believe in that in which they care to believe." The reporter always follows up on this with "Would you fight to the death for this person's right to believe in god?" I choke again. I usually answer this one with "I am fighting for the rights of all when I fight for separation of state and church."

I really don't mean either of those answers, but they do have their PR value, I suppose. I cannot grant *anyone* the "right" to believe in such a notion of god when this is destructive to the human community. I have read and studied enough to know what that belief system has done to mankind down through history. I earnestly feel that if the individual involved really understood what his or her god-idea was and what human degradation is cast into the word "believer," that the person could not be one. I must look on a god-believer as an intellectually inferior person. The essence of god-belief is the subjugation of reason to phantasy. In plain terms, it means that this person holds to be true that some kind of power which he cannot define rules him and takes cares of him. It does not matter what he does or does not do, since all is predetermined. It also means that this person really believes that he will live on in some form after death, maintaining all his life qualities of form, speech, intellect, *etc.* These notions are so absurd that the reporter may as well have asked me if I granted others the right to believe that a man can give birth to a baby if he so desires. (Remember *Life of Brian?*) No man has a right to believe he can give birth. This is patently absurd, being physically impossible. Likewise, it is physically impossible to "live" after "death" and the "right" to believe is bizarre — and immaterial. Whether they believe it possible or whether I grant their right to believe it, nothing can come of such an exercise.

I feel that no one has the "right" to ignore facts and proceed contrary to them. Anyone who does so on a consistent basis is a candidate for restraint. On a rare occasion when I do answer such questions honestly, the question-asker is horrified that I could deny the right to believe in god. So be it. Let them be horrified.

I don't "believe" in anything, as an Atheist. I do "accept" many things, however, because they can be substantiated. I cannot "accept" god notions. If I can live without belief systems, then so can anyone else. If they cannot, I must come to the conclusion that they are made of lesser stuff than am I. That is, I feel that they lack the intelligence to live without belief.

It is this position that brings me to the point at which I understand that the world must either be Atheist or theistic. *There is no middle ground.* There is no "living side by side in harmony." One position is correct and the other is incorrect. I am of the view that the incorrect position grabbed culture early and has hung on ever since through the simple process of capturing each new generation. We are now a backwards culture, worldwide, a culture where fundamentally-incorrect notions are held in esteem and where the masses scoff at correct notions. The correct, or Atheist, position must win its rightful dominance. In order to do that, we must capture each coming generation. If one has an incorrect position upon which to build, all erected on that false base will be futile. If a correct base is the foundation, there is a chance that all built on it will be wholesome until a mistake is reached. Our current cultures worldwide are built upon the rot of religion.

It is much like laying a column consisting of one brick on top of another in a single stack. If the first is level, there is a chance for the next to be so. If the first is not level, the next cannot be either. Each succeeding brick only has the chance of being level if the preceding one was. Thus, if the base brick is correct, there is the potential of all the rest being level until one is mislaid.

It is then imperative that once one comes to an Atheist position that everything possible must be done to see that the next generation starts off with that opinion or on that base position also — to keep the bricks going up straight, as it were.

Religionists have always been able to do this well. A United States Supreme Court justice (Jackson) spoke to this in *Everson v. Board of Education, 330 U.S. 1, (1946):*

> It is no exaggeration to say that the whole historic conflict in temporal policy between the Roman Catholic Church and non-Catholics comes to a focus in their respective school policies. The Roman Catholic Church, counseled by experience in many ages and many lands and with all sorts and conditions of men, takes what, from the viewpoint of its own progress and the success of its mission, is a wise estimate of the importance of education to religion. It does not leave the individual to pick up religion by chance. It relies on early and indelible indoctrination in the faith and order of the Church by the word and example of persons consecrated to the task.

It is essential, then, for us to capture the next generation with our movement. We cannot let each new generation fall into the same entrapment. Once we have one generation which is *free from religion*, we have the brick which is level. In reaching out to them, I must be honest. I will not state that the religionists have the right to their insanity. All of humankind has the right to be free from that.

We have our job ahead of us: education of the adults who educate the youth and honesty in our position, no matter how it hurts.

The Morality Quotient

February 1981

One of the things of which Atheists are accused most often is being amoral or nonethical. In order to understand that charge a little better, let's look at what morals and ethics are. Morals refer to the set of generally-accepted customs or conduct and correct living in a given society, *and to the practice of an individual within that society in relation to these.* The second part of this definition is the most important. We see that morals are rules that are laid before a young person, particularly, coming into society. That individual has two major options with respect to those rules: a) He or she can choose which one or all of the rules to follow; b) he or she can determine for themselves to what degree to follow those they have selected to follow at all.

Persons are judged by others in society on the basis of what rules they choose to follow and to what extent they follow them. Supposedly one who follows all the rules and does so with 100 percent accommodation to each is the most "moral."

In the United States, the rules which are then laid down for the determination of one's "morality quotient" (my own label) are based upon Judeo-Christian teaching and history. The immediate problem for an Atheist is then one of being presented with a set of rules that may be wholly unacceptable, with judgment by the rest of society hinging an adherence to them.

Since morality is a subjective matter based on the cooperation level of the individual, it then follows that if an Atheist chooses a low level of cooperation he could be labeled a-moral or less moral than others. That is why that label bothers me not in the least. Yes, to a great extent I am less moral than the (Christian) others, *but in relation to what standard?*

Now ethics are a different situation. Ethics imply adherence to a high standard of honest and honorable dealing, particularly with the business world. Ethics also refer to the methods used when dealing with others, again usually within a business context. As an Atheist, I consider myself most ethical. I am honest with my opinions and my method is one of straightforward confrontation of situations and ideas. I don't think that an Atheist, in general, could be then considered unethical on the basis of his or her Atheism alone.

Getting back to morality again: if morality is then subjective and on a level of percentage of individual compliance, then it seems logical that it must be discussed in terms only of a closed system — that is, within a single society or social group. One cannot calculate the "morality quotient" of an individual by dividing his or her participation or adherence percentage into the rule-set of a society not that of the individual.

This is exactly what the United States is doing in many areas of its foreign policy. We calculate the "morality quotient" for the citizens and leaders of Iran, for example, using our rule set in place of theirs. The resulting quotient is then not valid. The morality of the Ayatollah is probably quite high when calculated on the basis of a Moslem rule-set. We do the same with Israel, but they get a high quotient since their rule-set is almost identical with the one used in the United States. The U.S.S.R. gets a very low quotient since their rule-set is one based on materialism and is therefore almost the antithesis of the U.S. one.

We are told that children never laugh and play in the U.S.S.R., that the citizens still live in huts and poverty and have no modern conveniences at all. We are told that the people of the U.S.S.R. go around constantly with dour expressions and that they only live for the opportunity of escape from their rule-set to ours. We are told also that this is because our rule-set allows the subjectivism implicit in the definition of morality, while the rule-set in the U.S.S.R. *requires* perfect participation.

Nothing could be further from the truth. Yet, on the basis of such assumptions, we stand ready to "nuke" the world in an effort to free the people of the "Communist" countries (including many more than the U.S.S.R. itself) from their rule-set — and bring them under the umbrella of our rule-set which we perceive as superior.

The Judeo-Christian based rule-set is not alone *not* superior to a rule-set based on materialism; it is wholly unacceptable as a standard for the conduct of any animal, human or not. In addition, the Christian moral rule-set has guilt as one of its built-in catalysts to foster higher overall percentage of participation and adherence.

As an Atheist, I am basically anti-authoritarian and am therefore uninterested in following any rule-set that I cannot be allowed to establish myself rather than being handed one by default (being born into a particular society) against which I am to be measured. Atheism predicates a system of conduct based on *eclectic*, rational, construction of one's own rule-set from all the information which can be gathered. Is it so much easier to follow guidlelines which you create rather than those created by an outside authority, whether that is a deity or a state?

If, however, I am to be bound by circumstance beyond my control to fall within a rule-set not of my own construction, I would rather fall within one that is closer to the one that I would construct than one that is further away. The rule-sets in some of the "Communist" or "Socialist" states are constructed from more of the same building blocks that I would choose for myself than is the rule-set here in the United States.

While I prefer their morality (assuming a choice had to be made), I see it as being more compatible with our governmental precepts *as they were originally laid down* by our founding fathers. It is a strange situation indeed to be in a country of one's preferred political system, but have one's preferred moral-set exist in another state with an undesirable political system.

No wonder we Atheists have a hard time getting along with religionists. How backward! A totalitarian government with a liberal moral-set and a liberally conceived government with a totalitarian moral-set. As an Atheist I am trapped between the two. The Christian moral-set is tailor-made for a totalitarian or fascist state while the materialist moral-set is tailor-made for a truly democratic state.

We have a long road ahead of us to turn the systems around. My only hope is that we can beat General Haig and his ilk toward this end through peaceful means, rather than through a planned nuclear holocaust in which all Christians would delight.

Moron Majority

March 1981

Ever since the campaign which led to the election of our actor-President first began, the emergence of a new group has stirred comment on every side of the separation of state and church issue. That group is the Moral Majority, led by Jerry Falwell out of Virginia.

The good Mr. Falwell seems to feel that it is time for the United States to return to those good old days of pre-Constitution theocracy that our founding fathers knew so well. Those were the fine times, yes, indeed! The days of the Mathers who had us all "by the thread," hairshirts, scarlet letters, dunking stools, stocks, and an occasional lighting of the fagot (no reference to modern slang intended — although from Falwell's point of view, not a bad idea at all).

The Falwellian era should rival that of Queen Victoria in conservatism, to say the least. Americans will be given all kinds of freedoms. Let's take a look at a list of our expanded liberties under Falwell:

A) the right to hire a funeral director, fill out a census form, file a death certificate, buy a matchbox coffin, and order flowers for the next spot of blood you may find on your killer tampon;

B) the right to hire a good criminal lawyer for a murder trial on six counts of wearing a condom to prevent pregnancy;

C) the privilege of experiencing bankruptcy court with your doctor over the costs of keeping your dead relatives artificially alive for seven years, not to mention the cost of fertilizer;

D) the right to "love it or leave it" with a one-way ticket to Moscow, guaranteed proletariat class;

E) the right to have your child recite prayers each day in school to the god or gods of his/her homeroom teacher;

F) the right to ship your child to a "Christian" school "first class" via franking privilege, courtesy of your fellow taxpayer (be sure to pack him well against secular mishandling);

G) the right to have your children told that they were made out of mud pies by a lunatic who later drowned everyone except an old drunk and his family;

F) the right to be taxed without representation to pay for all of the above.

Can all of this become reality? Is it all really backed by the President, or is he just acting? Only his hairdresser and most of California know for sure. Strom Thurmond is setting up the Inquisitional tribunal in the background just in case, so if it is needed the coals will already be hot.

What do the mainline boys think of all this? They love it. While the nation turns its eyes to the Moral Majority and its soft shoe, the established churches continue the same old plan of ball control. The big three — Protestant, Roman Catholic, and Jew — are carving away at the wall of separation step by step as they always have, but now with less opposition. Now their former opposition is keying on the Moral Majority while leaving the main liners free to run.

Where are the Atheists? Well, for the most part, with the rest of the opposition — flat on their face, having been faked out by Falwell while the mainliners roll on. We see many new organizations, all under a variety of freethought pseudonyms, popping up to tackle Falwell, not paying any attention to the real ball carrier. Most of these groups are composed of those of mainline denominations who fail to see the true support that Falwell is giving them in the long run.

Millions are being raised to fight the decoy. Will this insure true separation of state and church? I don't think so. Separation means separation. It does not mean allowing the ones who can mix quietly to go ahead while stopping the shouter.

Our nation was captured for Christ in the 50's without a shot being fired. Now that Falwell and others are making waves to clean up the loose ends faster than the master plan calls for, heads are being turned. Where were these "liberals" when our national motto was changed from "E Pluribus Unum" to "In God We Trust?" Where were they when "under God" was inserted into our pledge? Where were they when it became mandatory for all federal judges to believe in god? They were right in there voting with the rest of the pack — and the Atheists were in the closet.

Don't be fooled by these so-called "liberal" or "humanist" groups out to fight the Moral Majority. They would impose the self-same "rights" on all of us in their own good time. God concepts should be the object of our fight, not denominational interpretations thereof or varying tactics for their aggrandizement. We saw the same kind of tactic on the part of the mainliners fail when they tried to pin all of their evils on the "cults." They loved the red herrings, Jim Jones and Rev. Moon. That attempt failed, only to have the same persons who screamed about Jim Jones *et al.* be decoyed by Falwell. I am ashamed of these "liberal" groups falling hook, line, and sinker for another dodge. Let us hope that they get over it like they got over cults. At the same time, be proud that American Atheists did not fall for either decoy.

It just goes to show that a stand on principle is the best stand. When one stands on principle, one does not run as high a risk of getting faked out of the game, especially if the principle is a narrow, but good one. The be-all, and defend-all groups get sidetracked very easily. The stalwarts stand.

Nuclear Fantasyland

April 1981

When I go for the morning paper over coffee these days, it is no longer the pleasant, informative prelude to the day's work that it once was. In fact, it is more like waking up to a horror movie. On every page there is glaring irrationality. Irrational thinking and actions, in which the doers would probably not be involved had they stopped to think first, hop out at you. For example, you can see an article on any given day in about any major newspaper in the country with more Pentagon, Senate, House, White House, or State Department talk about nuclear war. I just keep waiting for Gen. Haig to say against whom we should declare subversive war next. You can read about senators, presidents, congressmen, secretaries of state, talking about "limited nuclear war" fought on top of some poor agrarian nation that would just as soon be left in its poverty. There is no such thing as limited nuclear war. Once you start, you are talking about eradicating life on earth. Yet our "leaders" talk about such things as two old ladies may talk about a new dress over tea. It concerns me no end that grown men in three-piece suits can sit around over coffee and strudel and chat about megadeaths. Especially since one of those megadeaths would most likely be mine.

This is unthinking irrationality. I am convinced that if they really knew what they were talking about and looked at it from a realistic standpoint, they would be ashamed of themselves. Why does it go on then, with an overall passive acceptance from the media persons reporting it as well as the majority of the readers?

The answer lies in the thought structure of society. Americans have been reared on fantasy and emotionalism. Take, for instance, the old John Wayne movies. He gets shot in the arm by one of the bad guys and wraps his bandanna around it and continues with the chase. Have you ever seen someone who has been shot in the arm in real life? It is not very pretty. I can guarantee you that if you were shot in the arm with an old Colt "shootin' iron" you would not continue the chase. Depending on the muscle structure damage, you may not be able to use the arm again, period — or, if so, only after months of physical therapy. Many things in movies you cannot do in real life; we all know this. The point is, however, that they put these fantasy behaviors up for us to emulate. This is particularly true of children. How many times have you heard a young boy say, "When I grow up, I want to be just like John Wayne (or James Bond or one of a thousand others), and do all the neat things he does"?

If you look deeper into the John Wayne hero-type movie, you realize something that can "scare" you worse than the newspaper. What do all of those movies have in common? A male (or female) hero coming into a town, an island, a situation generically being one of "sin" or "corruption" or "vice," and then cleaning it up single-handedly. This is the same story as that of Jesus Christ in the Bible. The world is full of sin, vice, corruption, and good old blonde, blue-eyed, kind, tender, sweet Jesus saves the day. The only difference is that Jesus didn't kiss his horse in the end and ride off into the sunset. Over and over again you have the savior figure battling the forces of sin and vice and corruption. One of the most popular movies in the history of movie-making so far has been *Star Wars* and its sequel, a real box-office smash hit. In that classic you had the goodness of "the force" fighting against the evil black-suited villain. Is there anyone who has an I.Q. of any level who cannot see that "the force" in that movie is god? They may as well have said "god be with you" as "the force be with you," since the statements are identical. The reason for the box-office success of a film of that type is because it portrayed on the screen that which the majority of the audience had been taught in church or Sunday school or on their mother or father's knee. Yet I did not see one reviewer in any major paper in the United States see what was so obvious or say anything about the biblical message delivered so overtly by this film.

The same thing applies to television as well as movies. What does all this do? It prepares us to meet the final holocaust, the final battle between good and evil.

By this time I know you are thinking, well, this writer has flipped. He has been an Atheist under fire so long that he will be seeing Jesus leaping out of the toilet next. Before you pass judgment on my sanity, consider this. Our present Secretary of State (former general) Haig, at the time he was in command of the NATO forces in Europe, said in a press interview that he felt that a real corporeal devil existed; that the devil in the flesh was a real living being with horns, a tail, a pitchfork, and all the trimmings; that our first duty as a nation was to hunt this devil down and destroy him; that we must fight the devil at all costs — even including nuclear war.

This man now has his finger on the button. He actually passed Senate confirmation hearings. I'll give you three guesses as to who the devil is in his mind and what all the people of the devil's land have in common. Give up? The U.S.S.R is the devil and all the people in the devil's kingdom are *Antichrists* or Atheists. I cannot see any difference between this and what I see on the screen in *Star Wars*. He will gather the army of the lord to fight the forces of evil.

I am not implying that the U.S.S.R. is a paragon of virtue as a nation. What I am saying is that I don't care to be hunted down as a devil-Atheist or nuked because an irrational man leading an irrational populace wants to kill demons. I would not be concerned it I did not see the White House and Congress lining up behind Haig in support of this madness. I remember seeing an anti-war poster in a head shop once that read over a scene of a military cemetery with an endless row of markers: "Here lie the unwilling, led by the unqualified, to do the unnecessary for the ungrateful."

What I see now in America is a new poster spread across the front pages, TV's, and wide screens from coast to coast. It shows thousands of eager, wide-eyed Christians pouring out of churches. The caption reads: "Here stand the *willing*, led by *qualified* maniacs, to do what their God tells them is *necessary*, to the heretic who 'will' be *grateful*."

The only way to insure that this remains only for a poster is to assert your rationality as an Atheist wherever and whenever possible. If we all pitch in maybe we can start the tide going in the other direction.

Prayer Doesn't Help

May 1981

I had just returned from an out-of-town business trip. It was one of those unforgettable kind where one has a flight canceled and one sits in some airport for three or four hours waiting for the next one. I had hardly walked in the office door when the radio blared out "Ronald Reagan shot in assassination attempt." Everything at the American Atheist Center stopped. We all rushed to the television to see what had happened. There it was, big as life, a shooting scene in vivid color and even slow motion.

I could not believe that it had happened again. The Kennedys, Martin Luther King, our own Atheist Bill Moore, George Wallace, Vernon Jordan, Malcolm X, two attempts on Gerald Ford, Larry Flynt. My first thought was oddly enough not for President Reagan but for Dr. O'Hair, my mother. On how many public appearances had I been with her where hostile, jeering crowds threatened? How many times has she received actual death threats? Thousands! I have often wondered why she had not met the same fate as George Wallace as yet — so unpopular is the Atheist stand.

No matter what the stance, political or religious, and no matter what the position given or the remark uttered, violence is not the solution to anything. I personally disagree with virtually everything that Reagan or his party represents. I feel that his policies on state/church separation are all in direct derogation to the Constitution of the United States. I must, since I disagree, know the solution: vote him out. Help the opposing candidate. Help the candidate of my choice. Murder is not among those solutions. Yet things like the Reagan shooting have happened before in America and most likely will continue to happen in the future. They must be dealt with as other emergencies have been dealt with in the past. This one, however, was not. It had a new wrinkle — the wrinkle of religion.

No sooner was Reagan in the hospital than the business of the Senate came to a halt. I see nothing wrong with that. I should have recessed to wait for news about his health. They did more than recess, however; they prayed. And oh, how they did pray! They were led by a conservative Republican senator in a prayer for god to come down and heal their fallen leader and heal all of the others who were shot.

In a time when they should have been concerned with the skill of the persons attending on Reagan and the others, they were concerned with god. None of the wounded had even died and they were praying for their souls.

Why is it that every time the nation has a crisis of any kind, the solution is always prayer? What do our leaders think this will accomplish?

It will accomplish nothing. Reagan is alive because the Secret Service and the police did their jobs well. One Secret Service man almost gave his life for the President. It would have been a great deal better and made a lot more sense for the Senate to thank that Secret Service man for his willingness to give his life, if need be, for the protection of the president. He and the wounded policeman were the real saviors, not Jesus Christ.

At the time of the Reagan shooting, Vice-President Bush was on his way to Texas to address the state legislature, among other things. When he had to turn around to go back to Washington on account of the shooting, the legislature here did not just call off the session for the day. No, they got a local Baptist minister in to lead them in prayer for Reagan and the nation. The pages of the Austin newspaper were filled with photos of all the state legislators with their heads bowed in prayer.

What we have here is our government, on both a national and state level, *officially* endorsing prayer as a means by which to handle a national emergency. To what have we come since the days of our inception as a nation? Thomas Jefferson would not have reacted in the same way to such a crisis as the Reagan shooting.

Billy Graham and other ministers rushed to the side of Nancy Reagan in order to comfort her in this troubled moment. The doctor attending on her husband would have been a more suitable comfort to her. That is the style of a person such as Graham, however. Get them while they are down. Prey on the emotions with prayer.

All of this is immediately and unthinkingly accepted by almost the entire population. "Well, of course, what else would do in a moment like this but pray?" The Texas legislature even prayed that the man who shot Reagan might be forgiven by the lord.

I have no doubt that if the would-be assassin were to be fully "redeemed" in the lord, as they say, he would be set back out on the street to try again in just a few years. If he can be made to turn to Christ, a minister will be called in to beg for his parole.

I cannot imagine a more sick or degrading state for a nation to be in than to drop to its knees in any emergency situation and beg for divine intervention. We have sunk to a new low.

Prior to his shooting, Reagan called for a national day of prayer and humiliation to be held on May 7th. It is not yet that date at the writing of this article, but I am sure that a willing nation will obey his command.

Now is the time then, more then ever before, for Atheists all over this land to stand up and make themselves heard and say, "No prayer!" We must shout out a loud and clear "no" to religious insanity. If we don't, we will be left with a nation of trained sheep.

I am asking each chapter to picket the federal building closest to them — the federal post office, the federal court, the federal building, whatever is located where the chapter is — on this infamous day when the president has called for prayer. I expect all our members to be there with a simple sign: "No! No prayer!"

The Pope Has Been Shot

June 1981

The pope has been shot and suddenly the Roman Catholic community — and the politicians who rely on the Roman Catholic vote — gather round to weep and bewail this attempt on what they call "the Vicar of Christ on Earth."

It is regrettable that any human being is shot by another. The education for such violence on an individual level is given by the governments of the world. The example is with those governments arming to the teeth for a nuclear confrontation. As the nations posture and threaten one the other to wipe out entire civilian populations to a man, as those nations call for more and more billions for armaments, they encourage individuals to seek violent solutions for their arguments also.

If we have an ideological argument with another nation, shall we win that argument through the use of firepower and war or through the use of logic and reason?

So it is with the individual terrorist who is determined to have his voice and his ideology represented by a gun.

It is regrettable, particularly, that the pope has been shot since he could well be martyrized and his repressive theology given impetus from the event.

The pope is a menace to humankind. He is a threat to the human community in his desire to drag us back to medievalism with his neofascistic, reactionary, inhuman, and authoritarian pronouncements.

The pope is anti-life, anti-peace, anti-woman, anti-human sexuality, anti-science — ah! but when he was shot, he immediately sought out medical science for the cure. He did not wait for the intercession of the Virgin Mary to assuage his wounds. A mass was said for him after he was out of the operating and the recovery rooms, not before he was taken to the hospital while his body lay oozing blood in the Vatican. Prayer then was not efficacious — surgery was.

It is always thus. While denouncing the very disciplines which bring some amelioration of the condition of mankind, the powerful always make use of those disciplines — such as medicine — for themselves.

The pope needs to live, not to die. He needs to live because his irrational and inhuman ideas must be defeated in a free marketplace of intellectual confrontation. Women cannot be told to retreat to the home. The Inquisition, which he has reinstated, must be closed again. There cannot be censorship of scholarship, of the press, or of speech. We have such little freedom now; it must be enlarged, not reduced. The pope has assailed sex education, birth control, free inquiry, and secular education. He must be shown to the world to be the reactionary, the medievalist, the neofascist, the authoritarian that he is. This can be done only if he is alive and well so that we may do battle with him.

A dead pope, enhancing the doctrines he promulgated while alive, would be replaced with another of an even more evil stripe.

The would-be assassin was ill-advised. He adds stature and dignity to the pope and gives him an aura of mysticism. Later, it will be claimed that the pope survived because god was with him. Again, this is powerful symbolism to reinforce ideas which are basically insane. The assassination attempt makes it more difficult to deal with the pope, not less. The would-be assassin should be dealt with in proper fashion, and quickly. Meanwhile, American Atheists will continue the fight against the pope, enemy of humankind.

Closet Atheism

July 1981

I have just returned from a one-month organizing tour of the Eastern seaboard for American Atheists. I was accompanied by Mr. Gerald Tholen, National Chapter Coordinator for American Atheists. What I say here and now is derived from not alone first impressions in many cities, but from thought and analysis of those impressions as the tour wore on.

About two years ago, I set out on a mission to visit every chapter of American Atheists that had been formed up to that time and to try to found some new chapters in cities where the response level of mailings indicated sufficient interest. Over the past two years I have met my goal of visiting every chapter or of starting those new ones. I wanted to get a sense of Atheism in the United States from individual Atheists. I felt that I needed to know what as many individuals as I could meet in that two-year period thought about themselves as Atheists, what they thought about an Atheist organization, and what that organization should do or be from their viewpoint.

I must admit that I started out with some preconceived notions of what I would find. I have had those notions shattered. I thought I would find knowledgeable Atheists. That is to say, knowledgeable about the true meaning of the term "Atheist," its roots and its historical personalities. I have not found any really knowledgeable Atheists in that broad sense of the word. That may know a great deal in their particular field of employment and have applied that information to a system of religious dogma and found that the dogma system was of no use to them in the life they lead, but they have not tried to extend their Atheistic thinking into other areas. I have been in the homes of Atheist sexists, Atheist racists, Atheist bigots, Atheist anti-environmentalists, Atheist fascists, Atheist economic determinists, and a host of others. That is to say that Atheists, by and large, compartmentalize their Atheism like a religionist compartmentalizes his religion. A Baptist is a Baptist on Sunday, and any other day of the week he can be for or against anything else, regardless of how it may agree or conflict with his theology. As a Baptist, his little packet of dogma from the church only relates back to the church; it is religion for religion's sake. Most Atheists I have met hold Atheism the same way; Atheism for the sake of Atheism. They either can not nor will not apply Atheist thought outside of Atheism. I really do not have the answer to the questions yet whether it is "can not" or "will not," and I know that a great deal of difference exists between those two attitudes.

I feel that it is impossible to be an Atheist and at the same time be a racist, a bigot, a sexist, a fascist, or against environmental conservation. The life-style of Atheism simply cannot fit with one of these non-freedom, or non-community concern, viewpoints.

In a general way the compartmentalizing of one's Atheism leads to a very egotistical and narrow life view. Atheists, by and large, have a concern for themselves and their very close family members only. They could care less about the family next door or across the street. Until the hand of religion touches their life in a personal way, they are not willing to combat religion in any way, either generally or specifically. Atheists, in general, I find to have a view analogous to the religious view of salvation, which is one of paddling their own little canoe to heaven and to hell (in the literal and figurative sense) without anyone else.

Now remember, I speak of the vast majority of Atheists I have met all over the country. There are some exceptions, but they are very few — probably one percent or less. I am concluding from personal experience and what has been said to me personally by persons holding themselves out to be Atheists.

Pending any direct encroachment of religion into the lives of these Atheists, they prefer to keep their Atheism in the closet. As long as it is in the closet, it need not be applied to anything. Atheism for them is something to be discussed at meetings, or the dinner table, or in terms of something they have seen on television or heard on radio. They don't live their Atheism. It is a philosophy to discuss, rather than a life-style to live. Of what use is a value system based on rational inspection and eclectic selection of alternatives if it is put on the shelf to be dragged out at meeting or convention time? It is of no use; that is the answer. Atheism is something to be lived and to be used day-to-day in one life situation after another, or it is not Atheism at all.

We have now, for the first time in America, something new in the theological area. We have a departure from the thinking of the Baptist (to whom I referred earlier) to a new thinking based on extroverted rather than introverted religionist behavior. The electronic preacher is trying to get his congregation to act on their religious dogma system and put that dogma into action in terms of all areas of their daily life. We, in turn, are trying to convince Atheists to put their Atheism to work in all areas. The success or failure of either group depends on which group motivates its adherents to act in areas outside of philosophy in their thought system first.

If the evangelicals get more persons to become extroverted with their theology before we can get the Atheists to become extroverted with their Atheism, they win. That is — they win the country, the Constitution, and control of society, *including* the control of Atheists. We must use the same tools as do they in order to win the race. They tell their congregations what can or will happen to them if they do not act on their theology in order to scare them into acting. All television commercials work on this same principle. They scare you into buying the product by showing you an undesirable result if the product is not used. If you don't use spray deodorant, you will stink; if you don't use brand X, your underwear will come out gray; if you don't use toothpaste Y, you will have to go the dentist and experience pain while he drills out cavities.

The commercial sell technique of fear works on everyone. The commercial sell technique of fear certainly works for the evangelical leaders. They don't even have to project a valid consequence for the non-use of theology, and it still works. Why does the same thing not work with Atheists? I don't have the answer to that yet, either. All I know is that it does not work. On the other hand, telling Atheists that they are the most wonderful persons in society by just being Atheists without their doing anything doesn't work either, if the goal is to get them to do something — which it is.

So, here we stand in a race with theology. The nature of the beast of a religionist is in the favor of the theological side. A religionist responds to all the time-tested commercial sell techniques. An Atheist responds to no technique. How does the Atheist even catch up, much less win? The answer is that he doesn't.

Two years ago I started out with the assumption that Atheists were smarter than religionists and could see around commercial sell techniques, see that others responded to them, and that they had to respond too, based on their understanding of why others responded in order not to lose by default. That assumption was wrong. So, I said to myself, "O.K. They can't see around behavior modification techniques, so use the techniques on them." I tried that too, but it did not work. My religious counterparts tried and it worked for them, since they knew their people could not see around advertising techniques.

I have seriously misjudged the intelligence level of the average

Atheist. I know, now, that the Atheist movement can only succeed by returning to basics. Atheists have to be brought up to the point where they have basic reactions based on achieving the goal of avoiding unpleasant consequences. They must understand that they can do what their Atheism drives them to do in many areas of social and cultural outreach, as a group, without facing the consequences they would face individually. The root to avoiding individual consequences of Atheist behavior is in collective simultaneous expression of that behavior. Groups are far less likely, especially well-organized and cohesive groups, to suffer consequences of actions taken than are individuals. This is a fact of history. The only large groups that have ever suffered for their opinions are those in which the individuals within the groups were willing to tolerate the suffering. The Atheist problem is that the majority of individuals with the group are willing to suffer. As long as there are Atheists who are willing to accept the negative consequences of being an Atheist, those of us who are unwilling to accept them and know that we can have our Atheism in full public view without negative consequences will be forced by those willing to accept them to do so as well.

Closet Atheists hurt all Atheists, not just themselves. What I have discovered in my travels is that we have a majority of closet Atheists within the Atheist circle, in proportions far beyond what I had thought. A reversal of that situation is the first priority for the survival and happiness of those of us who are already out.

Prayer as Legislative Fiat

August 1981

The American Atheist organization has had as one of its principal occupations the litigation of issues involving the constitutional separation of state and church. The organization has filed and argued a large number of such actions since its inception. It is becoming increasingly obvious, however, that the organization and Atheist plaintiffs in general can no longer seek redress for constitutional separation violations through the courts.

In 1959 the case of *Murray v. Curlett* was filed and taken through the United States Supreme Court, which rendered a decision in June of 1963. That decision, theoretically, ended religious ceremonies in public schools. Since that time neither the organization nor any individual Atheist plaintiff has "won" (that is, after each side having its day in court in the setting of a *full* hearing on the matter at bar). In order to determine why this is the case, one needs to look at the very nature of constitutional litigation as well as the specifics of the last in this list of "no win" cases, which is particularly instructive.

Our country captured a unique place in world history when it was founded with a constitution that included the concept of separation of state and church. The First Amendment to the Constitution divides that separation into the "Establishment" and the "Free Exercise" Clauses. The government may not establish the *institution* of any religion nor interfere with the freedom of any *individual* to practice or not to practice any particular religion. Thus we have separation guaranteed on two levels: the level of government involvement with whole religious institutions or groups, and the level of government involvement with individual conscience with respect to religion. Our government has then established for itself, from the beginning, a standard of conduct regarding any potential interactions between it and religion generally or individually. What happens when our government violates its own standards of conduct in this area?

The answer to this question is that an individual citizen (or group of citizens) must call the breach of that standard to the attention of one branch of government (the judicial) and ask that branch to compel the branch in violation of the standard (legislative or executive) to cease violation by modification of conduct, internal rules, procedures, usage, or pronouncements. The burden is then on the individual citizen to police his or her own government by pitting one branch thereof against the other. No provision exists for self-policing. When such a citizen police action is taken, the cost to the citizen is often extraordinary and prohibitive. The defense to the citizen plaintiff is, however, financed from tax funds. In effect, that means that the citizen must pay for (either directly or indirectly) the sides of both plaintiff and defendant in any action he or she initiates. Thus you, as a citizen, must bear the financial burden of forcing your government to adhere to its own standards, while doing it the favor of paying for its defense as well. In this setting the government has no responsibility — only the citizen. It is easy to see then why one of the major components of the defense in separation suits is stalling. The longer the defense drags a suit out, the more attorney's fees they collect from your tax funds and the more you have to spend directly out of pocket. The same holds true with a suit brought by an organization on behalf of individuals.

Another aspect of separation litigation is that the judicial branch of government has set up internal rules of its own governing interpretation of legislative and executive branch action in the separation area. The judicial branch then violates its own internal standard by which it determines if a violation has in fact taken place in one of the other branches. This "violation" of its internal standards is most often in the form of misinterpretation of those internal guidelines. The guidelines themselves are all too often written in an ambiguous form, which lends itself to misinterpretation, or with the use of undefinable terminology. A good example of an undefinable term is "benevolent neutrality," which was used to denote the preferred relationship between state and church with respect to the part of the state in regard to taxation of church property. How can the state be both benevolent and neutral in the correct sense of either word at the same time? The answer is it cannot. Neither can the court assume such a position.

For a number of years the courts established various and sundry internal standards for separation determination based on the fact situation of individual citizen police actions. Then in 1973, in the famous *Nyquist* case, the Supreme Court laid down a standard test that was a succinct review of the many individual actions gone before. This "*Nyquist test*" has since been viewed as the best, or governing, internal rule or standard for violation determination in separation cases. The *Nyquist* test is:

> [T]o pass muster under the Establishment Clause the law in question, first, must reflect a clearly secular legislative purpose, second, must have a primary effect that neither advances nor inhibits religion, and, third, must avoid excessive entanglement with religion.

Since the compilation of this test by the Supreme Court, the lower Federal courts and especially the State courts have done their level best to circumvent it via misinterpretation or misdefinition. Notice that this test applies only to the Establishment Clause. If a given court cannot place a particular citizen police action into the Free Exercise Clause category, then it must deal with this test for Establishment Clause violations if found.

If an individual asks for taxpayer-supported facilities for practice of his individual religion, and a citizen complains, the court says that the providing of those facilities has to do with "free exercise" for the individual, not "establishment" entanglement on the part of government. In that way such an action is more easily disposed of by the court. The logic is that the state is not "establishing" this man's religion by giving him public property to promote it on, but is in fact guaranteeing him "free exercise" of his religion, as if he could not have that "free exercise" on private property. With this kind of convoluted logic it becomes obvious that it is easier for the court to dispose of "free exercise" questions or questions that can be defined, although erroneously, as such. In many cases, however, they are stuck with "establishment" determinations.

Such an establishment case is that of *Marsa v. Wernik*, which was recently decided by the Supreme Court of the State of New Jersey. The court in this case, involving the opening of Borough Council meetings with prayer, had no choice but to determine "establishment," since governmental officials actually participated in the violation. The court reached the conclusion that the actions of the council did not violate the *Nyquist* test by the following reasoning:

> (A) The prayer has a clearly secular legislative purpose of "calling on the consciences and moral resolves of those in attendance at the council meeting and to inspire their wisest and fairest participation through a few opening moments of prayer or reflection."
>
> (B) The prayer has a primary effect of "solemnifying governmental proceedings" and "in its contextual setting is not sugges-

tive of religion or religious ritual."

(C) The prayer does not foster excessive government entanglement, since, although it "is conducted by individual council members, and to that extent is under an official aegis, it does not purport to be otherwise officially sponsored or authorized; rather each opening exercise can be viewed as the beliefs or sentiments of the individual in his private capacity."

Let us look at the faulty reasoning behind this decision. Mr. Marsa is an Atheist and a member of American Atheists. He is a regular attendant at the Borough Council meetings as a businessman in his community. He is offended by the action of the council as an Atheist. Let's review the court point by point.

(A) The court says that prayer can be secular under the right circumstances. In a council meeting they feel that its purpose is that of acting as a gavel to call the meeting to order and set the tone for it. Looking at the terms involved, we find "prayer" defined by *The Random House Dictionary of the English Language* as "a devout petition to, or any form of *spiritual* communication with God or an object of worship"; or, giving the benefit of semantics, "invocation" is defined first as "the act of invoking or calling upon a deity, *spirit*, etc., for aid, protection, inspiration, or the like," "supplication," and third as "a form of *prayer* invoking God's presence, said esp. at the beginning of a public ceremony."

"Secular" is defined as "of or pertaining to worldly things or to things that are not regarded as religious, *spiritual*, or sacred; temporal."

Noticing the word spiritual in all three definitions as their nexus (another court term), how can one come to the conclusion that "prayer" (which equals "invocation" by the above) can be "secular" under *any* set of circumstances? It cannot. Prayer is not and cannot be construed to be secular.

(B) If this prayer "solemnifies governmental proceedings" and acts as a gavel, then why have a gavel at all? In fact, the Borough Council meeting is gaveled to order first; then a formal announcement of such a calling to order being in compliance with requirements of the Open Public Meetings Act of that state is given; then a roll call of members is taken; then the mayor asks for those who wish to, to rise for the invocation.

After all of this — the gavel, notice of compliance with the Open Public Meetings Act, and roll call — is a prayer needed? Would one not assume that the meeting had been called to order by the end of three official actions by the mayor? Should not everyone be quiet and set for the meeting by that time? Yes, they should. Even a roomful of children would be quiet, have their attention properly called, and be ready to listen well before the call for prayer. The prayer is then gratuitous.

(C) Until June of 1976, Borough Council meetings were opened by local clergy. After that, individual council members began giving the invocations. The court says that because individual members give personalized invocations, they cannot be said to entangle government. Prayer is by its nature an individual act. When you pray, you ask for god to grant you a wish that will redound to your benefit either directly or indirectly; otherwise, why ask for it? Even if a group leader says a prayer while others assume a reverential posture, each person in the group is hoping for a result from the prayer that meets *his* individual needs, even if it also meets the needs of a group incidentally. All that is really important to any group member is that his wish is fulfilled, even if the larger group wish (often given in a general way) is not fulfilled.

Therefore, the fact that the prayer is given by and composed by individual council members is of no significance to the act itself. Prayer is individual, no matter how it is presented. The entire history of religion points to individual "judgment" by a deity in reply to supplication and individual "salvation" or lack thereof.

What is important is government authorization or the placing of a governmental seal of approval on the prayer. The mayor goes through three steps in order to prepare the room for the prayer. The mayor gets the attention of all those present and even cites the legal aegis by which their attention is commanded prior to the prayer. The presiding government official, in an official manner, sets the stage and prepares the audience for the prayer as an obviously important part of the proceedings. Such preparation signals to me the importance placed on the prayer by the mayor and council members. It is then in fact authorized and approved as an appropriate action by the council in its official capacity. Marsa is not complaining about the content of the prayers, but their use generically. Preparation for the prayer and giving it an official place in the meeting agenda is the entanglement. The content of the prayer could only be properly addressed under A or B above and not under the third part of the *Nyquist* test.

The point to be gained from this is that religious persons in the United States are determined to make their religion a pervasive part of our culture from every official standpoint. Any tool for promotion of theology in general is a valid tool, including the state, from the standpoint of a religionist. Judges, as people, cannot rise above their theological upbringings or positions in their decision-making. The faith must be defended, even if it is watered down to the point of nonexistence first. We seem to be at the same old mentality of "we had to burn the village in order to save it" again, as we were during the war in Vietnam (which we called a police action in the nomenclature style of the court).

The lesson for Atheists is that until we can capture the power to define, litigation can only serve the purpose of raising public awareness on selected issues. You cannot fight an opponent capable of redefining or changing the rules every time you challenge one. Prayer cannot be secular in one context and nonsecular in another at the whim of the court and make Atheist police actions on government either effective or practical. The seizure of the power to define comes with numbers. Identification on the part of individual Atheists is the key to gathering the numbers, and cooperation between those numbers is needed to seize the power to define, so that Constitutional violations of state/church separation become just that — violations — instead of hallowed institutions.

Atheists as Outcasts

September 1981

Last month I commented on the case of *Marsa v. Wernik*, which has been decided by the Supreme Court of the State of New Jersey. That case involved the opening of Borough Council meetings with prayer or an "invocation." Since the time of the *Marsa* decision, The American Atheist Center has filed two new important Establishment cases in two different states in quick succession. These were filed in Arkansas and Mississippi on July 14th and 15th, respectively.

In order to understand their importance and why they were filed, we need to look at a little history. Five states of the Union have sections in their constitutions that speak to the rights of Atheists. These states are North Carolina, South Carolina, Arkansas, Mississippi, and Texas. In each state a "belief in God" is required as a prerequisite to holding public office. Back in 1979, the constitution of North Carolina was challenged in a suit filed by the Charlotte Chapter of American Atheists. That suit never came to trial, because the governor and attorney general of North Carolina both admitted to the unconstitutionality of the belief requirement. As a result, a "consent decree" was signed by all involved to declare the requirement of belief in god to be unconstitutional, and this decree was then issued by a Federal District Court.

A similar case filed in Texas has not been met with similar cooperation from that state's authorities. It has been opposed since 1977, and now rests in the Fifth Federal Circuit Court of Appeals in New Orleans, Louisiana. The State of Texas has spent tens of thousands of dollars of taxpayer funds fighting this case, and shows no sign of giving up yet. The Appeals Court itself has had a rather odd reaction to the case, however, doing something that it has very rarely done in its history. When the Texas case first reached the appellate level, oral arguments were heard and the court upheld the Texas constitution by a vote of two to one (with a three judge panel). The decision was sent back down to the Federal District Court in Austin, Texas, remained on the desk of the Federal District judge for about one week, and was recalled by the three judges of the Fifth Circuit Appeals Court. Since the "recall," both sides have been puzzled as to what the Fifth Circuit had up its sleeve. No word came from the court for several months.

While the recall of the Texas case was pending further action, The American Atheist Center filed the two actions in Arkansas and Mississippi. Article 19, Section 1 of the Arkansas Constitution says, "No person who denies the being of God shall hold any office in the civil departments of this State, nor be competent to testify as a witness in any Court." Article 14, Section 265 of the Mississippi Constitution says, "No person who denies the existence of a Supreme Being shall hold any office in this state." Both of these provisions can be seen to be clearly, on their face, abrogations of the rights of Atheists in those two states. Yet, preliminary indications are that both states are willing to fight for these provisions, no matter what the cost or how long the struggle.

To give you an idea of how the people of these two states regard these laws: In Mississippi a former attorney general, while in office, remarked that he thought the provision in his state's constitution was valid and that it would serve to see that only "good" men occupied public office. He felt and said that anyone who could look at the flowers and not see the wonder of god's handiwork was insane, and that the state had a legitimate right to keep insane persons out of public office. When American Atheists went to Jackson, Mississippi, to file the action on behalf of an Atheist and member in that state, the organization was unable to find an attorney in the Jackson area — or the state, for that matter — with the courage to represent them. One attorney came to the motel room of Dr. O'Hair and myself and said that he would be ruined if he associated himself with the word "Atheist" publicly in the state. He said that he must think of his family and children, and that he would never be able to practice his vocation of law again if he associated with "Atheism." To this date no attorney in the state of Mississippi has come forward to handle the case. As a result, the individual Atheist involved had to file *pro se*, tackling the case on his own until such time as counsel could be found. The local Atheist involved is in his eighties. The entire legal community of the state of Mississippi is afraid to challenge a law that is blatantly unconstitutional and are willing to be led by an octogenarian.

In Arkansas, official reaction seems to be that the provision in the state's constitution has not been enforced in recent years and therefore does not merit consideration for a change. From their view, discriminatory law is permissible as long as it is in form only and not in application. Form is, however, very important. If the state can deny a section of its population full rights on paper, it has set the tone for discrimination on all other levels of daily life, both business and personal, against that section by the general population. States such as Arkansas know that they dare not enforce such discriminatory provisions in their constitutions, since the act of enforcement would give standing to a member of the class discriminated against, to allow the courts to strike it. A state creates a law, allows it to become vestigial, and then claims that its vestigial character makes changing it unnecessary and gives grounds for resisting that change.

Only those laws which are meritorious in their own right and enforced or are enforceable should be on the books. If a law is ceremonial only and is not enforced, what is the purpose of its continued maintenance as a law? It is like an official at a sporting event insisting on keeping a rule in the rule book that is never enforced on the field of play and is considered to have no bearing on the outcome thereof. Yet, over and over again government entities argue for the retention of vestigial laws, with the argument that they must be kept because they are ceremonial and are not enforced.

A ceremony is inextricably entangled from a definitional standpoint with religion and operant conditioning. A ceremony is something that you do because those who have gone before have done it, not because you know why you are doing it or because it has any merit. Carrying out a ceremony is most often an emotional consideration. Why be sworn with your hand on a Bible? Why have "In God We Trust" as a national motto? Why have "In God We Trust" on the coins? Why have prayer in school? Why open a public meeting with a prayer? No one who participates in any of these activities can tell you why he does it. His only answer would be "just because!" or "why not?"

In the Arkansas suit, the state's first action after filing was to take the depositions of the two individual member litigants involved. Since the Arkansas constitution says that no Atheist is "competent to testify as a witness in any Court," how can the depositions be admissible? They cannot.

Once again this drives home the point that you cannot play a game with an opponent who can obey or not obey the rules of the game at will, while you must always obey them to the letter. The only solution is for you to capture the rules and make them steadfast and impartial. This can only be done through the power of numbers and coordination. Organized religion has the numbers and the coordination. American Atheists has neither.

Until we develop the coordination and gain the numbers, via dragging Atheists out of the closet, our chances of doing something about these irrational laws are slim.

Israel
October 1981

The Middle East is probably the most tenuously balanced area in the world today. A disturbance in that balançe could lead to global implications almost overnight. Much of the information from this area is so twisted that no one really knows what is happening at any given time. Some things are clear, however, in an overweening way. The basic one of these is that the problems faced by all concerned in the Middle East stem from religion.

Each participant in the balance holds particular religious tenets with ferocity. Those tenets overshadow their judgment of the problems in the area. Unless one recognizes the theological basis for the position of all concerned in the Middle East, one has missed the boat in terms of understanding what keeps the area in such turmoil.

The primary religion that has caused the most problem in the Middle East is, of course, as in most troubled areas, the minority one. Any time that a minority religion, in terms of numbers only, seeks to dominate a geographical area in which it is outnumbered by manyfold, there is conflict. If the greater numbers or majoritarian religion dominates, the minority is usually either ignored or persecuted, as the case may be, without the conflict spreading to global proportions.

What we have in the Middle East, with the theocratic Jewish state of Israel, is a small group of religious zealots (small in terms of the number of non-Jewish Semites in surrounding areas) who are determined to physically, militarily, economically, culturally, and religiously dominate. This domination of a geographical area in which the Jew is a recent import is based upon the claim of the Jew that the Old Testament stories of the Bible give them the status of "god's chosen people" — being "chosen" by that god to rule the area in question. They back this biblical imperative with the money and modern weapons of one of the two greatest military powers in the world today — the United States.

Those of the Jewish religion in the United States apply pressure so that billions of dollars of tax support is given each year to Israel, whether the United States can afford it or not, in terms of domestic considerations. Many non-Jews in the United States back this support because their own religion owes its origin to the Jewish writings of antiquity. What we have is some three million alleged Ashkenazic-type Semites, not all of the Jewish faith, (and *that is all*, by their own count) in this country who extort six billion dollars worth of military and other aid for Israel annually from our 215 million Non-Jewish.

Not alone could these funds be used for domestic programs for all Americans, but the exempted taxes and the interest involved could lower the tax burden for all our citizens.

On top of the monetary loss, these same three million (alleged) Jews pressure the broadcast industry so that it gives continued support to their position. When have *you* ever seen a program, on any network, giving either the Muslim or P.L.O. prospective of the Middle East situation? Never. It is not permitted. It is not permitted for the same reason that you have never seen an accurate presentation of the political concept of communism on any media, or an accurate presentation of Atheism. What you do see is a continued degradation of Germany (and persons of German descent). Often this is very subtle but there, just the same. Indeed, who is not sick of the repeated propaganda pieces of *Masada, Exodus, Fiddler on The Roof,* and Old Testament stories (always starring the non-Jew Charlton Heston)? One more "holocaust" documentary will set us all screaming and clawing the walls.

Let us look at the following example. Your ancestors came to the United States on the first boat of settlers. One of your great grandfathers started a farm, fresh off that boat. Every succeeding generation of your family was born and reared on that acreage. Then, one day an army of religious zealots came in militarily and took your land. They took the house in which all of your forefathers had been born for the last 400 years. The village down the road, where you had sold your crops for generations, they wiped off the map completely. It does not exist any more. At that point, would you fight for your land? Of course you would. Would those of your family who survived or who were taken prisoners be bitter and hostile to the new landlord? Of course they would. Now multiply that loss by a factor of twenty to make it more like the 8,000 years that your family had claim to the land. And, remember that the only claim the intruders would stress would be their religious right to the land.

You will then know exactly how the Palestinians feel about Israel. Have you ever heard that view expressed openly in the United States? No, because the dominant Judeo-Christian community here will not permit it. Yet, that is how the Palestinians see it. Should not that view be given equal time at any and every set of negotiations held by the parties involved to bring an end to the hostilities in the Middle East? Reason dictates so, I think.

As an Atheist, I am not impressed by biblical admonitions. That the Jews are supposed to be the "chosen people" of god has no bearing on the fact that they are causing my country to be involved in the support of the theocratic state of Israel. The nation in the world which pioneered the concept of separation of state and church cannot now turn to support of a theocracy — any theocracy, anywhere. I do not advocate support of the P.L.O. by the United States, either. We need to stay clear and assume a neutral position with respect to the religious claims involved. We do not.

The myths that were compiled to form modern Judeo-Christianity had their origins in the area we now call the Middle East. On the basis of those tales and myths, the United States will support a theocracy to the point of nuclear war. For if the spawning ground of the tales that we now call Christianity is violated, its adherents fear that it will fail. We find ourselves involved in a new twentieth century crusade, a crusade to regain the "holy land" through the mercenary services of the theocracy of Israel.

Someone must expose this idiocy. No one in the religious community can. So it is up to the Atheists.

Now, some of you have written this journal in the past referring to yourselves as Jewish Atheists. A spate of letters has been received at the Atheist Center objecting to any comments in this journal regarding Israel or Judaism, by persons designating themselves as Jewish Atheists. *There is no such thing as a Jewish Atheist.* The term "Jewish" refers to a religious stance, not an ethnic group. "Semite" is the proper term for the ethnic group. There are many non-Semites who are religiously Jewish also. (Sammy Davis and Elizabeth Taylor, to name two!) All "Jewish" customs are based on religious ritual. The true Jew has no secular holiday or custom or food habit. All of these are dictated by holy rote. Everything that an individual hails as making him "Jewish" is based on religious ritual.

I will, as an Atheist, publicly denounce U.S. aid to Israel and ask for the inclusion of the P.L.O. in any and all talks relevant to situations in the Middle East held by any party. I do not ask all Atheists to share this view, but I do feel that it is the only view consistent with upholding the secular nature of our country — what is left of it. I cannot stand idly by and watch my country plan a holocaust as a self-fulfilling prophesy of a myth. That is simply too bizarre. My intelligence and desire for self-preservation will not let me remain silent any longer.

Censored

November 1981

"Censorship" used to be an ugly word to most Americans. It conjured up images of Thomas Paine struggling to distribute *Common Sense* against British opposition. Just the mention of the word would bring the old hand-over-the-heart reaction of "not in America." Not so anymore. The new Christian movements across the country are finding out that censorship is a needed component of religious indoctrination. If our young people are allowed to read and see and listen to all things and explore for themselves, medieval church doctrines will be hard for them to swallow. What can be done? Simply remove any material that does not follow Christian dogma from the reach of children and insulate them from reality. What is real — that is, a true picture of the trials of everyday life — is being replaced with idealism right under our noses.

A 1980 survey of 1,891 school officials (sponsored by the Association of American Publishers, the American Library Association, and the Association of Supervision and Curriculum Development, covering the school years of 1978 and 1979) showed that one-fourth of those surveyed said one or more books, films, or magazines were challenged in their area during those years. Half of those challenges resulted in one of the following actions:

a) **Restricted circulation** of the offending material. For example, in Whiteville, North Carolina, the county library has an "adult" shelf. The library issues restricted cards to those children whose parents don't want them bringing home "adult" books.

b) **Removal of the material** altogether. The *American Heritage Dictionary*, for example, has been removed from school libraries in parts of Texas because it contains colloquial definitions of words such as *hot, hooker, coke, clap, deflower, tail, ball, knocker, nuts,* and *bed.* Some of the books and publications that have been removed from various school libraries across the country include such titles as *Sports Illustrated* magazine for its photos of swimmers in bikinis, *Brave New World* by Aldous Huxley, *A Farewell to Arms* by Ernest Hemingway, *Robin Hood* for its condoning of robbery, all of Charles Dickens' novels except *Oliver Twist*, *To Kill A Mockingbird*, *Esquire* magazine,

Catcher In The Rye, Ms. magazine, the play *Death of A Salesman*, all of Shakespeare except *Hamlet* and *Romeo and Juliet, The House of Seven Gables, Robinson Crusoe*, and last, but not least, *Huckleberry Finn*.

c) **Cutting offending parts** of any books, films, or magazines. For example, a principal in Romeo, Michigan, scissored the bosom from a recent *Time* cover photo of Cher Bono before allowing the magazine to be placed on the school library shelf.

d) **Destroying the offensive material**. Book burnings are now widespread. Christian groups in Michigan, Indiana, Kentucky, Tennessee, Texas, and Illinois, to name a few, have burned books and records and even color TVs to demonstrate public opposition to what they feel are "un-Christian" influences on society.

A full seventy-five percent of those reporting in this survey said that there was a change in their area in censorship and that it was on the increase.

The pro-censorship battle is being waged primarily in the school at this point. Parents, if they really try, can do a pretty effective job of insulating their children from reality at home. When they are forced by truancy laws to let their children out into the real world for so many hours each day, they must do either one of two things: control the environment into which they place their children as they do the environment of their home or remove their children from the public school system into a system that reflects the home environment. Many parents who can afford the move are taking the latter course of action. There are, on the average, three Christian schools *per day* being opened in the United States. Since a move to a private school (parochial or not) entails extra cost, the fight is also on for tuition tax credits or similar aid to parents fleeing public institutions. Government is being asked to either change publicly-funded educational institutions to meet Christian standards or provide "separate but equal" facilities at taxpayer expense.

If parents really desire a Christian environment for their children, it is their duty and not that of the state to provide that environment. Pressure is now so heavy on individual schools and school boards that many are running scared. Teachers are now beginning to carry tape recorders into the classroom whenever they present a topic for the day's lecture that may be considered controversial. In that way they can defend themselves against angry parents when a child reports a given incident to his parents at the end of the school day. If any misinterpretation is involved on the part of the child, the teacher has a record of exactly what was said, and more importantly in what context, during a given class period.

A very telling example of parent pressure on the classroom can be seen in Plano, Texas, where teachers are no longer permitted to ask students for their opinions on various subjects because to do so would be to deny absolute right and wrong. This kind of thinking has given rise to the creation of a new "devil" to be battled in the classroom, the devil of "secular humanism." According to fundamentalist groups, secular humanism is a philosophy which places man at the center of the universe, encourages free thought and scientific inquiry without deference to a supreme being, and offers no absolute standard of ethics. If any schools of which I am aware were actually teaching that, they would be outstanding in standards far and above schools anywhere else. I can't think of anything more valuable to be taught to our children than to encourage them into "free thought and scientific inquiry" in all areas.

Secular humanism is, in fact, reality. Anything that even borders on giving the child a real view of what actually happens in the world can be placed under this all-too-broad label. According to the Christian view, everything must have a label. All things must be either good or evil. Nothing is neutral. To the Atheist, mathematics is neutral, as it is simply a problem-solving tool. To the religionist, mathematics is evil, since it does not directly promote god ideas and bolsters the value of "proof" and "logic." This kind of black and white view of things comes directly from the thematic biblical admonitions of Christ when he says, "Those who are not for me are against me." Everything must fit into either the "for" or the "against" column to be dealt with under the Christian scheme. As Atheists, we know that life is not a simple black and white. We have not only many grey areas but a multitude of colors.

The secular humanism battle is extending now far beyond the schools, however. Television and radio are now coming under attack. Recently the chairmen of the boards of both Procter and Gamble Company and General Foods have withdrawn sponsorship and advertising from such shows as "Soap" (ABC), "Three's Company" (ABC), "Dallas" (CBS), "Saturday Night Live" (NBC), "Charlie's Angels" (ABC), "The Newlywed Game," and "The Dating Game." Network executives seem to be giving in to pressures such as these, especially since they now have the competition of CBN (the Christian Broadcasting Network) and thousands of Christian cable network productions. CBN has recently gone to playing old motion pictures of the '30s and '40s as a more "wholesome" alternative to shows such as

ABC's "Charlie's Angels." That is, of course, in keeping with the general Christian tendency to hold back the clock and return to those good old days of puritanism.

One of the most astonishing aspects of the whole censorship movement is a new version of the classic "Mother Goose" stories now in print entitled *The Christian Mother Goose Treasury*. This new version sold 520,000 copies in twenty-three months with such rewrites as:

Humpty Dumpty sat on a wall,
Humpty Dumpty had a great fall.
Humpty Dumpty shouted, "Amen!
God can put me together again."

. . . and:

Little Miss Muffet
Sat on a tuffet
Thanking Jesus for curds and whey;
There came a big spider
And sat down beside her,
To listen to Miss Muffet pray.

Where do the Atheists stand with respect to all of this censorship in the name of piety? Mostly they stand aghast and mutter comments like, "How shocking" or "That's incredible." While they look on, the Christians march right in. A zealous religionist has no qualms about marching right into a principal's office and demanding a book be removed from the school library. To them it is the right thing to do. They have never thought otherwise. In the same manner, many of them whip their children because their parents whipped them, and if a teacher won't, they can't imagine why not. Many religionists are willing to jeopardize their family financial situation in order to litigate on the issues of school prayer, creationism, tuition tax credits, corporal punishment, sex education, and many others. The consequences of long-term legal action are secondary; their Christian principles are first.

The problem we face, as Atheists, is how to fight extremism of the kind evidenced by the censorship movement. One cannot fight extremism from a middle-of-the-road-stance. If a fighter goes into the ring against an opponent who knows that a win is a must for his career, and continues with the attitude that this is just another fight, only a show, and the outcome does not matter, he will be beaten. To the religionist, winning is everything. Maintaining a principle is everything. To many Atheists, the principles of an Atheist life-style are transitory. They are alive in word but often not in deed. Religious principles are always flaunted without hesitation. When we, as Atheists, can proceed without hesitation to stand up for freedom of speech and freedom of the press and all the freedoms which make up freedom of the mind, then we have a chance. In the meantime, we will continue to stand aghast, in default, nose raised high, too good for the fray. We must match with equal determination and diligence those who seek, through censorship, to quell the spirit of free inquiry that brought most of us to Atheism in the first place.

The Hydra Head of Religion

January 1982

The American Civil Liberties Union (ACLU), although doing an adequate job of protecting civil liberties in some areas (such as criminal search and seizure, *etc.*), has by and large been an organization enamored of the establishment. Their presentation, especially on issues involving separation of state and church, can be characterized by the oft-repeated film scene of an old Victorian crone, dressed in black, looking over her spectacles at a pretty young thing entering the parlor, ankles exposed, and remarking, "Oh! How unseemly!" I guess I should be grateful that they notice at all.

Only a fraction of what is noticed is acted upon. This I can understand from a logistical perspective, knowing as I do the cost and complexities of litigation. That desire to remain "respectable" has, over the years, still cost the ACLU a lot and the public even more in terms of the decreasing circle of liberty we all find closing in around us.

The tactic of the respectable fighter is to come at you, instinctively (a product of family and school training) within the Marquis of Queensberry rules, only to go down swiftly from a kick to the groin. When fighting someone or something that is fighting for survival, it is more prudent to put some of those rules aside. The old adage of "fight fire with fire" still has some merit.

What the ACLU should have been doing all these years is to strike at the core or root or radical of the problem, especially in the state/church area. Instead, they have battled the peripheral consequences of key systemic flaws in our social, legal, and governmental systems, leaving the radical actions to groups of lesser financial ability and groups certainly without their "social" connections. The result of this has been that those more radical groups and individuals have taken a terrible beating in the courts, thereby laying down a foundation of bad legal precedent that the more conservative ACLU finds a now-impenetrable obstacle. They cannot get any further now with the courts than did the groups they looked down their noses at years earlier (and still do today) as being "scruffy fanatics." If the ACLU, with its superior numbers and financing, had lent a hand where it was really needed in the '50s and '60s, it would not have such a hard time now.

The ACLU attitude toward Atheists is a prime example of this. Back in 1959, when the case that eventually removed Bible reading and prayer recitation from the public schools was in its infancy, the then Madalyn Murray went to the ACLU for help. It was swiftly denied. They were too respectable to get involved with Atheists then, and they are too respectable now. When American Atheists challenged the right of the pope to give a mass on the Washington, D.C., mall at public expense, an ACLU attorney from the District was right in there on the side of the Roman Catholic Church and the right of the pope to have "free speech" in America, although the ACLU knew full well that "free speech" was not the issue in the case at the time.

The only conclusion one can reasonably come to is that the maintenance of its financial base is most important to the ACLU, and they therefore cannot afford to alienate monetary support by backing unpopular issues. To the best of my knowledge, the national ACLU budget now is about $11,000,000 ($6,000,000 in the field and $5,000,000 for the national office) annually. One could ask, however, what is the use of remaining silent to collect funds and to do nothing with them out of the fear of losing them by doing something unpopular?

American Atheists has reached out on many occasions to the ACLU for help and with help, but our hand has always been somehow too dirty to touch. We, therefore, have forged ahead with case after case on principle and have suffered many a defeat because we lack the ACLU level of funding and availability of legal personnel. Those lost American Atheist cases have been used to defeat the ACLU in its less-obtrusive actions now on several occasions.

We at American Atheists will continue to fight on a radical level with or without help from the ACLU or any other organization, but they need to be put on notice and need to realize that our loss is their loss.

Speaking about losses, we all have a lot to lose, perhaps in the near future, and those losses will be across the board — not discriminating against liberal or conservative. Just recently, the ACLU has come to a partial conclusion that the combination of their legal snobbery and the defeats of others has placed them in the position of needing to look toward legislative lobbying activity in place of the courts as a route to halt the march of the "New Right" in Congress. In fact, that realization has even brought the ACLU to the point of being willing to forfeit their tax-exempt status to enter into the activation of what they call the "National Bill of Rights Lobby."

American Atheists likewise realizes the mounting futility of legal action, but its budget does not permit it to enter into lobbying, and its tax-exempt status is crucial to its survival. ACLU, on the other hand, can probably operate quite effectively as a lobbying group. They have the numbers and the established funding base that American Atheists does not have.

Perhaps the movement of the ACLU into the lobbying area is a good thing. Groups such as American Atheists never got any help on the legal front from the ACLU anyway, and perhaps now our radical styles can operate unfettered while the ACLU targets Congress, which is an entity unreachable by the Atheist community at this stage in its development. If ACLU action in Congress can in the least slow down the moral majoritarians and their New Right allies, it will give Atheists the opportunity to concentrate on the legal front, with the ACLU being helpful in a noncompeting area. It will surely require a double punch of legislative and legal pressure to counter the forces of organized religion.

Some of the reasons why the ACLU has decided to move into legislative action are worth enumerating. We should all be at least aware of what is going on, even though our individual ability to do something about it may be limited to donating to the organization of our choice. Let's take a look at some of what the legislative and executive branches are up to.

1) President Reagan has granted pardons to FBI officials who were convicted of illegal breaking and entering under the pretext of their acting in the name of "national security." Reagan just recently issued an executive order expanding the power of intelligence agencies to mount some kinds of covert operations domestically, to step up surveillance of Americans abroad, and to "infiltrate" domestic organizations. The orders restore the authority of the CIA to conduct activities domestically as long as they do not affect *U.S.* policies, politics, or press; they authorize the CIA to infiltrate U.S. organizations, including those largely composed of aliens *thought* to be acting on behalf of a foreign power; and they authorize shadowing of Americans abroad and monitoring of corporations to obtain "important foreign intelligence" that "cannot be obtained by other means."

What that really means is that the "if-mommy-is-a-commie-then-you-got-to-turn-her-in" syndrome is back with us again. American Atheists fully expects to be one of the first groups on the list to be "infiltrated." That will be nothing new, of course. The offices of American Atheists have had their phone lines tapped so often in the past that at one point they had the tappers taking messages when the staff was away from the phones. That would be a welcome service again in these days of governmental cutbacks and runaway phone bills.

2) The U.S. Attorney General's Task Force on Criminal Violence recommended a change in legislation to encourage law enforcement agencies to conduct unconstitutional searches. It also proposed that judges have the power to imprison persons they deem "dangerous" for a period of time without a trial. This preventative detention could be used against almost any individual who needs to be "silenced" in his or her expression of an unpopular cause.

American Atheists president Dr. Madalyn O'Hair has gone to jail now many times simply for being an Atheist. These jailings have been under a series of bizarre interpretations of antiquated laws used simply as a harassment procedure. In the future, however, such "detention" could be done in an open and straightforward manner, although still accomplishing the same thing — harassment.

3) A move to resurrect the House Un-American Activities Committee has been cosponsored by 158 members of the House. In addition, the Department of Justice is proposing major changes in the Freedom of Information Act to broaden what can be exempted from public view. There is also a campaign within Congress to reestablish an "Internal Security Apparatus," and Reagan has taken the first step in that establishment, as mentioned above.

Too many new books and other publications, as well as documentaries, have surfaced since the passage of the Freedom of Information Act. An exposed intelligence apparatus cannot function. What we see here is a repeat of the trepidations of our government in 1917. At that time, the Russian revolution had every world power on edge for fear that the revolutionary sentiment would spread.

Our government is shaky now. There are major problems in many areas. They fear what the church fears, which is the estrangement of their constituency. Just as the pope hopes to "circle the wagons" with his new conservative policies and hold the flock together, our government hopes to displace the fears of domestic failure with the fear of external infiltration to maintain calm. Whether it's the communists or Libya, the spook of the enemy without keeps our minds off the enemy within — our own representatives.

4) Renewal of the Voting Rights Act of 1965 is facing stiff opposition in Congress. It is quite possible that an entire large segment of our population, the Blacks, could be disenfranchised.

5) Budget reductions have now begun to seriously hamper administrative enforcement agencies. The Justice Department now backs away from many civil rights cases it at one time would have litigated. In addition, the Senate of the United States has passed a rider to the

appropriations bill for the State, Justice, and Commerce departments to endorse organized prayer in public schools by removing authorization from the Justice Department to spend public funds to litigate against school districts violating the law in that area. Only Senator Lowell P. Weicker opposed with a filibuster. Asked about right-wing attacks on the Constitution and Federal courts, he said, "They cheapen everything . . . when they use the Constitution as a garbage receptacle for every one of their philosophical quirks" (*New York Times*, 11/30/81).

Good "Christian" activities such as arms buildup can be financed, but not upholding the law, especially when it comes to the Constitution. Money is no object to maintain our "national technical means" (in the jargon of the State Department, "spies" to all of us lay persons) for domestic as well as foreign work.

6) The Legal Services Corporation, which provides legal representation to the poor, is being fought by the Conservative Caucus and other rightist groups. Equal access to justice has never been a real factor in our justice system. Those who have the funding are always more represented than those who lack financial strength. It may now be even more difficult than ever before for the poor or minorities to fight back.

7) The Family Protection Act is now pending in Congress. This Act would withdraw federal funding from school systems which do *not* institute periods of prayer or silent meditation. It would require textbooks to depict women solely in domestic roles. The purpose of the bill is to create a legal atmosphere under which a Christian-value-based "nuclear family" concept can be government-promoted, while discouraging "deviancy" therefrom. It is a selective protection act, "protecting" the rights of those who choose to conduct their personal family affairs in a particular style only.

8) A new mood is in Congress to prohibit federal courts from even hearing claims of unconstitutionality from individuals or groups in certain subject areas. The most prominent of these subject areas is school prayer, although busing and abortion run a close second. Limiting or excluding federal court review in any legislative area would alter our basic form of constitutional government. What we would have left is a two-part system with no checks and balances. With only the executive and legislative branches left and the judicial pushed out of the picture, a strong personality in the White House with majority backing in both houses of Congress could take over, Khomeini-style. The founding fathers set up a well balanced system at first in order to prevent such an occurrence, and it has fared well for over 200 years

now. Only Senator Edward Kennedy has spoken up against actions to limit judicial review of Congress in the Senate so far.

9) Jesse Helms and others of his ilk are pushing a "Human Life Bill" which would give a fetus full constitutional rights from conception, making abortion or *birth control* methods illegal. The "Right to Life" amendment to the Constitution proposed earlier has not fared well in the states. This bill is an attempt to circumvent the mandated constitutional amending process. All of the concern over abortion rights is based on biblical doctrine rather than freedom of conscience considerations.

10) Sen. Strom Thurmond is backing the return of the federal death penalty and the expansion of its application to crimes other than homicide.

All of the new right-wing religious efforts in Congress are really nothing new. They have been going on *sub rosa* for many years now. The difference today is that these actions are flaunted instead of being carried out in closed-door meetings or during social contacts between government officials and church leaders. The question is what can be done about it by those of us who realize the danger at hand. The answer to that question is a difficult one.

Currently, the "liberal" community is fragmented. On one side are the respectable groups and on the other side the non-respectable groups, with each side claiming the reverse. The churches, too, are rent with schisms, but with one very important and overriding difference. Whenever the root, or core, of their religiosity is challenged, they can work together and do work together. Though their petty theological differences keep them at one another's throats on the surface, try challenging their tax exemptions, for example, and see how quickly they band together. The religious community has always had a deep and abiding solidarity and fraternity when it comes to fundamental or radical (speaking in the mathematical sense) concepts that form the basis of their belief system or political or economic strength.

The Roman Catholics may hate the Protestants for theological reasons, but when it comes to aid to parochial schools, they will work together in the ultimate analysis to keep the money coming in. The Roman Catholics may be split internally on other issues, but when it comes to the celebration of a golden jubilee for Cardinal Cody in Chicago, despite the recent exposures of his misuse of church funds, they can all stand together. Denominational differences play no part in the ability of the religious community in general to sit back and allow a nativity scene to be ruled as having no more significance than a mere ornament on the tree to keep it on public property. The Jews can fight for the nativity scene (representing the birth of a character they no more believe in than do Atheists) to remain on public land, under the legal theory that it represents the "nuclear family."

In distinction to this, the ACLU defends the Nazi marchers in Skokie just to show the oposition that they are able to stand up for an unpopular cause, even with most of their monetary support coming from Jewish persons, rather than out of any real concern for civil liberties. It would have been better for the Nazis not to have been represented by the ACLU in terms of their own internals, and I am sure that they could have cared less about the Nazis' rights.

We cannot fight a well-oiled machine-type opponent that has the ability to muster fraternity, solidarity, and synchronization at the drop of a hat out of seeming chaos, unless we can be fraternal and synchronized, too, when we need to be.

Each organization can and should maintain and retain its individual autonomy. At the same time, we need to be able to strike together when the time comes. A victory for one of us is a victory for all of us, and a loss for one is a loss for all. The religios community knows this, and they use it to their advantage. Are we less smart than they?

The basic difference among the multiplicity of "liberal" groups is with respect to tactics. Why not let those groups who desire to give the right-wing forces back some of their own medicine do so? Other groups that want to work within the "rules" solely can do so as well, as long as they realize that in some cases, they must stand together when basic issues on which their very freedom to operate are at stake.

Failure to do so in the past has so weakened our collective positions now that no individual group may be able to succeed. We have a finite base of persons in the United States to whom upholding the Constitution, especially in the separation of state and church area, means anything at all. If we divide their support too much, it may mean an overall failure.

We at American Atheists, despite our strong stands on many issues, have always known that solidarity on basic issues is needed. We support and urge that solidarity, and are willing to work toward it in the areas in which we all can agree and in which we all can benefit. We do, however, remain cautious when it comes to working with other groups who have used what they deem our "nonrespectability" as a recruitment incentive for their own group. We don't even object to that, since the persons who respond to such incentives may not be helpful in our ranks anyway. That does not mean, however, that on an administrative and executive level between groups, we cannot co-operate on specific and perhaps mostly legal issues, where our combined strength in terms of numbers and finances is needed.

Even within each group, the lack of solidarity in the rank and file membership is staggering. Every Roman Catholic knows his rosary and every Protestant his catechism, but every Atheist will give you a different definition of Atheism should you ask. Ask a religionist what separation of state and church means, and you will get a uniform answer that it means government not interfering with the church in any respect. Ask an Atheist the same thing, and the answer will vary considerably and not even be basically the same. This internal solidarity must be fostered by each group on its own, however, through education of its rank and file. It was indoctrination that did the trick in the religious groups, but I remain convinced that education can do the same for us.

What can be seen from all of this is that we are under a strong multifaceted attack in a number of areas. Though multifaceted, the attacks are rooted in the irrationality of religion. It is from that religious base that all of the attacks sprang. The various "liberal" groups are out there facing this hydra of religion and each cutting off one head or putting a band-aid over one if its bites, but they fail to kill the beast. The solidarity I speak of is the need for all groups to realize the basis of the individual assaults on freedom of the mind, some of which I have enumerated here, and to be able to strike together at the basis, the irrationality of religion, as a combined force. Even if we all strike at different times and with different styles, as long as we aim for the same spot, the heart, we should succeed. We are not doing that now; we need to start doing it.

Evolution/Creation in Arkansas

February 1982

The issue in the evolution/creation debates which are now in the legislative bodies throughout the several states is *not* an evolution/creation debate at all. The root issue is never mentioned in the cases, in the proposed legislation, in the evidence tendered, in the reporting of the cases, or in any analyses given anywhere. Even approaching the root issue is anathema to all.

The religious community understands the need to have a rhythmic reinforcement of ideas with the youth. This is effectively done with the adults, every Sunday in churches. The religious know, however, that the child must be seized and the parent cannot be left with the job of indoctrination. The church knows how to do this best and also does not, in actuality, trust the parent with its important concern of capturing the next generation. Therefore, since 1963 when the Murray-O'Hairs dealt a blow to the rhythmic reinforcement of religion in the public schools by the outlawing of religious ceremonies (Bible reading and prayer recitation) there, the religious have been attempting to reintrude religion into the institutions where the children are, by compulsion and under truancy laws, in attendance on a regular basis. Since the schools are representatives of government, religion accepted and taught in the public institutions is doubly reinforced through governmental approval. Whereas the prayer and Bible reading was overtly religious, now the religious feel that it is necessary to be more covert, *i.e.,* transcendental meditation, moment of silence, releasing of children during school hours to attend religious classes. The entire exercise is get to the children before they are mature enough to realize that they are being indoctrinated with religious insanity. A third grader will accept that the earth was created at 9:00 A.M. on October 23rd, in the year 4004 B.C.; a third-year college student will not.

The creation/evolution conflict is illustrative. The effort is to coerce the acceptance of an evangelical religious fundamentalist literalist interpretation of the Bible, where the children are held by the state and forced to listen to the instruction through the instrument of teachers representing the state, but using texts prepared under the influence of religious nuts. It would not matter, really, what was taught — creationism, transubstantiation, life after death, efficacy of prayer, virgin birth, Old Testament, or New Testament — just as long as it is reinforcement of religion. In this instance, the religious feel that their best chance is to try with creationism, masquerading their theology as science, utilizing some questions on which the scientific community itself has insufficent data to answer. The religious pretend that since all the answers are not in through the scientific method that the real answer is god, not more research and experimentation.

The case in Arkansas gives an illustration of the methodology of religious coercion and concern. When reading the case, "virgin birth" could be substituted for the idea "creationism" and the case would still be instructive.

The religious are hell-bent in six other directions to capture the child. They are intent now on (1) destroying the public schools through criticism of curricula, of teachers, of administration, of philosophy of public education (example: assault on "secular humanism") and of tax costs for support of public schools and (2) while attempting to destroy public schools they are erecting their own school system rapidly, demanding that the schools may be racist or exclusionary on the basis of religion, not alone tax-free and free of government standards, regulations, or accreditation. Meanwhile, every effort is expended to (3) control the curricula of public schools (examples: the intrusion of such courses as creationism, return of prayers, religious instruction), (4) censor textbooks and intrude religious books and materials into public school libraries, (5) control the teachers in presentation of material and in general (6) give recognition to religion and god, even in the most vague terms. The mainline religious groups do not really fight this effort by the fundamentalists because any bolstering of the god idea in general is good for every church. God is reinforced and god is the master of all the religious denominations.

The fact that creationism lost in Arkansas is irrelevant to the overall fight. Twenty minutes after the decision came in, the Mississippi legislature met and passed an identical law. Now those who oppose such religious intrusion must begin all over again, this time in Mississippi. It is a war of attrition, with the slender resources of time, energy, and money of the sane spent to fight the successful forays against children by the insane. If after a hundred-year battle, the religious give up on creationism, they will choose another base — the shroud of Turin, perhaps — and attempt to have that included both in history and science books as absolute authentication of the so-called resurrection.

Because of this, it was felt to be urgent that American Atheists have the complete text of the Arkansas creation/evolution case. If one reads one's local newspaper, one will never find out what happened in Arkansas. The national wire services contained only sketches — none of the real problem. Therefore, the complete text of the decision is printed in the February 1982 issue of the *American Atheist*. Read it and learn.

Attorneys And Atheism

March 1982

A principal part of the activity of The American Atheist Center is legal action to uphold the constitutional principle of state/church separation or to utilize such activity for litigious education of the populace at large. Attorneys which American Atheists have employed or encountered have been of two types. (1) Attorneys who are timid, supportive of the legal system of which they are a part and from which they derive their livelihood. Their basic fear of the nation's legal system is so well developed that they are unwilling to acknowledge or do not understand its faults or its abuses, which makes it effective in suppressing minorities such as Atheists. These attorneys are "company" men or women. (2) Attorneys who are not unaware of why and where the system fails, but who simply do not care to be the one to expose the failure or press for modifications. There is a desire to maintain the "equilibrium" and "the respect" of their peers. These attorneys will not "rock the boat."

Timidity, lack of social concern, and fear lead to an ineffective, even lackadaisical, pursuit of the question involved in the cases they handle for American Atheists. Deep inside, perhaps somewhere in the fabled subconscious, they have decided that no matter how much they would like to win, they had better just "put on a good show" and lose "with dignity."

Our desire to wage a principled legal battle in the face of unprincipled opponents precludes these attorneys from being daring or bold within the legal structure which they erroneously perceive to be one of decorum and decency. When "boldness" does come out, it is in the form of little forays accomplished by written barbs (never oral, as they lack the courage to face the judge or their opponents in open court). It borders on or is actually downright insulting to the courts, but usually on a collateral issue dealt with in a brief. Universally, these have been cheap shots which bring the opprobrium of the court down upon the American Atheist litigants rather than on the attorney — and they are posited in such a way as to have this effect. Few attorneys are capable of the art of rhetorical insult and most often these small forays simply come off as crude.

Other attorneys are money-hungry or fame-hungry. Attorneys frequently want their names in the media or their coffers filled. This type wants to soak the Atheist movement for all it can pay on the Atheists' genuine desire to seek redress of civil liberties or equity at law with what counsel is available. The only legal contractor to come forward can ask what he likes for the job when competition is lacking. The Atheists are then caught up in the marketplace practice of *caveat emptor* — let the buyer beware.

What is needed instead of American Atheists going to the open marketplace for an attorney of uncertain quality and ethics is for a group of concerned and dedicated Atheists with legal training and status to volunteer free services, prorated among the group in respect to hours and effort. This group should be headed up by an in-house attorney at The American Atheist Center who is coordinating all the efforts. The Center should be monetarily responsible only for the salary of the in-house attorney, actual filing and court costs, and printing of briefs, which can be done at The Center's in-house printing plant. These attorneys must be motivated to stand up for the truth and rights of Atheism, for justice and equality for Atheists under law, and for "common sense" in the courts. (The continuing Supreme Court nonsense term "*benevolent* neutrality" in state/church separation cases defies both logic and common sense.) They must be eager for systemic rather than cosmetic changes in the legal system, striking at the root — the radical in a mathematical sense — to eliminate adjudicated inequities.

They must have a conviction which causes a desire to make the legal system in which they labor representative of a better base at the same time they lay a predicate for the present and future protection and survival of Atheistic and other human rights. This must be paramount, instead of monetary, power, or fame considerations.

We ask, simply, that American Atheist legal counsel be principled.

I know of no attorney representing the side of reactionary religion — or a state apparatus designed to support religion as religion in reciprocation supports the state — who allows funding out of his or her own pocket or extra time needed to prepare a case to deter from the objective: the preservation and enhancement of religious prerogatives. Attorneys for the state or for religious groups always give freely of themselves far in excess of that for which they are compensated in an effort to preserve existing situations, whether harmful to the rights of another or not.

Therefore a consistency of purpose is also a "must" for an American

Atheist attorney. Separation of state and church **must mean the same in every instance** and be applied with the same intensity of purpose, for separation means *separation* as envisaged by Thomas Jefferson, who spoke in terms of a "a wall of separation between church and state."

The National Office of American Atheists wishes to find and band together an affiliation of such persons. Perhaps, some say, they do not exist in our culture now as I feel once they did. But, knowing that we need a score of Clarence Darrows, I cannot agree. I know that some such arbiters for *common sense* justice must exist. Call it "faith," if you will (although we generally eschew the use of the word), but there must be a positing of some "faith" in our fellows.

We will no longer proceed with either type of representation mentioned above. If that means no litigation, it is better by far that we abstain from such litigation than to place ourselves in an inextricable position of disadvantage for all times at the hands of a precedent-based legal system by engaging in action at far less than our full potential.

If we know what we need, it is folly to take less.

We, at National, reserve the right to hold Chapters to this policy as well. Any sub-unit of a national movement which engages in litigation that does not strike at principle and thus serve to strengthen the whole, but instead puts American Atheists one foot deeper in the hole of legal precedence of which we can already hardly see the top, must be **disenfranchised or abandoned**, if necessary, for the long-term good of the total organization.

You may call this position dictatorial, stubborn, or even fascist, as you will. It is designed for the best now and futuristically for all Atheists and for Atheism as a life-style in our culture. It comes from the most pure of motives. The liberty of each individual, of course, cannot be denied, and as individuals all of you are free to proceed as you like on an individual contractual basis with whom you desire to continue. But, before you do, however, I urge you to consider all of the ramifications of such action which cannot help but affect others.

National Office cannot support the contemplated or adventured actions of Chapters which fly in the face of National Office directives or positions. Often a Chapter sees what it feels may be a "win" in a local court on an issue in another case setting. This cannot be applied nationally and does not ameliorate the systemic conditions nationwide that leaves the same offense extant in other courts. An example of this is the requirement of an oath, "So help me God," in a court in order to give testimony. If the case is one of divorce or contract or traffic violation or tort, the court can well rule that in this instance the person refusing to give an oath may take an affirmation. Nothing is gained as a principle to apply in all courts. Individual relief only is attained. A case of divorce, of contract, of traffic violation, or of tort cannot be appealed on the basis of the court ruling or not ruling that an affirmation may be given instead of an oath. This does not mean that the National Office does NOT support your right to speak up in court and to do what can be done in such a single instance. In fact, *National Office demands that you do*. But it cannot be utiized as a cause célébre for a Chapter because it is not one. It is not a root or radical issue. It is *en passant* the showing of individual courage of an individual Atheist. We are happy to see this.

In strictly state/church separation situations, Chapters must adhere to national directives. Recently one Chapter agreed to participate in a "Christmas" pageant, to erect an Atheist booth of the same size as twenty religious booths depicting the so-called passion of Jesus Christ. The place of American Atheists is NOT in a Christmas pageant. The duty of a Chapter is to have the religious symbolism removed from government property or government sponsorship or financial aid revoked, instead of sanctifying the religious celebration by becoming a part of it. There is no room in government for support of religion or of Atheism. Jeffersonian separation means complete neutrality of government and the continuance of government only in secular activities.

Arguments concerned with funding in what have been enormously expensive cases have constantly arisen. This is especially true when attorneys, who are quite ordinary and unknown, are involved. Attorneys have been changed in mid-stream with attendant loss of fees. One Chapter, cheated out of large funds, finally completely abandoned a good case. In several other Chapters, attorneys have gone to those persons who have volunteered to be litigants and attempted to pump money out of them with neither the ligitants nor the attorney advising National that this was occurring. In other instances, attorneys have persuaded individual Atheists to undertake cases without National approval, and these cases have come to naught. On the other hand, when, with National approval and involvement, very expensive and prominent law firms were hired on the basis of monetary concern only, several cases have been won.

For many years, Great Britain dominated the world with the simple admonition, "England expects every man to do his duty." Rome maintained its Empire with its soldiers carrying the standard of S.P.Q.R. (*Senatus Populusque Romanus* — for the Senate and the

People of Rome). Although we are uninterested in dominating the world, American Atheists needs persons of such loyalty and dedication. National expects every Atheist to accept the burdens of support as well as the blessings of freedom for which The American Atheist Center stands.

We exhort Atheist attorneys to contact the National Office and to offer their services for local issues at their local levels. We ask American Atheists everywhere to become plaintiff litigants when necessary. And we ask all American Atheists, wherever situated, to support The Legal Fund.

Culture Shock

April 1982

During the past six years or so, The American Atheist Center has labored to found and intellectually nurture chapter organizations in the diverse states. The initial impetus for such chapters had come from members who felt the need to associate with other Atheists. These have blossomed into fifty-two functioning groups in thirty-one states. In attempting to organize the unorganizable — independent-thinking Atheists — problems and successes both major and minor have been met. We have had the good fortune to uncover some fine and distinguished Atheist minds, some very brave people, some warm and personable fellows. There has been a small scattering of neurotics, opportunists, theists, and persons with other axes to grind — and we have learned a great deal in handling them. But, reviewing the history of the chapters, the National Office has been much satisfied with all of the accomplishments, the solved problems, the honest efforts, and the good people.

But then, the Murray-O'Hairs went to Australia in December of 1981, and there suffered a cultural and intellectual shock.

In this issue an analysis of the Australian historical and current situation is made. There are many open Atheists in Australia. The holding of the position is not one of censure. We met officials, educators, persons in high office, famous personalities, all of whom wore their Atheism on their sleeves. Fundamentalism is not rampant in that land as it is in our own. Little or no notice is paid to religion, and few persons go to church. This is the millennium to which Atheist groups all over the world have aspired. The formula of "forget religion — it will wither away in due course" has been applied in Australia and would seem, on the surface, to have won the day. Yet, it is in this country where the churches (Roman Catholic principally, but also others) have won a most enormous and significant victory which can change the entire culture of the nation. In first legislative enactments and then in a judicial showdown, the churches have won the right to have their schools completely and totally supported by tax dollars. In this they have laid a foundation to capture the rising generations and through the most advanced educational techniques to bind the minds of the children to the insanities of the religious past. We were all disquieted by the discovery, full of justifiable apprehension, and intellectually uneasy with our new knowledge. It was then that we went to Sydney and checked into a hotel at Bondi Beach. But we were out of the way at that very beautiful resort beach, and the Rationalist Association was kind enough to find a driver for us so that we would be accessible each to the other and so that we could also be shown some of the sights of the area. That driver, a retired civil servant, A. F. Parkinson, was to change our entire perspective concerned with our Chapter outreach.

He was an odd man, with thick glasses, slow and deliberate body movements, and a small speech impediment. He was solicitious of our comforts and was kind. However, he (even though he said he was an Atheist!) was convinced of reincarnation. He practiced transcendental meditation two hours every morning and believed that various small physical ailments of age which had afflicted him had been cured by his practice of TM. He insisted that the government of the United States had endorsed TM and that many governmental officials has testified as to its beneficial qualities and had lauded "his holiness Maharishi Mahesh Yogi" for the rehabilitative qualities of his TM program in American prisons.

Finally, we simply could not take the campaign to convert us to TM and declined his excellent chauffeuring services. But in the course of his remarks in regard to Atheism in Australia and the rationalist and humanist organizations there, he emphasized over and over the magnitude of the victory that the churches had won in Australia in the financing of their schools — and in this he was right and we were in agreement. He went on then to point out that during the entire fight, the Atheist/rationalist/humanist community continued to meet in little meetings and continued to seek out speakers who could address those meetings while the Atheists sat passively taking it in. Where were they, he demanded of us, in the fight? What had they done? What good was it for a small group of Atheists to meet month after month for thirty or forty years and listen to speakers from the Unitarian church, the philosophy and history faculties of colleges, and various minority persons who now and again were in the news? How did this teach the great mass of persons in Sydney anything about Atheism? He and his friends had grown old in the meetings and the group shrank and became less and less effective through the years. What good was it to read booklets written a hundred years ago? Why worry about Bible contradictions and the history of the Inquisition? No one in Sydney even knew the Atheists existed. They made no impact. They were not in the fight against financing of the Roman Catholic and other church schools. The most they had ever done was to listen to someone who was in the fight — but they didn't themselves act.

It was on our way back to the United States, as we sat in that DC-10 for nineteen hours, that we came to realize why our uneasiness. Parkinson was right. It was — basically — as simple as that. Instead of Atheists sitting in a small room calling in speakers month after month to educate them further, they needed to be out educating the general populace as to what Atheism is. We had been in error in our own attempted structuring, for our Chapters were doing exactly the same — and forty years from now the members would simply be older, but still sitting and still being fed the pablum of what a "booger" religion is. *By that time the Roman Catholic and all other churches would be fully financed by tax money, and a hope for a sane world would be lost.*

Our Chapters needed to be centrs of learning where enthusiastic Atheists could acquire knowledge and go out to tell their communities of the benefits of Atheism. Chapter Directors should be speaking at lunches or meetings of fraternal organizations — the Elks, the Moose, the Masons; of business, union, and professional organizations — bankers, teachers, contractors, plumbers; of social cause groups — women, peace, population control. They should be speaking at PTA meetings, asking to be permitted to come into school classrooms, again and again and again knocking on the doors of the local television and radio stations, journals, and newspapers.

We know now what we need to do — and we will implement the necessary changes The United States cannot be another Australia. Here, American Atheists will not permit it. So — stand back! There are going to be some changes made.

"Ph.D." in Ignorance!?

May 1982

One of my duties as Director of the national American Atheist Center is the handling of an increasing number of public appearances. Due to the sometimes uncertain health of American Atheists' President, Dr. Madalyn O'Hair, I have found myself chosen to speak before more and more college and university groups. My most recent engagement was before a class at a North Texas junior college.

What I find on the college level is an ever-growing hostility to the topics of Atheism and separation of state and church. I have been appearing at the college level for some five years now, and the situation seems to be worsening. Apathy among students is a much more easily understandable phenomenon than hostility toward a particular position or life-style. After all, what is the goal of attending college in the first place? It is the attainment of a "degree" which is a stamp of your worth on the open market as you enter the job market, much like the grade markings on a side of beef determining the appropriate price per pound. With the economic situation in this country growing more harsh by the month, it is only natural that students would concern themselves with graduation with the proper qualifications for that "good-paying" job to the exclusion of much other than sports and sex. Those few students around the country who are attempting to form University Student Atheists (USA) groups can attest to this "blinders on" view of hallowed college days by the vast lack of participation in any of their programs.

In addition to mere apathy, however, the actual hostility toward Atheism, humanism, "secular humanism," and the like among students is much more alarming. Part of the root of the cooler and cooler receptions Atheist speakers on campuses receive may be that the parents of this generation of students are turning to more traditional values. This can be seen not only from the election of Ronald Reagan, but by increased parental support of returning to the basics in the public school system, which include basics such as corporal punishment, book censorship, "creationism," classroom prayer, dress codes, and the like. Who is to say? One group of sociligists will tell you that students reflect parental attitudes and another group will say that students generally turn from parental authority and assume attitudes in direct conflict with those taught at home.

The North Texas junior college class is a good case in point. First, no matter what the topic one discusses, the questions posed in the question-and-answer session are always along the same line, most often having nothing whatsoever to do with the topic. Even before the questions are put, a speaker can sense the feeling of the audience. In this particular class, I could tell that the prevailing attitude (before I said word one) was "Atheist = amoral = no veracity = Whatever this guy says is Atheist propaganda so I can fall asleep now and avoid the rush." After I carefully explained what an Atheist was, clarified the agnostic differential, and even went into the philosophical base of materialism, the instructor (no less) stopped me to ask about my brother who had found the lord and what I would do if I were dying of some terminal disease. My assurance to him that I would not have the least interest in crying out for god at a time of illness drew the usual"Yeah, uh huh, that's what you say now" verdict from the students. It was then that I noticed that every woman in the room, save for the lone Atheist in the class who had invited me, had enough makeup on to put on a circus. The questioning from the students then turned personal as it always does. "What do you think happens to you when you die?"I replied that my dying would be the same as a leaf dropping off a tree, just another step in a natural cycle. Well, you would have thought that I had grown horns on the spot! The negative reaction from the leaf analogy rippled across the room as if a sudden cold draft had come up. Another question was "What about all the miracles?" which was posed by a woman who seemed quite sincere about their existence. I said that no miracle had ever been scientifically verified to my knowledge and that they were all attributable to natural phenomena. The look I received back was one of "Well that's what you say!"

All in all, I think that the class was struck with horror that someone could actually exist in modern America who did not "believe in god." The idea of being on your own, emotionally and intellectually, was so foreign to them all that they viewed me as a freak. That is exactly what the problem is, in a thematic sense, with all of the student groups. Atheist speakers are viewed as freaks and the attention they receive is the attention of curiosity, not that of academic interest or sincerity. It is a hard feeling to try to explain to those of you who do not engage in this type of activity as I do. To be put in the initial position of a freak, like in a sideshow, and then to need to convince the audience otherwise (often in a very short space of time) is a unique feeling.

If you're waiting for a solution, I don't have one other than to keep going and keep convincing one small audience after another that we as Atheists are not freaks, we are not insane; we are "normal" people, and our views need to be respected. The fact that precursor Atheist organizations did not go out into the field and try to make the general public understand about Atheism has helped to being us to this position of hostility through ignorance that I face today. The fact still remains that there are too many of them — the uneducated with respect to Atheism — and too few of us. That is why it is more important than ever for all of you "rank and file" Atheists to take the time to explain Atheism to at least one person each day. It may take a generation or two of that sort of grass roots outreach, but it is time well spent.

While you take that generation or two, we here at The American Atheist Center are going to continue to try to do it in "double time."

"Reds"

June 1982

The Soviets know how to play geopolitics in a much more sophisticated manner than do our national (so-to-speak) "leaders." When it comes to the theopolitical field, they are in many aspects superb theological chess players. Having built into its constitution a complete separation of state and church, the nation has felt comfortable enough to permit churches to function — knowing as it does that without state tax exemption, state financial support, state favoritism, churches can only remain static and small.

Knowing full well that the Christian religion is both used and rewarded for being used by the United States in its ideological confrontation with the Soviets, that nation in May pulled off its own black propaganda coup. The United States is adept at black propaganda and recognized the ploy, so that the White House stepped in to ask Billy Graham not to go to Moscow to participate in a meeting of several hundred of the "Clergy against Nuclear War." The temptation of "carrying the words of Jesus" to "Atheist Russia" was too overpowering to Graham in his basic fanaticism, and he eschewed the warning of the White House.

Courteously received and having been shown that there exist in the U.S.S.R. literally thousands of churches (albeit small ones) Graham was enthused about "incipient religious freedom" in that nation. The news media of the United States, speaking to the ploy instead of the basic issue, fell upon the subsequent words and reports of Graham in regard to religion. That was *not* the name of the game. What the Soviets were doing was reaching out for another group of allies in respect to disarmament and the precluding of a nuclear war. It was incidental whom that group represented as long as it could be enlisted on the side of peace. What citizens of our nation do not understand is [1] that Russia was decimated in the First World War and the revolution immediately associated with that war and [2] that she lost 20,000,000 people and several great cities in the Second World War. The United States, bounded by two oceans, knows nothing of the destructiveness of a war on its own territory. No civilians, no cities of our nation have ever been plain bombed, firebombed, or nuked. The magnitude of the Russian lives lost has never been equalled in all of the combined countries of the West in any war. Russia wants and needs peace. Hence, she reaches out, if need be, to the utmost enemy, the clergy. And, she stages the outreach by inviting a leader thereof into the heart of her nation: Moscow. That is astute geopolitical and theopolitical moxie! The United States cannot pull off the reverse by asking Atheist leaders of the world to meet in Washington, D.C. to discuss peace by asking a foreign Atheist leader to address them. The United States is precluded from doing this because it has set up "Atheism" as a real fundamental enemy so inherently evil, so allied with Satan, that the thought of such rapport is totally untenable politically. The U.S.S.R., therefore, could and did play one-upmanship with élan.

Billy Graham, whose ignorance is surpassed only by his basic fanaticism, even after the event could only see the hope of a Graham crusade across the wild tundras of Russia with himself as a Don Quixote of our era carrying "the word." The spectacle is pitiful.

Meanwhile, back in the United States, Graham was under fire by his colleagues, perhaps as much out of envy as out of Soviet hatred. The government was aghast.

Recent media reporting of the plans of the Republican party for the November [1984] election indicates that a religious issue is planned to dominate the domestic scene during that autumnal imbroglio humorously known as the democratic process of free elections. After surveying and resurveying, the right-wing Republicans, now in possession of the nation, have found that they have "overwhelming support" (reported as being 65% of the nation) on one issue and one issue only: return of prayer to the public schools. Reagan and his cohorts are failing across the political front in all areas, hence a tried-and-true emotional issue is not only needed but has been found.

The escalation of the issue started on two fronts. Within days of Graham's return to the United States, his reports of religious freedom in Russia were attacked from all quarters, and a campaign began in the press to show that Russia was beginning an internal campaign to crush religion and reinforce Atheism. This was a clear signal then for the United States to begin an internal campaign to crush Atheism and reinforce Christianity in the United States.

Suddenly the old McCarthy issue of "All Atheists are Communists" was being resurrected, while the President himself opted for the return of prayer to the public schools. In conjunction with the president's declaration, a test was instituted to see how quickly a constitutional amendment could be passed. That the place chosen was the state of Tennessee has particular significance in the plot. The largest Bible publishing house in the world is situated in Nashville, and it is orchestrating an enormous campaign to sell, in millions of copies, a book which will assault the Murray-O'Hairs and the American Atheist organization as not only tools of communism, but as communists. Due to be released in June, the building of the campaign is scheduled to peak in November. That the charges are a tissue of lies matters little or nothing: the F.C.C. phantom petition (*see* Vol. 24, No. 5, May 1982 issue of the *American Atheist*, an article titled "The Phantom Phenomenon, Christ-insanity Strikes Again") has settled that to the benefit of the radical right. Atheists in the United States may have their characters besmirched with impunity — public figures such as the Murray-O'Hairs being "fair game" in such an exercise. A Roman Catholic priest, alleged to be the "Madalyn Murray O'Hair" expert for that church, was placed "on loan" to Tennessee (from his Massachusetts base) to help effectuate the legislative coup. A bill to return prayer to public schools was introduced into the Tennessee congress on March 11th, and by April 6th it had passed both houses soon to be signed by the governor: a three week romp. The handwriting is on the wall.

The "Good" Book

July 1982

In an interview early in his bid for the office of president, Reagan was adamant: the only guide which the nation really needed was the "good" book — the Bible. He made it known that he did not subscribe to the "theory" of evolution, that Nancy's place was in the home, that parochial schools should receive the largess of government, and that abortion was an evil upon the soul of the nation.

All of his utterances on these issues, heavily related to religion and that peculiar activity thereof which is yclept "fundamentalism," were either muted or ignored by the media as they focused on his charisma, his innate charm, and the doctrine of economic chaos which they chose to label Reaganomics, touting it to the heavens. There were only two groups in the nation involved with his aside and *sotto voce* religious utterances: (1) American Atheists who were appalled and spoke loudly about that side of the president (albeit being then the voice of the turtle abroad in the land), and (2) the fundamentalist, radical religious right. The former watched, evaluated, and warned; the latter schemed, conspired, aided, and abetted. The former could only scream aloud, "Don't you hear what he is saying?" while the latter poured millions of dollars and man-hours into his campaign. The smug media was complaisant when in the early weeks of his term in office he did not turn immediately to embrace the radical religious right. Speaking of "politics as usual," it was only in an aside that the media deigned to notice or comment that the religious NCPAC group had chastised Reagan for not amply rewarding its activity. The phenomenon of six "liberal" senatorial aspirants to re-election being ousted from office was analyzed as being primarily a disgust with "liberalism" rather than the machinations of a compact group of religious nuts working in concert, using sophisticated but blackguardly techniques and money.

When Reagan's appointments to power emerged in the next year or two, James Watt, a fundamentalist madman, was esconced in the Department of Interior; Roman Catholic Alexander Haig was firmly entrenched in the State Department; and Bob Billings was decimating public education from inside the federal Department of Education. That was only the tip of the iceberg. But, the media (with the exception of cartoonists) continued to ignore the religious base from which flowed the political implications. The basic primitivism of the president himself was not explored, but for, again, the most casual asides concerned with his "deep commitment" to "religious ideals." But, the radical religious right knew him well. The leaders and groups of that stance had taken time out to learn his positions and to explore in depth the shallowness of the man. They found access to him easy, and they consorted there in the White House with the most respectable religious representatives who understood that the madmen were advancing old-line religion as well as their fundamentalism as they intruded more blatantly into the political process. It was almost like having the Jesuits in power again. There was no more need for backrooms, or intrigue. Any takeover could be overt, and proclamations were broadcast that the religious had an equal right to political power.

The election process in our nation rolls around every two years and Reagan began early this year to woo the religious radical right again —this time with action, not promises. He directed his staff to prepare a bill to be introduced into Congress to give financial relief to parents who send their children to parochial schools and another bill to outlaw abortions. He turned back an I.R.S. ruling which would require religious schools *not* to be racist. And he had a White House bill presented to Congress to return prayers to the public schools.

In this decade the attack has been directed against science, education, women, and peace — with the President of the United States in the vanguard of the attack. His witting lackeys in the United States Senate and the House of Representatives, completely devoid of either courage or intellectual acumen, rush to do his bidding.

Our founding fathers abhorred the Bible and repudiated it. The finest words of Thomas Paine were the scathing unmasking of this vile, and abominable, unspeakably obscene, and disgusting book. His *Age of Reason* was a scathing attack on this anti-human, anti-life, anti-female accumulation of printed offal produced by diseased minds. Indeed, the first six presidents of the United States took pride in being deists, which is to say: *repudiators of Christianity, the Bible, and the church systems of the then new America.* They were joined wholeheartedly by Benjamin Franklin, Col. Ethan Allen, George Mason, Lafayette, Stephen Girard and a host of others. Church attendance was down to 3 percent, and there was hope at the time that religion would entirely disappear.

Now for the United States Congress to resurrect and eulogize a book which has caused more misery to all of mankind in every age since its hallowing, than any other idea or document is a crime against humanity, against education, against science. This abject subservience to fear — for it is fear that motivated the vote — of reprisals from the religious nuts of our nation can no longer be tolerated. The Bible is the worst of human thought, not the best. It is the excrement of primitive man, now to be discarded, not resurrected.

Our Congress sinks constantly lower. In the terrible years of McCarthyism it put the shameful and disgraceful motto "In God we trust" onto our currency and coins, befouled the national pledge of allegiance with the insert "under God," and embarrassed our nation in the world with an enforced "day of prayer." McCarthyism is behind us, but now the Brave New World of 1984, locked into religious hysteria and non-think, threatens us ahead. It is the responsibility of American Atheists to stop this erosion of our original founding ideas: get to your senators and representatives and to your (ugh) president, and tell them of your shock and dismay. It's our country being befouled — it is our duty to stop it.

The Prayer Gambit

August 1982

On May 6th of this year President Reagan held a combination press conference and prayer meeting in the Rose Garden outside the White House with about 120 religious and conservative political leaders in attendance, among them Jerry Falwell. At that conference he announced his backing of a constitutional amendment to put "voluntary" prayer back in the public schools.

In his speech Reagan said, among other things, "I have never believed that the oft-quoted amendment (the First Amendment to the Constitution) was supposed to protect us *from* religion, it was to protect religion from government tyranny." This line is synonymous with the thinking of many "liberal" separation-of-state-and-church groups today. American Atheists is the only group willing to stand for freedom *from* religion as a necessary corollary to freedom *of* religion. There is not much that we can do *now*, however, about an administrative interpretation of the First Amendment as running only in one direction. That leaning has been standard White House procedure at least since Eisenhower. We did not correct this interpretation then, so we have to live with it now.

That fact is important, but not so important as the real motive behind Reagan's endorsement. Falwell summed it up to the press in the Rose Garden when he said, "Obviously, the purpose of the constitutional amendment is to circumvent the Supreme Court and to put it [the issue of prayer in public schools] out of their reach." This proposed amendment is nothing but a wolf in sheep's clothing.

For some years now, in both the Carter and Reagan administrations (more in the latter), various members of Congress have been pushing the notion of Congressional curbing of Supreme Court jurisdiction in some key areas. Those areas have been selected far more for their emotional appeal to the voters-at-large than for their face value. They are: busing to achieve racial balance in the schools, abortion/right-to-life, ERA, and aid to parochial schools. In each of these areas, attempts have been made in either the House or the Senate to pass legislation to limit in some way the jurisdiction of the Supreme Court or Federal Courts in general, concerning review (especially appellate review) of these matters. In effect, some congressmen have been asking their colleagues to vote for a breach in the tripartite form of checks-and-balances government set up by our Constitution.

Our founding fathers established a judicial branch of government to have review powers over the legislative branch (the Congress) and the executive branch, principally as a safeguard for minorities. They knew, as history has demonstrated to us, that a minority group, such as Atheists, by simply being small in number cannot influence Congress or the executive branch and are therefore left to seek redress for any grievance or civil right abridgment through the Courts. Therein they have a forum, at least by original design, that does not depend upon their numbers or political muscle to get a fair hearing. If that forum is closed down or restricted in certain areas, to what should minorities turn? Violence? A good modern example is our own black community prior to the passage of some of the civil rights acts.

If these few conservative congressmen succeed, will we then have, in effect, a two-part form of government? The answer is a shocking yes. A government of legislative and executive fiat with a circumvented judiciary will mean simply majority (or should I say "moral majority"?) rule. In 1943, after a series of federal cases involving schools, the Supreme Court said,

> The very purpose of a Bill of Rights was to withdraw certain subjects from the vicissitudes of political controversy, to place them beyond the reach of majorities and officials, and to establish them as legal principles *to be applied by the courts*. One's right to life, liberty, and property, to free speech, a free press, freedom of worship and assembly, and other fundamental rights *may not be submitted to vote; they depend on the outcome of no elections*.

We need to maintain a high court that retains this position at all costs. If we lose our forum of dissent, we lose our civil rights as well.

The issues around which to rally the muzzling of the courts have not been chosen lightly. This goes double for the prayer issue. Can you name a representative in your state legislature who would dare go on record as voting against "voluntary prayer" in public schools? I can't think of one in Texas. That particular part of their voting record would be used by their opponent in the next election and would cost them their seat in almost any district, especially some of the rural ones. Federal legislators are, on the other hand, a little less vulnerable to demagogic pressure than someone who is elected by a small district instead of an entire state. If the Reagan prayer amendment is to be stopped, it must be stopped in the federal congress. An amendment to the Constitution requires two-thirds of both houses of Congress plus the ratification of the legislatures of thirty-eight states. If the federal congress lets the prayer amendment loose on the states, it will be ratified faster than any amendment in the history of this country. It will not be defeated as was the E.R.A. Why do I say this? Why am I so pessimistic? One example will suffice. The Huntsville *Times* recently published an article done by the *Washington Post* news service on Louisiana parish schools that ignore the 1963 decision on religious ceremonies in public schools. In that article students, teachers, and administrators were asked their opinion and here is what some of them said:

1) Mother of a student — As for the Supreme Court "To heck with them. I'm not going to let anyone tell me when my child can pray. If we're breaking the law, so be it."
2) A school board member — "Just because the Supreme Court says it, doesn't mean it's the law. The people are the law of the land. . . ."
3) A school board president — "We're closer than Washington to what the people in this community want. The courts have gone too far. They've reached the point where they're trying to regulate everything about our lives."
4) A school board member — "I'd rather be right with God than the Supreme Court."
5) An 11-year old female student — "I like it [prayer]; it helps us on our tests."
6) A 17-year old male senior — "It [morning prayer] gives you a chance to get your thoughts together. You don't have to pray. If you're an Atheist, you can sit and think."
7) A fifth grade teacher — "We are a nation governed by rules and laws. If you break them, you pay the penalty. The Supreme Court says I'm breaking the rules, but I'm working for the good of the *majority*. I'm willing to pay the penalty. We're not violating anybody's right here. What are we going to do next? Take God's name off our coins?"

In these answers are embodied all of the standard misconceptions of the June 1963 decision of the Supreme Court in *Murray v. Curlett*. The Court ruling did not outlaw voluntary *private* prayer by individuals. Nor could it have under our Constitution. The Court outlawed "religious ceremonies," going on to say that a "prayer" was an integral part of a religious ceremony; if you have a religious ceremony, it must contain prayer. Thus, Reagan's proposed amendment for "voluntary prayer" in public schools *is not necessary*. Students can now, at this moment, pray over their lunch tray, in the hall, between classes, before they begin a test, and so on. The Supreme Court spoke concerning organized or group prayer in schools, *whether the prayer was voluntary or compulsory*.

Number 6 above speaks in an off-hand way to the notion of volunteerism. Can an Atheist child just sit and think? No, of course not. The emotional and peer pressure is so great on a school child to do as the rest of the class does or as the teacher directs or leads that "civil disobedience" is not a practical alternative for a student. Any student who failed to participate would be the "dirty little Atheist" and would immediately be ostracized. Few youngsters have the stamina to cope with their studies and complete ostracism at the same time.

Number 7 speaks directly to "majority rule." Only a few days ago, on one of our local cable channels, I happened upon Jerry Falwell speaking from his pulpit in Virginia. He was talking about prayer in school, so I stopped to listen for a moment. I cannot quote him from memory exactly, but in general he said that he knew of many public school teachers who lead their class in prayer each and every school day, sometimes with the knowledge of administrators and sometimes not. He urged those teachers to continue that practice. He quipped something very close to "what are they going to do, put them in jail?" Then after a moment of pause he said, "Wouldn't that be a wonderful thing to go to jail for?" — a direct encouragement for teachers to violate the law in favor of their religious convictions.

Then the Huntsville (Alabama) *Times* reported again on July 1st that the governor in that state, after forming a "family lobby" with his wife and son for the bill, was ready to sign into law a bill allowing "willing teachers to lead willing public school students in any prayer or a suggested offering of written by the governor's son. . . ." In Louisiana, an official legislative attempt to back up the sentiments of the teachers', students', and administrators' remarks above was overturned by the Fifth Federal Circuit Court of Appeals in New Orleans, standing by the 1963 Supreme Court ruling. In fact, since 1963, there have been forty major challenges to the Supreme Court ruling in both Federal and State courts. All have been unsuccessful.

Since every Federal legislative attempt to curb Supreme Court jurisdiction on school prayer (or any of the other emotional issues I have cited) has failed, and since state or local legislative attempts to circumvent the Court on the issue have failed, a constitutional amendment attempt is the only thing left. So far only two members of Congress have realized the true issue at hand, that of preserving our checks-and-balances system of government. Those two were Sen. Edward Kennedy of Massachusetts and Sen. Lowell Weicker of Connecticut, the latter leading a Senate filibuster on the busing issue.

If Congress chooses to curb high court jurisdiction in one area, they can, one by one, do the same in other areas until many minority causes that have been so dearly won will go down the drain. Without a protest forum, what are we to do as Atheists? The prospects are bleak indeed. Congress can make exceptions to Supreme Court jurisdiction constitutionality, unfortunately. I view this as the one of two major flaws in an otherwise magnificent document. Article III, Section 2, Paragraph 2 of the Constitution states, "In all other cases before mentioned [". . . to all cases, in law and equity, arising under this constitution. . ." (Paragraph 1)], the Supreme Court shall have appellate jurisdiction, both as to law and fact, with such exceptions, and under such regulations as the Congress shall make."

Congress has not chosen to take full advantage of this checks-and-balances loophole in prior sessions. With a combination of right-wing religious and political figures in power now, the situation could change rapidly. Preserving a forum of dissent for Atheists is now in doubt. That issue is of far more importance than daily school prayer itself. The vehicle of school prayer is, however, the most effective means of getting the job done by those who would have a true "One Nation *Under* God."

Can we stop our Constitution from being split up? I don't think so, not at this point. Immediately after World War II our country plunged into a course of action designed to reach this ultimate end of a complete "majority" rule of theocracy. No one was around then to say no. No sufficient obstacle has been placed in the path of the progress of theocracy in some thirty years now, mostly because the "liberal" community refused to recognize the gravity of *small* steps in a theocratic direction. Now that we are in the large step stage, it is too late to wake up. Everyone who ever said:

A) "'In God We Trust' on the money doesn't hurt anything. Don't nitpick."
B) "'One Nation Under God' doesn't hurt the kids. Don't nitpick."
C) "Who cares what our national motto is? 'In God We Trust' is as

good as any other one. Don't nitpick."

D) "Tax exemptions for churches are not subsidies. They just protect the church from government. Don't nitpick."

E) "A little prayer in school never hurt anyone. Don't nitpick."

F) "All Atheists have to be Communists; you can't be a Communist and believe in God. Don't nitpick. Anti-communist legislation which puts God on top of our nation is for your own protection."

deserves everything that they are sure to get; they have had it coming for years. What bothers me is — that I have to take the medicine too — and I am not sick.

"And A Little Child Shall Lead Them. . ."

September 1982

In my position as Director of the American Atheist Center I don't often get to engage in any leisure activities of any sort. But, now and again, I may get the opportunity to go to the cinema. Recently I did just that when I went to see the new "hit" science fiction movie *E.T.* After sitting in that theater and watching that picture for a couple of hours I was so disgusted and so turned off by what I saw that it took me hours at home to calm down. Why was I so upset? Why was I the only nonsmiling face in the crowd exiting the theater?

The answers to those questions will necessarily leave those of you who have not seen the movie in the dark. For those of you who have, I will be general with my comments. *E.T.* is another typical anti-science, anti-logic, anti-computer, and anti-intellectual movie that is part of a torrent of such films flowing out of Hollywood. Essentially the plot in *E.T.* is that an "extraterrestrial" (from another planet) being drops into the backyard of a suburban family and is discovered by the middle, in age, of three children. In the meantime, scientific teams are portrayed as working in a clandestine fashion in the area knowing that something had "crashed to earth" near the house of the subject family. *E.T.*, as the boy names the extraterrestrial, soon becomes endeared to the hearts of the children who are convinced that no adult could understand or appreciate their find or the value of their friendship with it. The scientific teams take on the role of the *enemy* from which the kind, loving, emotional children have to hide this "being." They can communicate with it through love. Science is "wicked" and cannot love and can only reason, so science will hurt their "being." Well, sure enough, *E.T.* gets sick, and the dirty scientists find out whose house it is in and come with machines and medical equipment and computers to try to save its life. But, they kill it with their "wicked" science and "foul" technology. The little boy, in a bed right next to his "friend" from another world, is tortured because the boy has "communed" with *E.T.* to such an extent that he feels everything that the "being" feels, in a textbook display of psychological transference.

All is not lost, however, because after they start to pack up all their scientific instruments of "torture" the little boy goes to look in the freezer in which they have stored his little friend's remains, and it winks at him. Knowing that it is still alive from "his love and his love alone," the little boy plots the kidnapping of the body and, with the aid of his friends from school, gets *E.T.* back to the woods and to a rendezvous with a spaceship come to recover their stranded comrade. The spaceship was summoned by a homemade transmitter fashioned by the extraterrestrial out of old toys from the little boy's room. Take that, you mean old scientist know-nothings!

It is hard for me to believe that such things are portrayed on the movie screen in the twentieth century. (We *are* in the twentieth century, aren't we?) The moral of the whole story was that human emotion and faith are somehow superior to human intellect and problem-solving ability. One is not a "whole person" unless he or she can love, show compassion, render tenderness onto all creatures, and "a little child shall lead them" in that path. The best way to put what is being presented, I think, comes from a debate that Dr. O'Hair, our editor-in-chief, had with a fundamentalist minister some years ago in the Northeast over the existence of god. At one point in the debate the minister pulled a rock out of his pocket and said, "Are you trying to tell me that we all came from this kind of brute matter? Yes," he said, "brute, unfeeling, unthinking matter." All of us Atheists in the audience sat just as stunned as I was stunned by another in a series of antiscience movies. What is "brute" about matter? What is "brute" about a rock? Science does not deal in that kind of terminology.

The theme of all things being possible through faith and emotional outreaches of one of the faithful to others and then to a deity is common throughout all of the teachings of the world's major religions. Very often this is why a child is used to fulfill prophecy or to bring god's words to the village, since a child is pictured as pure emotion — innocence and faith having not been corrupted by adult education or insight or knowledge. The adult is to take the example of the child and be as a child in front of the deity — unknowing, innocent, trusting. Our films reflect this biblical teaching over and over again. Does the "bad guy" ever win? No! If a wife cheats on her husband in a film, who gets venereal disease by the end of the film? She does, because that is the "wage of sin." The tall, strong, blond, blue-eyed hero comes into town and cleans up the crime (or "sin") and rides off into the sunset content to kiss his horse instead of a woman. It is simply a reenactment of Christ coming to save the Jews, "god's chosen people," with his goodness.

Our children are sent to see these things over and over again. They appear on TV over and over again, and no one catches on to what they are actually watching because it becomes so commonplace. The conditioning is almost subliminal at times, or, at least it was in the past. Not so anymore. Now, Hollywood is coming right out in the open with bold attacks on science, medicine, education, and technology. *Poltergeist* is another good example of such a film. It is a ghost story where science is thwarted again, and the ghost has to be subdued by a psychic (or should I say psycho?) — and not even an ordinary psychic but a dwarf psychic. The suburban family in this movie even has a twenty-foot-tall uterus appear on the wall in the kid's room and attempt to suck them all down to "hell." The worst part is that audiences just don't use such things anymore as diversions only. A goodly number of the persons actually believe in the ghosts, or spirits, or souls.

"What harm can come of this, anyway?" I hear you say. "This guy will be seeing Bible quotations on toilet paper next," you think. Well, let me give you an example of what such conditioning can do. Dr. O'Hair and I were in a local restaurant for dinner just the other day. We were both recognized by a man with two young girls in his care at the next table. We are often recognized in public as "those Atheists," since we have weekly "American Atheist Forum" television programs aired on cable channels here in Austin, Texas. Everything was all right until we finished eating and got up to leave. We were only about six feet away from the table when this man jumped out of his seat, causing his chair to fly and land on the floor upside down behind him, and came running after us with glassy eyes. He shouted, "No matter what you have done, god can forgive you. Repent now, and you will be healed." My initial reaction was "Dogs heel. People don't." I don't know why I thought of that. We got rapidly out of the way (knowing that the man was unstable and dangerous) which is what we always do — not saying a word in retort. Everyone in the restaurant just turned around and was shocked at the spectacle. The point is that when a man grows up with the likes of dwarfs defeating ghosts, then why can't he confront "evil on the hoof" in the form of an Atheist?

Many Christians really believe that they can use their righteousness or their faith as an offensive tactical weapon against what they perceive as evil. They think that they can stand behind the shield of righteousness while they hurl their faith at you. This can be very dangerous and lead to rash and unpredictable behavior. Every film has some aspect of good *vs.* evil, and good is always the victor. We all know that in real life evil is the victor far more often. Many more crimes go unpunished than criminals caught.

If we are conditioned to believe that through faith and emotion we can fight all the bad things we run into in life, we are being given a false sense of security that can in reality lead to more trouble in the long run. When a man with a gun asks you for your wallet, give it to him; don't try to shield yourself with your faith while he puts a bullet in your brain. The conditioning is spreading even into the U.S. national and international policy. With faith on our side, we feel that we can be the victors of a nuclear exchange with the dirty Russian Atheists. I have news for a person with that kind of view. No one ever wins a nuclear exchange. Everyone dies. If the conditioning can proceed, however, long enough over a wide range of generations, will we finally come to the point when we will pull that nuclear trigger because we really feel that our faith is the winning trump card?

Built into our culture is a continued reinforcement of religious values and concepts from which one cannot escape even with a leisurely pursuit like going to a movie. Once you become turned on to the different kinds of reinforcements and subliminal conditionings and can recognize them, you sometimes feel as if you are the one who is a little "off base" and not those who go along in a herd manner never realizing what they are being taught and why. I can sit down and turn on the TV and no matter what channel or what program that is in the story-entertainment category (excluding documentaries, hard news, educational programs, etc.) I choose, I can find savior themes, good doing battle against evil, anti-science, pro-war, pro-violence, anti-life, anti-intellectual themes running through all of them.

The point of all of this is that what used to be a simple afternoon escape from the problems of the day for a few hours is not so anymore. We are surrounded and engulfed by religiosity everywhere we turn. As Atheists we must learn to recognize it, teach our children to see through it, and attempt to do what we can to make others recognize it as well. Our entertainment needs to be just as much in touch with reality as our daily lives. In reality there is pleasure as well as work or pain, and we must force ourselves to recognize it and take advantage of it without being sucked into the mold of the mass who prefer to go outside of reality for their pleasure. I can get just as much enjoyment out of a film depicting what really goes on in the life of a family, with emphasis on their good times in a natural state, as others think they can from a contrived battle of good against evil. Reality provides such a wide range of intellectual stimulation and personal emotional moods to experience and share that we may never find the end of possible combinations. As an Atheist, I don't need any more than that.

Change and Fear

October 1982

The *American Atheist* is an Atheist magazine, dedicated to the explication of the Atheist viewpoint. In it, we — the editors — are currently featuring articles concerned with the disastrous nuclear arms race, the possibility of nuclear war, and the need for disarmament. Most Atheists are in agreement with what we print, but occasionally we receive letters in violent disagreement, dressing us down in vehement terms. The thrust of these letters when analyzed is that it doesn't matter to the Atheist writing if they are "pro" or "anti" arms, "pro" or "anti" nuclear war; they are still Atheists and they consider this to be an improper subject to be addressed in an Atheist magazine.

I would first like to point out that if there is a nuclear exchange between the U.S.S.R. and the U.S.A., there are not going to be any Atheists left. They will die — as will everyone else. Since the primary command of nature to our species is survival of the species, it is important for Atheists to take a position in respect to that survival.

I don't believe that anyone can be an Atheist and be either pro-war or pro-nuclear buildup, because Atheism is reason in the flesh. If we currently have enough nuclear weapons to blow up the world and everything in it two thousand times, it is highly irrational to continue the buildup. The idea of stockpiling and devising more and more lethal weapons of greater and greater sophistication is insane. It is just as insane as the idiocy of the virgin birth. Atheists who hold this viewpoint of the need for an Armageddon still have an emotional and anti-intellectual lag of religion deeply engrained in them. They have some mystic and religious-like fear of the U.S.S.R. which is equivalent to the religious fear of Satan — or the Antichrist. The U.S.A. is regarded by them as equivalent to the sacred Christ in their ideology. Passionate patriotism takes the place of their former fervently-held religion. The substitution is very obvious when viewed from the position of Atheism.

As long as humankind was living in the bushes, free roaming and taking from the land as best as it could, there were no difficulties with control. It is when "civilization" (from the Latin *civis*, member of a state, nation or group who owes allegiance to its government) began that the problem arose of *how to control the members of the group*. This has been the central problem of humankind ever since. The history of every nation and of every group has been a history of the struggle between the controllers for domination of the controllees under each sovereign. Every theory of "government" has been devised to best exercise that control. In the world today we can clearly see the fascism of most South American countries, South Africa, and the Philippines; the communism of the U.S.S.R. and China; the capitalism of the United States, the socialism of Australia and most of Europe, and the developing socialism in most of Africa.

The controllee, and that is *you*, fellow Atheist, is a dog on a leash. You have been thoroughly housebroken to the rules in your nation, if that nation is Japan, China, England, the U.S.S.R., Australia, Canada, or Finland. And, you have been taught to lick the hand of the master who holds the leash and to proclaim to the world that the system of control over you is better than the system of control devised in the other nations.

The citizens of the U.S.S.R. are under as many laws and restrictions as are you. In the U.S.S.R., the controllee must get up and go to work in the morning, pay rent, struggle to own a home (or apartment) and automobile, purchase food and clothing, rear a family, care for the elderly, struggle with health problems, and try to get some relaxation and joy out of life. That is absolutely no different than what happens to a controllee in the U.S.A.

The fear on which your controller (the government of the U.S.) plays is that your way of life may be totally and completely different if another controller takes over. The government of our nation posits that will be by force of arms — since you are told you are so devoted to your form of controller that you would never voluntarily change it. You are not supposed to notice that all the countries of Europe have been effectuating a change from capitalism to socialism without force of arms. France and Greece are the two last nations to vote in socialism and Mexico is well on the way with its nationalization of the banking system there.

If you awoke tomorrow morning and were under a different controller — let us suppose a fascist terrorist such as those in power in South America — you would get up, put on your shoes, go to work in the morning, pay rent, struggle to own a home (or apartment) and automobile, purchase food and clothing, rear a family, care for your elderly, struggle with health problems, and try to get some relaxation and joy out of life. Very little would be different for you. If you awoke tomorrow to a socialist government, the same daily living problems would confront you.

The Atheists who advocate a build-up to a nuclear exchange which would devastate the earth are fearful of a change in their lives, and it is the change that they fear.

The U.S.S.R. is not an Antichrist determined to change your life-style. And it is significant that the Reagan administration's quarrel with that nation is primarily that it is not a religious land, working on the supposition that religion makes our brand of control system more palatable.

Your editors feel that this is intellectually immature. You change all the time. Aging is a great changer. In addition, healthy and reason-controlled human beings are rubber balls. Pitch them down and they bounce back. If my grandmother could be born into a culture which had her riding in a carriage drawn by a horse, using coal to stoke her kitchen stove, and before she died, she had adjusted to jetting across the world and using an electronically controlled kitchen . . . then everyone in the world can adapt to change.

The Few, The Proud, The Elite

November 1982

As Director of the American Atheist Center, one of my many duties is to oversee the admission of new members into the organization, American Atheists. The organization has a standard membership application which interested persons are asked to complete and submit with the appropriate fee. On that application are a number of terms that one may apply to one's life philosophy. A wide choice is given ranging from "Atheist" to "Objectivist" to "I evade any reply to a query" to "my own appellation as given: ______."

Over the past period of about six months, it has come to my attention that persons applying for membership in American Atheists are in increasing numbers choosing any other life-style designation of the choices given than "Atheist." I believe there to be a reason for this that is justifiable in the minds of those who choose to label themselves as other than Atheist. That reason is very simple in that it, and the labels themselves, can be denoted in one word. That word is *fear*.

Fear is one, if not *the*, mainstay of established religion in America. You may think when I say "fear" that I am speaking of the traditional fear of burning in hell promulgated by the fire-and-brimstone, tent-hopping variety of minister. That is only partly true. A greater fear is the fear of being out of place, of not being accepted as a part of the whole — the whole family, the whole school, the whole job, the whole town, the whole community. Everyone must belong to something or somebody, or so we have been enculturated to believe.

In the lasting words of John Donne, the lesson has been taught and learned well by generation after generation:

> No man is an Iland, intire of it selfe; Every man is a peece of the Continent, a part of the maine; if a Clod bee washed away by the Sea, Europe is the lesse, as well as if a Promontorie were, as well as if a Mannor of thy friends or of thine owne were; any man's death diminishes me, because I am involved in Mankinde;
> And therefore never send to know for whom the bell tolls; It tolls for thee.

Donne was no Atheist. In fact, he was one of the outstanding religious fanatics of his day. But he does make a valid point about our culture. The problem with Atheists or near- or pseudo-Atheists is that they yearn to become a part of the wrong whole. They are fearful of establishing their own order, free from dogma, to have whatever comforting loyalties and solidarities they wish just as well as those they hold hypocritically within the prevailing establishment.

At this point in our nation's history, we are at a new high of Christian resurgence. Resurgence for what? To reestablish the fear of nonconformity to minimize the losses suffered by attrition in more lenient times. The pope is probably the best example of this in his return to medievalism. In that push for return to "basic" or "fundamental" doctrines of the church, he is not asking of the Catholics any more than Falwell is asking of the Protestants. Returning to basics means returning to conformity. Fundamentalism cannot be only piecemeal with any given congregation. The nature of religion demands full participation in it by all concerned.

Fear has even spread into our economic system. All commercial advertising is based in whole or in part on fear: fear of having your natural body cooling processes stain the clothing under your arms. (Oh, what if someone saw me sweat? The indignity of it all!); fear of not having the latest model car; fear of "body odor" or "Am I using the right soap?"; fear of "grey underwear" or a "dull" kitchen floor.

So, you see, I do understand why many newcomers to an Atheist organization prefer another appellation than "Atheist." They prefer those other labels for entirely the wrong reason. They don't prefer "humanist" over "Atheist" because it better describes them, but because it is innocuous. If, on the other hand, all whom the label "Atheist" fit came forward and used it with pride, there would be a new "whole," a new "body" of which to be part, with which to belong, that would not disturb their encultured security.

Atheism is a label under which you can and should maintain your individual autonomy, but at the same time be reinforced by the ideas and achievements of others freely — instead of in a rhythmic dogmatic way as in the church. You can still be a part of a group — just a different kind of group.

Eclecticism does not necessarily rule our collectivism of thought. Many individuals can all come to the same conclusion about the same thing with input from widely various sources with their quite distinct backgrounds. Atheism is a very fine example of that. Persons from many different social, political, educational, monetary, and religious backgrounds have all, for the most part independently and eclectically, come to the same conclusions about religion — leading them to the rejection of its principles. If that isn't a strong basis for unity, I don't know what is. What better or stronger feeling of "belonging" could you have than to belong to a group of people who achieved the same result from the widest possible number of standpoints?

It's a very special group, and I have a very special sense of solidarity to it that I don't have to most of the mainline culture around me anymore. There is nothing the matter with that. The Black community is slowly coming around to being proud to be Black. They have formed a solidarity around being Black. As Dick Gregory said, "Let them call me *Mr.* Nigger!" Let them call me *Mr.* Atheist.

You may feel that you are downgrading yourself by giving up a larger "identity" or a smaller one when you come out as an open Atheist, but that identity will not always be the smaller. Christianity was the smaller at one time, too.

Whenever I see those Marine advertisements urging young men to join "the few, the proud, the Marines," I think to myself "the few, the proud, the Atheists."

'Tis The Solstice

December 1982

The season has come round again, and it is once more time for the Christian community to go into their "heat season" to ward off the cold. Each year, in December, we hear about the birth of the alleged "Jesus" echoing through the halls of church after church. The commercial spirit is rekindled by the merchants urging you to buy some useless utensil for an ungrateful relative. What does all of this have to do with humanity's well-being? Nothing much anymore, but at one time the winter season was indeed a very special time for people. In our primitive beginnings we were frightened by almost everything — certainly almost everything that moved, especially at night. It was the fright spawned by ignorance of those natural and often cyclical things that went on around us.

So, when the days began to grow shorter and the nights longer and the "great ball of fire" in the sky that warmed things like our fire warmed our cave began to come around less and less, we got frightened. Primitive man asked "Would it return?" It did, and then it was time to rejoice. All of the early cultures built festivals around this time of year with various "sun gods" being heralds for returning with light and warmth. Horus to the Egyptians, Mithra to the Persians, Dionysus to the Greeks, Bacchus to the Romans and Jesus to the Christians. In the case of the Christians the transition from "sun" to "son" was a rather obvious one and easily made. The traditions of ignorance played into the hands of the newcomer of perpetuation systems for that "state of bliss." If one "sun" could bring life and warmth back, so could a substitute "son," and so Christianity was off and running.

Other things caught primitive minds about the season of the return of the sun. Certain things in the woods stayed green or had berries (or both) while everything else died from the lack of the sun. Mistletoe was held sacred by the ancient Druids, but they didn't kiss underneath it. Mistletoe, appropriately enough, is a parasitic shrub which fits it admirably to a worship system. The Romans did use it for kissing, though, and it played an important part in the Roman Saturnalia festival. In fact, slaves were even allowed to kiss their masters on that feast day if they caught them under the mistletoe.

Human characters, besides the mythical Jesus, got into it rather late in history. Nicholas was an early Christian bishop in Asia Minor who was renowned for his generosity to children. When Dutch seamen carried back stories of his good deeds, December 6th was set aside in Holland as a day on which children received presents. The Dutch transformed his name to "Sinter Klaas," as well as his appearance. It was not until 1809 that Washington Irving portrayed the American Santa Claus as a chubby, jolly, elf-like character.

Winter was not the only seasonal change month that primitive man noticed, and hence festivals sprang up around other seasons and the natural events associated with them as well. Eggs, for example, were regarded by many cultures as a symbol of continuing life and resurrection. They were handed out as prizes by the Romans to the fastest runners during their spring festival. The Chinese colored eggs, especially red, during the spring.

The Romans once celebrated the killing of wolves with a festival to the triumphs of Lupercus, a god who protected farmers from roaming creatures. As a part of the rites, maidens made up love missives and deposited them in large urns to be drawn by the men of the village who then courted them. When Christianity took over the holiday, Lupercalia was renamed Valentine's Day in honor of an alleged Christian martyr beheaded by Emperor Claudius II about the year 270.

May Day was another springtime celebration partaken of by the Romans. This one honored Flora, the goddess of flowers. In medieval England the May Day custom was for everyone, regardless of social station, to go out on the first day of May and to "fetch the flowers fresh."

From as long as 2,000 years ago harvest festivals have been a part of every culture. Our Halloween, or All Hallows' Eve, has most of its customs brought over by the Irish in their immigrations of the late 1800s. Our pumpkin replaced their turnip for jack-o'-lanterns lit with candles to ward off the witches, demons, hobgoblins, and evil spirits that were supposedly allowed to roam the earth on that night. It was also the Irish who initiated the "trick or treat" custom hundreds of years before it came to America.

Over all, most cultures have celebrated natural events associated with the changing seasons and what happens in those months, particularly in agrarian times. Remember, farming was the principal occupation of whole countries for a lot longer than factories. The industrial revolution came very late in human history. Essentially then, holidays have been celebrations of natural events that all cultures and localities share — that is, until Christianity and other major religions got a grip on the world. Now even the word "holiday" means holy day.

Let's get back to the Christian December 25th for a moment. Even that date has been in some dispute throughout church history as the day of the miraculous birth of this alleged savior. I mean, if the Christers are going to invade the lawns of our city halls with nativity scenes every year, they at least ought to be certain on which day the "blessed event" took place.

Historical evidence is not at all accurate on this point, but some historians think that the church in Alexandria, Egypt began commemorating the *baptism* of Jesus on January 6th around about the year 200. That date on the Egyptian calendar marked the festivals for the sun god at the time of the Winter Solstice. In later years that same date, January 6th, was known as Epiphany on the calendars of the Eastern Mediterranean church. Epiphany is from the Greek word meaning "manifestation." It commemorated the birth, adoration of the Magi (wise men) and baptism of Jesus *all together*. It was not until about 274 when the Roman emperor Aurelian decreed that the birthday of the unconquered sun (not son) be celebrated at the Winter Solstice — calculated by the Romans on their Julian calendar as December 25th. Then at some time just before the year 336, the church at Rome established the commemoration of the birth of Jesus — the *son* — on that same day. The evidence for that was found in a chronography (an almanac for the use of early Christians) which included an entry for December 25th in the year 354 as: "Christ born in Bethlehem of Judea."

In the year 381 in Constantinople (now Istanbul in Turkey) Pope Gregory of Nazianzus gave an epiphany sermon speaking of "Christmas" or the "mass of Christ" as recently past. Remember, Epiphany was on January 6th. Then, in Antioch (a city in south Turkey — capital of ancient Syria from 300-264 B.C.) about the year 386, in a sermon on December 20th a bishop there spoke of an upcoming festival from which all others come, the Christmas celebration. The same sermon referred to the visit of the Magi. Five days later, on the 25th, the same bishop's sermon said that the December 25th festival had been known among the Antiochans for less than ten years. But in his sermon of January 6th, 387, he stated that the name Epiphany should not be applied to Christmas, as some held, because Jesus became manifest to others and began his ministry after his baptism.

The separation of the two dates, December 25th and January 6th, was not achieved back in Egypt until at least 432. The opposition to Christmas lasted until the sixth century in Jerusalem, when the nativity was separated from January 6th and celebrated on December 25th.

There are still some Armenian Apostolic Churches in the United States today whose congregations commemorate both Christ's birth and baptism on January 6th. Most of the Eastern Orthodox Churches, especially in Slavic countries, observe Christmas on January 7th and Epiphany twelve days later, because they continue to use the Julian calendar (established by Julius Caesar in 46 B.C., which fixed the length of the year at 365 days with 366 days every four years), which is thirteen days behind the Gregorian calendar (named after Pope Gregory XIII, [1572-85], according to which the ordinary year consists of 365 days; a leap year of 366 days occurs in every year whose number is exactly divisible by four — except centenary years whose numbers are not exactly divisible by four hundred, *i.e.*, 1700, 1800, etc.) which we now use. Trust a pope to make things more complicated. You see, January 7th to us is December 25th (thirteen days back) on the Julian calendar for them.

The point of all of this history lesson is that some 400 plus years after this "savior" was supposed to have been born the early church decides to come down on a birth date for the founder of their faith. It seems to me that a date of such importance could have been nailed down a lot earlier. How convenient it was when they did decide to pick out December 25th that every culture was celebrating some kind of natural event around that time! Even the people in the southern hemisphere have their Summer Solstice at that time. All that had to be done was to rename the event.

That is why it is very important for us, as Atheists, to take the mysticism surrounding holidays (holy days) away and celebrate what is really worth celebrating, which is life. Just being alive is wonderful. Celebrating the cycles of life has intrinsic value to all humans and is something that goes far beyond our specific cultures to give us something every one can be happy about. To do so, however, reaffirms that we are part of the animal kingdom. The seasonal events that mean something to the wild animals mean something to us as well in a common way. The church will never allow that because it denies their special creation stories.

I don't think that we, as Atheists, should be celebrating the Winter Solstice in the same spirit as our very early ancestors, either. They rejoiced out of ignorance. We can rejoice too — but out of our knowledge of natural phenomena and the ever-increasing part we play in the cycle of life on our planet and not out of relief from fear of the unknown. We should look around us at this time of year and say how wonderful it is to be a part of the cycle of nature and how can we make that cycle work better for us and all the other organisms on the planet. Instead, the majority of the population takes this season as an opportunity to reaffirm their desire to be apart from the cycle of nature and to isolate themselves to paddle their own little canoes to "salvation," unconcerned about future generations or the cycles that brought them this far up the evolutionary chain.

I don't plan to swap life for an escape from life into fantasy this Winter Solstice or any other. I do plan to put up my conifer, decorate the house with pine cones and mistletoe, drink too much, eat too much, sing, and enjoy what life has to offer with my fellow animals. I think that's a whole lot healthier than pledging my mind to submission under a myth in some dark hall, don't you?

1963 — 1983

January 1983

This is the normal time of year for Happy New Year greetings from most journals, and the staff of The American Atheist Center (which produces this one) offers you that sentiment as well. We do, however, have an additional event about which to be happy, for 1983 is the twentieth anniversary of the existence of the American Atheist organization.

American Atheists was founded by Dr. Madalyn O'Hair in Baltimore, Maryland, on July 1st, 1963, following the eight-to-one decision by the United States Supreme Court in the case of *Murray v. Curlett*, which removed religious ceremonies from public schools. Since that founding, American Atheists has enjoyed a slow but steady growth, despite many setbacks that would surely have caused the permanent closure of many other groups. Those setbacks came as a result of the fascistic stance of religionists, organized and unorganized, in all walks of life, as they did battle against the idea (as they saw it) of organized "ungodliness."

For many years the American Atheist organization was sustained monetarily, psychologically, and physically by Dr. O'Hair and her immediate family — with Atheists, by and large, being too frightened to join in any way. One of the most immediate stumbling blocks to the success of the organization was to convince the rank and file of Atheists that it was O.K. to have their name on a "mailing list" without fear of loss of citizenship for the exercise. It is not hard to realize why that attitude prevailed when you take into consideration that America, in the early 1960s was just shaking loose of the McCarthy hysteria of looking for communists under every bed.

I think that one of the greatest services American Atheists has performed in these twenty years is to let Atheism stand alone outside of association with any political ideal. As the name of the organization states, we are AMERICAN Atheists. That accomplishment alone was a long hard fight, one which the new radical right religious movements of today are attempting to turn around — to bring us back to the "good old days" of the 1950s with their McCarthy terrorist tactics.

The organization has had great success in increasing the self-worth of individual American Atheists by making them proud of their Atheist heritage and aware of the great men and women with whom they share their reasoned stance. My personal goal as director of the national office, The American Atheist Center, is to see the day in this country that all individual citizens can openly and proudly flaunt their Atheism without fear of reprisal, discrimination, or abuse of any kind. In many ways, that is a similar ultimate goal of almost every minority "cause" group in the United States today. They all want equality and true "liberty and justice for all." We are all approaching that goal.

I feel that the day of recognition of Atheism as a viable and, in fact, superior life-style is in our almost immediate future. The purpose of an American Atheist organization is to bring that future to fruition as quickly as possible. The way to do that is by forming a growing, well-informed, educated American Atheist constituency nationwide which, working together, can reinforce each other against the continued and now heightened onslaught of public criticism orchestrated by the radical religious right forces, while reaching out to educate that public a little at a time. Toward this end the *American Atheist* magazine, now beginning its twenty-fifth year of publication, has endeavored to bring information on every conceivable aspect of Atheist news and thought to its readers.

Perhaps the highlight of this journal's recent history was those issues produced from February 1977 through October 1980, with four-color process covers by a commercial printing house in Austin, Texas. Aesthetically, those were the apex years of this journal's publication, but in terms of content the *American Atheist* continues to improve issue after issue, providing a wide range of information to you in a number of subject areas of concern to you as an Atheist. More important, perhaps, is the fact that this journal will not compromise in "telling it like it is." This is one of the reasons why, throughout its publication history, it has had no or very little advertising. With advertising comes a dependency on advertising dollars and with that, in turn, comes the ability of the large advertiser to dictate the content of the journal. The ability of this journal to speak openly and directly on issues of concern to Atheists will never be compromised by the advertising dollar; that is where you, the reader, are the safeguard of the purity of the publication. It is with your continued generous support of American Atheists that the publication of the journal continues.

Unfortunately, the *American Atheist* is no longer produced in four colors, due perhaps to our uncompromising editorial position in the face of the stark economic times in which our nation finds itself today.

We do feel, however, that this journal has been and will remain the outstanding real source of information and education (and not from the fact that it is the only one) on a monthly basis for Atheists in the United States.

The American Atheist organization continues to gain strength and recognition. When it first started back in 1963, it was not possible to complete a chore so small as to mail this journal into many cities in the United States due to the level of hatred against us — and the determination of the postal services as they were then constituted to "lose or destroy" our mail. Currently, we now mail not only to our own fifty states, but also to Canada, Australia, Mexico, Europe, and the Far East. The journal can now be found on newsstands in several major cities. In the beginning, Atheists were not allowed to advertise in any media — radio, television, magazines, or newspapers. We are now able to do that in every area of the country. The journal is now in some 400+ libraries across the nation, with the major proportion paying for the subscriptions. We have come a long way indeed.

When the First National Annual American Atheist Convention was held in Austin, Texas, in April of 1970, not one hotel or motel facility in the city would host the meeting at any price, and the convention was held in a city facility where discrimination was prohibited (after a good fight!) by law. Now, not a week goes by at The American Atheist Center that another solicitation does not pass over my desk, as Director, from another major hotel asking for our convention and meeting business.

Just a day or two ago *Time* magazine called The Atheist Center asking for our input on an article being prepared on separation of state and church issues surrounding the winter holidays in the United States. *Time* magazine would not have seen The Center as a source in beginning years —in fact, there was no "Center." Now, we chuckle to note that we are quoted as "officials at The Atheist Center say" when our research is quoted by the news media over and over again throughout the nation.

At that First National Annual Convention in 1970, when the media showed up with portable TV cameras, the handful of members in attendance dove under the tables in the room, covering themselves up with the tablecloths for fear of being recognized on the evening news that night by employers, relatives, or friends. At the Twelfth National Annual Convention, held in April of 1982 in Washington, D.C., over 350 members in attendance picketed the White House with red, white, and blue signs, happily outnumbering, as they did, a religious counter-demonstration across the street.

So, as a common cigarette commercial says, "You've come a long way, baby!" Now, 1983 has the potential of being not alone a banner year for Atheism, but a doorway to the future. The radical right religious groups in the country are losing ground rapidly, as evidenced by their failure to unseat targeted candidates in the November elections, as they had done in the previous election. The American Atheist Center is now well into its third years of production of the "American Atheist Television Forum" series for cable outlets across the country. The American Atheist Press has embarked on publishing paperback books which will now make it possible to bring you the best of over 150 years of Atheism in America.

Plans are being drawn now for a new American Atheist Center complex to be constructed on acreage outside of Austin, Texas, during this new year. With that new complex will come even greater outreach. We have, indeed, even a new motto for our organization as we begin the third decade: "*Unity Today — Power Tomorrow.*"

With your continued support and the new and more efficient means of information distribution today, this journal and the American Atheist movement in general has nowhere to go but up, nowhere to reach but out, and nothing to conquer but the world. And we're ready for it.

The Media and The Message

February 1983

The American Atheist organization was established as a watchdog group to monitor the level of compliance with the First Amendment of both religious and government institutions. That task has been a very difficult one, to say the least. It is ludicrous at best for a small, often struggling, underfinanced and socially outcast organization such as American Atheists to think that it can take the government of the United States to task. When you have a governmental system established upon certain principles in the early stages and then have it stray from those principles itself as time goes on, it is quite difficult to lead such a massive bureaucracy back into a path of compliance with its own rules. One is immediately confronted with an "Alice in Wonderland" scenario where you play a game in which you are stuck with a given set of rules, and your opponent changes them or makes them up as he plays to suit the advancement of his side of the contest.

American Atheists has found itself in just such a ludicrous position for many years now. But we are not alone. Other "causes" and minority groups find that they are presented with the same problem of needing to bring an entire system gone astray back into line, along a reasonable rule set within which they truly have "the right to redress for their grievances." The exercising of that "right" has been chiefly accomplished in a long standing way by minorities through the judicial system. Politics is a game for the wealthy, either personally or collectively. It is ever increasingly so due primarily to the factor of increased population. More people means more congressional and legislative representation. This in turn requires a politician — or politicians in the case of lobbying groups — to expend more funds to reach those wider numbers of voters. Cause organizations have been left out in the cold in this race, since most do not have strongly enough defined voting blocs of persons who can be rallied around single issues at the polls in a day and age when just getting people out to vote at all is a cause struggle in itself. Most causes also do not possess the economic power required to reach all of the "key politicos" they need to reach in the same way that industry and other "for profit" concerns can.

So we have a legislative branch of government pretty much out of the reach of many minority cause concerns. With the "squeaking wheel gets the grease" approach of an over-burdened legislative branch, those without the money or the numbers to squeak loud enough simply don't get off first base — or even onto it, in most cases.

The executive branch is even harder to penetrate, requiring even more money and a greater number of "connections" — usually connections in the legislature. A group that can't deal effectively in legislative circles is certainly not going to get anyplace in executive circles.

What is left over then is the judicial branch. Access to that means of redress of grievances has a limiting factor as well. That limiting factor is the need to go through an intermediary who knows how to get your grievance aired within the constraints of a bizarre and often unpredictable set of arbitrary and capricious rules. That intermediary is, of course, your friendly law firm. Most law firms worth contacting these days ask at least $100 per hour of anyone regardless of perceived ability to pay. The legal fees are often so massive for a constitutional law struggle within the state over several years of litigation that it is all that a given cause can do to meet the bill. American Atheists is not alone in that posture. What then can you do if you are cut off from presenting your case to the legislative and executive branches of government and are limited to your access to the judicial branch?

In some cases the answer is that you turn to violence. Let no one be mistaken that violence and terrorism are caused by an inability of governmental and societal institutions to listen. When a group, especially a very small one, is placed in a position of not being heard at all, it is only a matter of time before they grab some judge or other official and place a gun at his or her head and say "now you *will* listen to me." Why Atheists either individually or collectively have not come to this point by now is an amazement to me. Most other groups in the position of Atheists in the United States have had a riot or two to their credit by now. It must be our rationality that keeps us subdued.

In our case, instead of violence, we do the only thing we can do, given the circumstances. We go into the judicial system as often as we can, representing ourselves, or with paid representation that is often not worth paying for, depending on the strategy of making such a nuisance of ourselves that the complained-of entity will simply give in in order to shut us up and get us off their back. Along the way we can use this "litigation" most of the time knowing when we go into the fight that we have the proverbial "snowball's chance in hell" of winning, as a vehicle for gaining media attention. The more media attention we can get, the more persons we can muster to our fold, and thus the larger monetary- and number-base we can amass in order to someday place ourselves in the reach of other than judicial redress of our grievances. If we "litigate" long enough, and get attention that way long enough to get a base of operation established, then we can begin to be influential in making policy, the ultimate aim of any "cause" group. We do not stand alone in this *modus operandi*. Many other groups do the same thing, all in a waiting or holding pattern when it comes to large substantive changes that we seek of the system being realized in that golden hour when we have "power" in the real sense of the word.

One of the problems with our scheme is that the media is not always cooperative. As the population grows and more and more minorities and thus more and more causes spring up, it gets harder and harder to get that media attention. We must do things now that are much more "controversial" than we had to do several years ago to get "coverage." Just filing a suit does not do the job like it used to do. Now we have to file a suit against a city council, for example, and picket their meeting the same day as we file, to make the papers at all. Competing against crime, economic troubles, hair-trigger geopolitics, and domestic political circuses for air time is getting pretty tough. In order to keep your place in the media, you have to keep giving those government entities one poke after another while trying to be as original as possible in the way in which you poke them. It's like playing with a snake. You want to irritate it with a stick long enough to keep the gathered crowd amused — but not enough so that you get bit. It is a delicate balance indeed.

The media also changes personnel as often as most of us change our underwear. The pattern seems to be that a young person, right out of college with a journalism B.A., comes to a station or paper and gets on the staff and is kept until they gain enough field or street savvy that they think they are worth more money. At that point it is more economical for the station to get rid of them and get the next greenhorn in line — at a very low entry pay, of course. With the exception of such institutions as, say, Johnny Carson's "Tonight" show, almost every time a representative of American Atheists goes back on a show the second time, the host, producer, director, etc., have all changed. In fact, the producers, hosts, and directors change more often than the "talent," *i.e.*, the persons who appear to be interviewed.

This constant turnover presents a problem to all those seeking media attention. Just as soon as you get the persons at a given station or newspaper to know you and you get them willing to cover you on some regular kind of basis, everything changes hands. One then has to work one's way back into the good graces of a new editor or producer or director and has to prove oneself again as a worthy and competent guest. A particular variation of this problem for American Atheists is that most of the media only knows of us through the name of our founder, Dr. Madalyn O'Hair. Since her landmark Supreme Court case on school prayer was in 1963, now twenty years ago, the new college-age persons coming into the media don't know who she is and frequently don't know that there even is an Atheist organization in the United States. We are trying to do something about this now by issuing a comprehensive media booklet listing all the representatives qualified to speak for American Atheists across the country, along with their pictures and biographical data. This speaker's bureau list is being sent to the producer of every radio or TV talk show in the nation that takes guests of our type. It is also going to newspaper editors as well. We hope to have a good response by sending thousands of these out. We will be following up with updated versions as well. The new personnel in the media and the fact that they don't know any better has caused a flurry of talk shows and interviews across the country with clergy being called upon to comment on separation of state/church issues in which they have a vested interest.

Getting on the air is, however, only part of the battle. The next major problem after getting on the air or getting an interview granted is to get your address out. Most media sources will cover you in a way in which interested persons hearing or seeing the coverage have no idea how to find you if they desire to help. Media likes to be paid for advertising; they don't like to give it up for nothing. Most of the time the only thing good that comes from a particular media engagement is a show of an address where people can write. This is because the format of almost every interview or talk show is a "confrontational" one. The show or interviewer is not at all interested in eliciting educational information from us. They are there only for a scandal — either real or contrived (and often the latter), a news story, or a fight, and not for an orderly progressive presentation of a position. Time and time again I, personally, have had a talk show host fight with me on the air in place of an opponent or in place of an audience that was not hostile enough to be to the host's liking. This is the classic "devil's protagonist" position. Even a sympathetic or outright Atheist host will say "Now, you understand that I must play devil's protagonist tonight" and proceed to tear into us with often more hostility than does the opposition.

The media, being socially entrenched, bows to the opposition over and over again. A good example is the following repeated scenario. I get up at 5:00 in the morning, get dressed suitably for television, pack a bag, get out to the airport, get on a plane, fly for eight hours while changing planes three or four times, and arrive in a city just in time to take a cab from the airport to the station in time for the broadcast. There I find a minister, priest or rabbi. They are fresh and clean-shaven, rested, and prepared with answers to questions that they have been given in advance by the show host or producer. They know all of the local people in the studio, and the host goes to their church. The station gives them free airtime every Sunday for their service. So, I come in with a wrinkled suit, a five o'clock shadow, windblown hair, a suitcase out in the hall, and am confronted with a hostile interviewer, the fresh clergyman who has been through "makeup," and often an audience or callers who have been whipped up against me by a promo run before I arrived of which I knew nothing.

There you have your media opportunity. That is typical of the kind of opportunity with which we are presented. Why the clergyman? Why the audience that has nothing to say and knows nothing about the topic that you will try to present to them? "Equal time," that's why. We are told that the station must keep a "balanced" presentation of views and that we cannot be on the air unless we have an opponent there. Now the fact that the opponent gets constant free airtime from the station, is local and can get on any time (and does usually once a week), and has a church on every corner where persons can hear his point of view four or five times a month at a minimum, while we are most often from out of town, makes no difference. Then why, when a religious representative comes on a show, are not the Atheists called in to provide opposition equal time for them? Well, "it just simply does not work that way," they say, and "longstanding station policy is hard to change."

Counting all of its Chapters, American Atheists must have at least 1,000 to 1,200 radio, TV, and newspaper appearances each year. Some Chapters are more active in this area than others — most notably Denver, CO and Tucson, AZ. Despite the stumbling blocks that are placed in our path we seem to be heard fairly well. We also have the "American Atheist Forum" cable TV series seen by 2½ million persons each week in seven major outlets around the country. This is our best form of media outreach because it is one in which we control the format of our presentation.

On a recent, nationally distributed PBS television talk show, our founder Dr. O'Hair had 28,000 calls in one hour placed to the station by potential questioners. That is proof positive that the public is interested in what we have to say if we are given a chance to say it. Other cause groups have had similar response on hot issues when given a media chance. Those kind of figures are never publicized, however. The FCC, for example, has received 17,500,000 letters of protest against an alleged petition that American Atheists is out to ban all religious broadcasting from the nation's airways. We have no such petition, we never have had, and never will. Just the rumor of it was enough to generate that kind of reply from the religious community. The media deliberately soft-pedals this, letting the rumor persist and sometimes feeding the fire as well, so that more letters will come, and the FCC will be influenced to give more consideration to the religious demands for expanded airtime and broadcast frequency power. If 17,500,000 letters had been written about Reagan, on any topic, the nation would have known about it from every media source. Since the letters are in opposition to Atheists, nothing is done to stop the rumor, ugly as it is.

American Atheists is stuck in the same position as many other causes, and we must just weather out the wait for the sun to come out on the day when we have that needed power and money. Until then, we just have to keep up the same scheme of getting media attention as we can and/or making ourselves an irritant as often as possible to any part of the system that fails to follow its own rules. That is why our new motto, "Unity Today, Power Tomorrow" is so appropriate. You will be seeing that on many things we publish throughout the year.

You can help individually with your letters to the editor, to your congressman, and with your monetary support of American Atheists during this holding pattern period. We will try, in turn, on a national level, to make the best use of what media time we can get, all the circumstances being as they may be.

Justice and The Trickle-Down Theory

March 1983

Just a little while ago I received a letter at The American Atheist Center from Robert Zauner, the new Chapter Director of the Northern Virginia Chapter of American Atheists. Bob is an attorney, and he sent with his note a copy of President Reagan's remarks at the annual convention of religious broadcasters held at the Sheraton in Washington, D.C., January 31st, 1983. I sat and read through the text of that speech carefully, and I grew more angry as I read, line by line.

Over sixty years now, since about the 1920s, the federal courts and the Supreme Court of the United States have been arduously laboring over the defining and delimiting of the "meaning" of the Establishment and Free Exercise Clauses of the First Amendment to the Constitution. The litigation over separation of state and church issues has been long and hard and well fought by a variety of groups over these many years. The Seventh-Day Adventists and the Jehovah's Witnesses have been more responsible than any other religious group over the years for trying to maintain separation of state and church. These two groups have sponsored numerous cases on the free exercise question. The Jews and the Baptists have been much less active — although more active than some of the rest of the denominations. One case has built up upon the other to form a set of guidelines for the lower courts by the United States Supreme Court and federal appellate courts for what is and is not "constitutional" when it comes to religion and the First Amendment. Considering all the circumstances and the complexity of the fact-situations of the various cases over the years, the Supreme and Appellate Courts have done a pretty good job in establishing those guidelines so far.

During all of this legal process, the religious leaders of our nation and the politicians sympathetic to them have been eroding those judicial guidelines in terms of the practical and logistical applications thereof. A good example of this is the battle over religious ceremonies in public schools. The Supreme Court in two major decisions laid down a fine and succinct outline of constitutionally-permissible activity in the public schools-only to have that outline overstepped on the local level over and over again, but politicians and religionists obfuscate the clear thinking of the courts with semantic games — such as the redefining of the word "prayer" with the synonymous terms of "meditation" (silent or transcendental) and "silence" or "thought" (moment of — or secular).

In real terms, then, all of the perspiration and inspiration of the courts has become functionally advisory in nature. Getting the local yahoos to heed that advice has been quite a different story. The moral to the story is that the religious never give up. Fanaticism, in all of its "glory," is basic to Christianity and the Christian ethic. There is little difference between being willing to die *en masse* in a crusade or for a Jim Jones and being willing to sink your teeth into the posterior of a principal or a school board member until Junior has the "right" to be forced to pray or watch prayer or has the "right" to be *free* of intelligent reading material. Religious tenacity and fanaticism make good bedfellows. The intellectual and scientific set has, on the other hand, traditionally disdained the "street fighter" image and style, preferring the Johnny-come-lately armchair type of combat. In the street, they obviously lose the day.

The blame for the failure of judicial wisdom to trickle-down to the rank and file lies with the court itself. Criminal (as distinct from civil) law attaches penalties, either monetary or physical, to noncompliance. Civil law makes it the providence, for the most part, of the injured party to sue again to force compliance on an issue that has already been decided in an overall manner on the appellate level. If some teeth could be put into the civil law, such as fines or imprisonment, then perhaps civil rights and state/church separation issues could be more easily and permanently resolved. Say, for example, that a fine of perhaps one hundred dollars a day were levied on a school district or principal where religious ceremonies were conducted in the schools in violation of standing court decisions. Would this not help preserve the efforts of the courts which took a great deal of time and money on both sides in the first place? Teeth have been put into *religiously based* law already, as we see in the blue laws. A store owner can actually be fined or jailed in some states for selling certain items or for being open on Sunday. If the religious community can have punitive enforcement of blue laws, why can't First Amendment separation of state and church guarantees have punitive enforcement as well?

This issue is a central one on which is focused the future of *effective* separation litigation. Chief Justice Burger has recently proposed a division of Supreme Court jurisdiction with a coequal appellate review court which would handle the many intrastate disputes now clogging up the Supreme Court docket — a great number of which are separation cases. The reason so much of the high court's burden is now separation cases stems from the fact that no teeth were ever put in their earlier decisions, and now they must handle the state by state religious attempts at circumventing them. Congress may eventually have to get into the act to resolve these issues. In order to resolve them properly, they would have to give some of that badly needed bite to judicial review in civil and civil rights matters. Politicians, being what they are — essentially populists — are not about to vote for the same kind of enforcement for separation of state and church as they are for, say, blue laws. Can't you just see Congress voting to withhold federal revenue sharing funds from any county that uses county school buses to transport parochial school students? How about fines for teachers who teach biblical creationism in any public school science classroom? There have been, and still are, laws to prevent the teaching of evolution alone, however. The shoe has never been on the other foot.

How does all of this relate to Reagan's speech before religious broadcasters? In the course of his remarks Reagan made it "perfectly clear" (remember that presidential line?) that he would, as part of the executive branch of government, fight to his last breath the putting of that shoe on the other foot when it comes to separation issues. As I have said earlier, politicians have been classically receptive to the whining of the religious voter, but never before to such a degree in our nation's history. Most of the support for religionist positions has come from congressmen — on the state level than federal — and executive department heads, but not so much directly from the White House. Sure, the White House has approved of the actions of the department heads and others, even Congress as a whole with things such as "In God We Trust" on the currency. That approval is a far cry, however, from blatant proselytization for violation of judicial separation standards by the Chief Executive himself. This is a recent phenomenon. The religious community has not had the luxury of a Chief Executive and many tenured congressmen being willing to openly and loudly stump for them in past decades. This luxury, particularly during the 80s, is one that we as separationists can ill afford. Now is the time for Congress to become involved in coming to the aid of the courts by putting those badly needed teeth in the civil statutes. Instead, during this critical period, Congress is gearing up to fight the courts — led by the religious zealots among them. In addition, we now have a Chief Executive to fan the fire. Needless to say, the religious community is taking full advantage of the situation.

Let's take a look at some of what Reagan had to say to his cheering audience of religious broadcasters. Early on in his speech Reagan said,

> In a time when recession has gripped our land, your industry, religious broadcasting, has enjoyed phenomenal growth. Now, there may be some who are frightened by your success, but I'm not one of them. As far as I'm concerned, the growth of religious broadcasting is one of the most heartening signs in America today. . . . The American people are hungry for your message because they are hungry for a spiritual revival in this country . . . they're saying, "We want the Word of God. We want to face the future with the Bible."

He went on then shortly to drop the bombshell of the entire speech when he said, "Thursday morning [February 2, 1983], at the National Prayer Breakfast, I will sign a proclamation making 1983 the Year of the Bible." (May I ask why there is a national prayer breakfast at all?) And on January 29th, 1983, Reagan has declared May 5th, 1983, as a "National Day of Prayer" in an effort to "bring renewed respect for God."

A small group or two tried to keep Reagan from making that proclamation through a court injunction. The cases were dismissed. Had they not been, the president needed only to claim executive privilege to cause their default. American Atheists has tried to sue prior presidents over separation issues and failed for the same reason; the president is in and of himself a branch of government. He can proclaim what he likes. Thus one can see one of the immediate advantages of having a Chief Executive on your side if you happen to be in the religious camp.

The driving force behind Reagan's aid to the religious cause was not revealed until a little further into the speech when he said, "I've always believed that this blessed land was set apart in a special way, that some divine plan placed this great continent here between the two oceans to be found by people from every corner of the earth. . . ." Holy predestination!, as Batman's sidekick would say. Obviously he has never heard of continental drift. He missed completely that the most unique thing about the founding of this nation was the separation of state and church wording in the Constitution. A state church had been the foregone conclusion of government for centuries before our deistic founding fathers made this "great continent" a special one indeed by making its government free from the hand of the church. The courts have been recognizing this fact, though reluctantly at times, over these past sixty years or so.

The president went on to say,

> I happen to believe that the one way to promote, indeed to preserve, those traditional values we share is by permitting our children to begin their days the same way the members of the United States Congress do — with prayer. The public expression of our faith in God through prayer is fundamental — as a part of our American heritage and a privilege which should not be excluded from our schools. . . . When the Supreme Court ruled that school prayer was unconstitutional almost twenty-one years ago, I believe it ruled wrong. And when a lower court recently stopped Lubbock, Texas high school students from even holding voluntary prayer meetings on the campus before or after class, it ruled wrong, too.

The president of the United States has no business speaking against the U.S. Supreme Court or any other court in its interpretation of the Constitution of the United States. That is an area reserved for the courts, and the principle of separation of powers dictates that interpretation of the Constitution is their province and theirs alone. In the 1940s the Supreme Court spoke directly to this issue when it said,

> The very purpose of the Bill of Rights was to withdraw certain subjects from the vicissitudes of political controversy, to place them beyond the reach of majorities and *officials* [emphasis added] and to establish them as legal principles to be applied by the courts. One's right to life, liberty, property, to free speech, a free press, freedom of worship and assembly, and other fundamental rights may not be submitted to vote, they depend on the outcome of no elections.

I cannot believe that we now have a president who is willing to reshape the entire mechanics of government as they have been functioning for over 200 years now to serve theological ends. The power of the office of the president of the United States should not be used to fulfill the private special interest of a religious maniac now occupying that office. The welfare of all the people of the United States — and that includes Atheists — is paramount.

That is not the worst of it, yet. In closing, Reagan made it very clear that he is willing to commit the United States militarily to the enforcement of *his* values worldwide — if that means by nuclear force as well. Listen to what he had to say very carefully.

> This year, for the first time in history, the Voice of America broadcast a religious service worldwide, Christmas Eve at the National Presbyterian Church in Washington DC. [VOA officials in a *Washington Post* interview of February 4, 1984, said, "VOA is mapping plans to increase its religious programming into the Soviet Union from the current forty-five minutes a week to one hour, with each segment to be repeated six times a week." Until now only religious "news" was broadcast. From henceforth full church services will be broadcast.] Now, these broadcasts are not popular with governments of totalitarian powers [I wonder who he means?]. But make no mistake, we have a duty to broadcast [Duty for whom?]. Alexander Herzen, the Russian writer, warned, "To shrink from saying a word in defense of the oppressed is as bad as any crime." Well, I pledge to you that America will stand up, speak out and defend the values we share [Which values, Christian ones?]. To those who would crush religious freedom, [Even Billy Graham did not find evidence of that in the U.S.S.R., and he was quickly silenced for saying so.] our message is plain. You may jail your believers. You may close their churches, confiscate their Bibles and harass their rabbis and priests, but you will never destroy the love of God and freedom [Note the connection; what does one have to do with the other?] that burns in their hearts. They will triumph over you. [Shades of Churchill!] Think of it — the most awesome, military machine in history [We're not?], but it is no match for the one, single man, hero, strong yet tender, Prince of Peace. His name alone, Jesus, can lift our hearts, soothe our sorrows, heal our wounds and drive away our fears. He gave us love and forgiveness. He taught us truth and left us hope.

Now if that does not sound like the call to Armageddon or the Crusades, act V, I don't know what does. All of us, as Atheists, had better begin to take a long hard reevaluation of our level of commitment to our cause. If we don't put our differences behind us and get organized and get moving during the '80s, it may well be too late for all concerned. We can't afford to let the kamikazes for Christ take the rest of us with them.

An Atheist "Fairy Tale"

April 1983

I would like to tell a little story this month to Atheists one and all. Once upon a time in the Eastern woodlands of America there was a very historic and very conservative state. The name of the state was Tennessee. Now at one time, long, long ago, the elders of this very pretty state decided that they would like to have a constitution. This was a very long, big, and important paper that set forth all of the rights and privileges of all the citizens who dwelt in Tennessee. A part of that constitution was not like all the other parts, though. All the other parts of the great paper gave many rights to the citizens, but this part took a right away from some of them. It said, "No person who denies the being of God, or a future state of rewards and punishments shall hold any office in the civil department of this State" (Article IX, Sec. 2).

Now most of the kindly, hard-working citizens of the state thought nothing of this part of the great new list of rights. They had all believed in God all their lives and did not know anyone who did not believe. "Someone who does not believe in god! Oh, how silly. No one like that lives in our pretty little state," they thought. But ah!, over in the deep dark woods in the southern part of the great state of Tennessee there dwelt a big tall handsome man, Sir Harold of Church. Sir Harold lived in a big castle in the little village of Columbia. Rumor had it around the village that a fire-breathing dragon lived under Sir Harold's house and that he used the fire from its nostrils to roast little Christian children he caught on their way home from school when they wandered near his castle. Everyone in the village knew that he was an Atheist. No one knew exactly what an Atheist was for sure, but they remembered their grandfathers' old tales about how wicked and naughty they were. They had all been told around their hearths at night to be good little boys and girls and go to the church down the lane whenever the kindly vicar rang the big bell, lest they become like Sir Harold. They knew that the "Church" in his title was meant to fool them and lure them to his web like a wily spider.

Well, one day Sir Harold found out about the part of the great state paper of rights that denied him one of his rights when it gave the others of the village so many. So Sir Harold went far, far away, to the far-off state of Texas where the queen of the Atheists lived. Everyone in the village knew of this and trembled in fear, for they had heard of this land of Texas down at the south edge of the land where the world dropped off over the edge. That is where the evil Atheist queen lived in a cave with her henchmen. Sir Harold came back from Texas with evil spells brewed up by the wicked Queen Madalyn of Hair and her black-eyed evil son, Jon, Duke of Murray, and tricked the goodly elders of the great state of Tennessee into changing that part of the great paper of rights so that people like Sir Harold could hold office.

"A wicked, evil, nasty Atheist hold office in our nice little state of Tennessee? Oh! Woe is me!" said the members of the village to each other. Sad as it was, it was true. Well, the leaders of Sir Harold's village were not going to give up without a fight, and neither were the leaders of other villages and towns and cities all over the great state of Tennessee. They all gathered together and put pressure on their elected representatives in the great, wise legislature of the state, whose job it had been all these many years to sit in judgment on the great long paper of rights and uphold and defend it against all the enemies of the state. The people from far and near cried out, "We must save our children from the wicked Atheists. We must armor them against Atheism with a shield that they can use against those like Sir Harold who may leap out of the woods at any time to gobble them up."

It was then that one of the kind, old, and wise senators proposed a bill in the legislature that would require all the teachers in the little red school houses in all of Tennessee to make all the children have a minute of classroom silence to be spent in "prayer or meditation" each day. In that way each child could recharge his little shield of faith around him each morning in school so that he could ward off any of the nasty, dirty Atheists that might try to gobble him up or fool him to leave the path on the way home. The Senate of the great state of Tennessee voted and passed the bill, and so did the younger and less wise House, and the good Governor signed it into law. "Hurrah!" the people shouted with glee. "Our children are saved from the Atheists." But it was not to be so.

Along came the knights of the ACLU. They had been known in the past to fight for the wicked. No one quite knew why; that was just their job. They swooped down on a poor old federal judge who had been placed in Tennessee by the great president, far, far away, who lived in a great white castle and looked after all the people in many states and who was all-wise. They badgered that poor old judge until he could not take it anymore (as was their style, as they had ganged up on poor unexpecting judges before), and he gave in and said that the new law was unconstitutional. One of the reasons the judge gave was that the legislature had spent so much time arguing loud and long over the wording of the bill that it was obvious that they intended to establish prayer in the school houses. The great mysterious Constitution of the United States that had been given (so the tales told) to the wise President in the "before time" (the time before the state of Tennessee was at all) had some words in it against the establishment of religion in all the land. The people thought that this part of that mysterious Constitution from the "before time" had been forgotten. The saga had been told from generation to generation that the fathers of all the land to the edge of the world had put together this great document with the aid of god almighty himself. The purpose of this great document, the saga said, was to preserve the relationship between men and god and never let men go astray. The part about establishment of religion was there because the fathers of all the land did not want any of the bad people like Sir Harold or the wicked Queen Madalyn to come to the schools disguised in the mask of a "secular humanist" and beguile the little children into the path of Atheism. So they thought, in the before time, that they would ban all religion from school so that the children could learn the true faith from their kindly village vicars and not be tricked in the school house by any Atheists in sheep's clothing masquerading as secular humanists.

The wise men of this time in Tennessee thought that such a thing must be changed now, however. In the before time the fathers of all the land had not been tricked by the likes of Sir Harold and Queen Madalyn to change their great paper of rights. The wise men of Tennessee had been tricked, and now they had to make amends.

So the good Senator from the village of Camden changed the bill made to protect the children just a little, so that it now called for the teachers in each little school house in the great state of Tennessee to make all the children in each classroom have a "minute-of-silence" each day. All of the good little children of Tennessee would know what to do during that minute to recharge their little shields against the Atheists. Their parents would whisper to them what to do so that the old judge that had been fooled by the knights of the ACLU could not hear. In a like manner, the wise men of the Senate passed the new bill *with no discussion* this time so as not to draw the wrath of the knights of the ACLU down on the poor old judge.

One Senator did not vote for the silence with all the rest. He was the Senator from the village of Murfreesboro. He said that he didn't think it was a proper function of the Senate of the great state of Tennessee to meddle with the law of the land given by the fathers in the before time. The papers all over the state printed this Senator's name in big fat letters on the front page so that all the citizens would know that he did not stand with them in their hour of need. They would make him sorry later on, they vowed.

After the Senate had passed the bill for the little children, the House, which is younger and a little less wise, had to vote on it, too. The House voted 89 to 6 to go along with the older, wiser Senate. The papers did the same thing with those six bad Representatives that they had done with the one wayward Senator. They put their names in big, big letters out for everyone to see. Out of the six Representatives who voted against the minute-of-silence for the children, two of them were extra-naughty. Representative Cobb from the city of Nashville and Representative Bragg from the village of Murfreesboro were the two extra-naughty ones. Remember that Murfreesboro is the same village that the bad Senator was from. That village would have to be shown a thing or two by the other villages and towns because its Representatives were no good and did not care about the little children. Cobb suggested to the other members of the house that they make the new law read so that teachers could be punished under the civil laws if they attempted to influence their students' thoughts instead of just keeping them silent for a moment. All the other good House members saw that this was a trick right away and voted against it. They knew that if the wording was changed the way the wayward Cobb wanted, that no one would vote for the minute of silence because they would be afraid of hurting the kindly teachers who are good to all the little boys and girls of the state. And besides, and golly gee, everyone knows that teachers are never wrong! "How could someone suggest that teachers would influence their students' thoughts?" That was a mean thing to say about the loving teachers of the great state of Tennessee. Bragg suggested two changes in the wording of the good minute-of-silence bill. One was to allow the teachers to keep the children in a period of silence for up to an hour each day. Oh! How terrible! "Our kindly teachers would not do such a thing," said the other House members and voted that suggestion down. The other one of Bragg's suggestions was for the bill to require a moment of silence in homes and businesses as well as for the children in each little red school house. The other House members knew that that was a fiendish thing that would anger all the mommies and daddies who would have to interrupt their busy worktimes each day for something that they did in church on their day of rest each Sunday. Perish the thought that the House members would do anything that the mommies and daddies who elected them may not like! So the other House members voted that suggestion down too.

Now all that remained was for the Governor to sign the new law into force and all of the children of the great state of Tennessee would be saved from the nasty Atheists like Sir Harold of Church for ever and ever and ever.

Meanwhile, the woods and closets of Tennessee were full of sinister, piercing little sets of eyeballs staring out of the dark, menacingly taking in all the commotion surrounding Sir Harold and the children. To whom do these eyes belong? Why, they are the other Atheists. They all agreed with Sir Harold and the wicked Queen Madalyn from the South, but they dared not show themselves or come out of the closet, for should they be revealed, the same fate might befall them as had befallen Sir Harold. What was this horrible fate? They would become part of the dreaded unloved of the state. No one would invite them over for tea. Their children would never laugh again or play in the sunshine. The daddies would be kicked out of the Moose lodge and never again be allowed to use the secret handshake. They would be mocked in the village square and everyone would whisper, "Look, there goes one of those people who think. They use their heads instead of their hearts to guide them through life. Oh! how hard their lives must be!" they would say.

All of the other Atheists did not understand that Sir Harold did that because he was very happy and free and full of joy. He read and thought of many things and explored many things of which the other people in the village were afraid or which their vicar told them were bad. He never thought of any of his actions as "sins" or of repenting for them. Sir Harold could do as he pleased without needing to figure out if something was or was not a "sin." He was not really so bad as any of the other villagers made out, and the smoke from underneath his house was not a dragon at all but just an old leaky furnace. He had never really eaten any children. Those bones they saw him with one day were from his interest in the early men that lived on the land way back before the fathers of the land, before the before time. He knew that people had been around back then too, and he studied them — unlike the other villagers who thought that the world was only a few thousand years old. Sir Harold read and explored the lands past the end of the earth. The other villagers would not even think of such a thing.

The moral of this story is that if all those piercing little sets of eyeballs in the closet had come out to help Sir Harold anywhere along the line, he could have made all the people of the village happy on the *inside* too like he was, instead of just being happy on the outside and full of fear and trepidation about what they did not understand on the inside. The whole village could have been a happier place to live, *inside and out*, and all the villagers could have lived together in *true* happiness for ever after. Instead of that, they stayed in the closet and allowed themselves to continue to be part of the "unloved" and to be counted among the "unthinking." In that manner, they created their own unhappiness and condemned themselves and their children and their children's children to life in the closet for ever and ever.

Are The Only Alternatives Dead or Red?

May 1983

It sounded like "birds of a feather," with the pope first stating that Atheism "is at the root of every present evil," and the president of the United States following that remark with his statement that "There is sin and evil in the world. And we are enjoined by scripture and the Lord Jesus Christ to oppose it with all our might."

Hardly anyone would have believed, hearing them, that it was the twentieth century. But, it *is* a century of technology, science, and education, and the columnists, editorial writers, and cartoonists of the hard media were immediately upon the president's remarks, characterizing it often as a "Darth Vader speech," or as "cold war rhetoric."

Adam Clymer, of the *New York Times*, in his "Analysis" column stated that obviously Reagan had taken the advice of conservative Paul Weyrich who had told him "to hew to the social issues," which is advice in exact opposition to that of the majority of his party. And, the president went to it with glee. The audience was handpicked for it, being the Forty-first Convention of the National Association of Evangelicals. Seeing the black and white of an international issue, the speech clearly staked out the opposite poles of a "God-fearing America and a Godless Soviet Union." Hitting every emotional issue — abortion, prayer in schools, tuition tax grants, and the freeze — Reagan identified himself as one of the "many God-fearing, dedicated noble men and women in public life." And, Clymer saw this as a clear statement of his candidacy for office in the 1984 elections. In fact, Clymer went to and was told by a "high-ranking Republican strategist" that the speech "could fairly be interpreted as another in a series of signals that a candidate is talking."

The question is then, could the candidate run on these "social issues" again?

In the *Wall Street Journal*, Alexander Cockburn, who is normally a columnist for the *Village Voice*, in his "Viewpoint" column, excoriated the president for his advocacy of Judeo-Christianity.

> I must enter a protest against the use of the "Judeo-Christian Tradition" as an advertisement for freedom or uplifting human

> values. To take the "judeo" part first, we need only glance at the Old Testament to find a deity of savagery, interminably urging his chosen people to acts of genocide. . . . Readers whose memories of Holy Writ have grown hazy may care to consult the disgusting tenth chapter of the book of Joshua (who slew all life in one country) or the crazed twenty-eighth chapter of Deuteronomy, with fifty-four verses of curses from God on those straying from his word.

Moving to the New Testament, Cockburn notes that,

> It could fairly be argued that two of the greatest blots on what the president would no doubt call the "Judeo-Christian era" were slavery and the subjugation of women. Jesus accepted both, and so did Paul. We may add to this the Christian tradition of persecution of heresy, which produced some of the bloodiest pages in human history.

It was hardly the kind of column one would ordinarily find in the staid *Wall Street Journal.*

But then Lars Nelson from the *New York Daily News* was equally as harsh: "The Reagan administration's view of the world has always been a little dippy but in recent days it has gone from bats to worse." He was particularly incensed with the president's story of a father who stated,

> I love my little girls more than anything. I would rather see my little girls die now, still believing in God, than have them grow up under communism and one day die no longer believing in god.

And, he quoted the president's analysis of that:

> "There were thousands of young people in that audience," your president continued. "They came to their feet with shouts of joy. They had instantly recognized the profound truth in what he had said."

The thrust of the column was that we obviously are back to "better dead than red" and that this is bats in the belfry.

The Knight-Ridder newspaper chain is a large and conservative one. But, its columnist John McMullan was constrained to ask in headlines "Is Reagan A Zealot?" In analyzing the speech he states,

> The president misreads history. He also stretches his scriptures to cover his political intentions. . . . Once the tiniest breach appears in the wall of separation (of state and church), where will it end? There's no question that history of humankind, and of America in particular, has been entwined with religion. Indeed, religion was once deemed a function of the public school system in the colonies. But the founding fathers knew what they were doing when they later erected the wall. . . . If Reagan would read a little more history, he would know that many of the red blots on the pages stem from sanctimonious nations and rulers waging war against "infidels." He is setting this nation upon a dangerous course when he quotes scripture and characterizes Russia as "the focus of evil" to win the Christian evangelicals' support of his defense program. Such pandering to religious bigotry offends us . . . it is unworthy of a leader of a nation founded upon religious pluralism.

William Rusher, the publisher of *The National Review*, was coldly furious of any criticism:

> A careful study of president Reagan's address to the National Association of evangelicals . . . is absolutely central to any understanding of the man or his presidency. . . . The central proposition of the speech is Reagan's declaration that "We" — meaning the American people — "will never abandon our belief in God." . . . Reagan shapes not only his domestic initiative but his concept of the world beyond our shores in the light of the American society's commitment to God. . . .

He further scoffed at "the liberal press."

It was all too much for columnist Anthony Lewis. " 'Primitive,' " he raged, "that is the only word for it. What must the leaders of western Europe think of such a speech?" Rusher must admit, with Lewis, "This is not a platform — on which every last American citizen comfortably could agree." But, Rusher wound his editorial up with *his* conclusion that *he* believes Reagan has "the enthusiastic support of the vast majority of the American people" and is "their leader," in this matter of "good and evil."

Historian Henry Steele Commager before the speech sadly commented that,

> Reagan has no ideas, no understanding of the Constitution, no understanding of economics. No one can take what the president says seriously anyway. Logically, the only conclusion you can make is that the Marx brothers are in charge of the economy, the Defense Department and the State Department.

His evaluation of the speech itself has not surfaced. However, it is instructive that the *Washington Post* newspaper refers to Reagan's press conferences as "The Believe It Or Not Show."

Tom Wicker labeled his protest "Dangerous Doctrines." This columnist appears in many papers across the country, and he led off with the statement,

> President Reagan has proclaimed and presumably bases his policy upon two dangerous doctrines. The Soviet Union is "the focus of evil in the modern world" and "an evil empire," while Americans are "enjoined by scripture and the Lord Jesus Christ to oppose . . . with all our might" the "sin and evil in the world."

The danger "lies in Reagan's vision of the superpower relationship as good versus evil, and his near-proclamation of holy war. . . ." Calling Reagan's view "smug," he charges him with having shaken off the strongest restraints on human conduct.

The *Washington Post*, hardly a friendly people's paper, hit the hardest with a cartoon:

William Safire, a national conservative columnist, called the president's speech "astonishing." He analyzed the president's message to be "that the essential contest in the world was not between life and death (in nuclear war) but between God and Satan." He felt the president sounded more like a "hellfire-and-brimstone evangelist than a political man, much less a president." He sees Reagan as calling "the moral man" to be militant, while "Most voters who take their participation seriously want political philosophy in action, not spiritual instruction from the president." He urged Reagan, "Let clerics be clerics, and let the president be president."

And Patrick J. Buchanan, who is fanatically conservative and a Russophobe, was forced to characterize the speech as "a fiery sermon from the bully pulpit," while he noted with some satisfaction that the preachers interrupted the president two dozen times with cheers and applause." Buchanan was right on target that Reagan

> constantly reminds the American people that, in the last analysis, this is a struggle between right and wrong, good and evil, light and darkness. . . . Reagan recognizes and is acting upon the notion, . . . that the American people will not long sustain, with economic sacrifice and surely not with the blood of their sons, a struggle they do not recognize as between good and evil.

And, of course, Buchanan's remarks give it all away: "Better Dead Than Red."

The *Washington Spectator* is of the considered opinion that "Reagan's views of the world were largely shaped by his experiences with the Screen Actors Guild in the late '40s. Quoting Patrick Owens, Washington correspondent for *Newsday*, the *Spectator* goes on,

> Reagan led an anticommunist faction that collaborated with congressional investigators and accepted the blacklisting of hundreds of the union's members. Reagan interpreted a drive by radicals as an attempt by communists to take over Hollywood, an idea encouraged by the industry.

The *New York Times*, which is quoted, adds

> Thus, to Reagan, communism *per se* is evil and almost all communist movements are controlled from Moscow. The Soviet Union is bent on world domination. Almost every serious

> challenge to American interests in the world is manipulated by Moscow. The Soviets cannot be trusted and seek to lull Americans into a false sense of security. It is a raw view, one that does not allow for real differences within the Kremlin about policy, that differentiates little among socialist and communist movements, and that leaves little room for mellowing of Soviet behavior or the development of common interests between America and the Soviet Union.

The upshot, says a *New York Times* editorial, "is a costly arms race."

Arthur Schlesinger, Jr., writing for the *Wall Street Journal*, being a historian naturally would reach back into time for his analysis:

> Mr. Reagan's sincere conviction . . . marks the fervent revival of the interpretation of the Cold War as a holy war. This is how John Foster Dulles used to explain the Cold War a generation ago. . . . Reagan now portrays it once again in apocalyptic terms. . . . This conception . . . raises problems. It eliminates any thought of accommodation or compromise . . . war to the death. Mr. Reagan marks out the world's final dividing line as between those who reject and those who worship God — the ultimate bad guys vs. the ultimate good guys. . . . Reagan . . . insists on "administering a religious saliva test to the world." He sees the U.S. as the "focus of virtue." Inordinate self-righteousness, the conviction that one is the appointed partner of the Almighty, is a perilous thing. In this area Mr. Reagan displays insouciant self-confidence. He appeared at Orlando to have no doubt at all about where God stands on the vexed issues of the age. God is *mit uns*. God is a Cold Warrior. God is against the nuclear freeze. God is against abortion and for the squeal rule. God is a Reagan Republican.

He concludes, "To mistake transient political preferences for the considered design of the Almighty is not only presumptuous; it is truly dangerous." Quoting from a theologian, he is ominous in his tone,

> If America perishes . . . the primary cause would be that the strength of a great nation was directed by eyes too blind to see . . .; and the blindness would be induced . . . by hatred and vainglory.

What Reagan invokes is what the *American Atheist* has tried to point out to you for many years: the world is *not* in a struggle, as Schlesinger would put it and as a number of journalists and politicians see it, between "totalitarianism" and "democracy," but between religion and Atheism. The United States does *not* want to compete economically, politically, or culturally with the U.S.S.R.; she wants to destroy that nation, even at the expense of self destruction, because, in the bitter end, "I would rather see my little girls die now, still believing in God, than have them grow up under communism and one day die no longer believing in God."

We are back to "Better Dead Than Red," with Reagan leading the howling pack of religious nuts heading us all straight to their self-fulfilling armageddon.

Twenty Years

June 1983

When the Supreme Court came down with its decision in the case of *Murray v. Curlett* in June of 1963 I was only eight years old. One of two sons of (then) Madalyn Murray, I was plunged at that tender age into the midst of heated public controversy that has never ceased. I have, literally, grown up in and with the American Atheist movement. This year American Atheists is celebrating its twentieth anniversary. I would like to give you, the reader, my impressions of the twenty-year struggle through which the American Atheist organization has been. My view is from *the inside looking out* and may therefore be quite different even from the view of some of you long-time supporters who have been with the organization from its inception.

My look at twenty years of organized American Atheism must revolve around a single term. It is unfortunate indeed that twenty years of work (and damn hard work at that) should come down to a single term. A number of perceptions ultimately can be couched in simple terms in life, and organizing Atheists is no exception. That single term is *survival*. For that is the very thing that this unique organization has been doing, essentially, when all things are considered for the past twenty years. We have been in what I call a survival mode. This survival mode has two parts to it, and I will get to both of them in a minute.

First, however, I would like to point out that the trials and tribulations of organizing groups of individuals are not unique to an Atheist organization. Organizing is organizing no matter for what or with whom. The logistics of banding a group of like-minded individuals together to accomplish certain goals are the same across the board regardless of the "likeness" which establishes the common denominator for the group. Political groups, social groups, ethnic groups, sexual-orientation groups, age groups all have the same steps they must go through to set up and run an organization. Even religious groups must do the same kinds of things. The group must first define itself, which means to set up a limiting criteria for membership. It must then establish goals or aims and purposes, *i.e.* principles. Call them what you will, the group must decide on what it wants to accomplish. It must set up a work flow and a division of labor among the members. Most importantly of all, it must create a uniform policy of public action based upon its principles and execute that policy in a planned way. The public policy of any organization must be controlled by that organization and the exponents of its policy — *not* by those on the receiving end, the public. Of course, in order to execute anything, funding is required, and the logical place to obtain that funding is from the membership of the group at large. All groups function in this manner. Almost all groups have a fairly easy time going through these logical logistical steps toward marketing their "product." With a cause organization the "product" is an idea, instead of something like soap in the case of a business. Business techniques are very useful, however, in marketing a non-businesslike "product" like an idea.

Now what does all of this have to do with twenty years of American Atheists? Plenty. Most cause groups have no problems with setting up and executing the logical progression of logistical steps from formation through achievement of goals. Some have tremendous problems in accomplishing their logical progression. One of those groups has been American Atheists. Why? It is because American Atheists is a group defined by a set of individuals who have a life-style and idea sets which are unacceptable to the rest of "society." Those groups that organize around culturally-acceptable idea sets or life-styles are the ones that have no problems. A joggers' club, for example, has little problem. Even a political organization has little problem. The problems begin, classically, with a group whose members share a view of life in general that is based on premises contrary to the majority of the society in which they find themselves. It does not matter if the majority is "right" or "wrong" in their view, as long as the group members' views differ substantially from what is considered the "norm." Emphasis needs to be placed on the word "substantially." Minor deviation is tolerable. Major deviation is not tolerable. In the case of American Atheists, we have the market cornered on a major deviation from society as a whole. So, American Atheists can then be said to be a deviant organization from a sociological perspective. That classification into which we fit well spells out why we have had problems with the basics of organizing.

At each step along the way in the normal progression of organization, from inception forward, there has been substantial interference, applied both from external points and — unfortunately — from internal positions as we have been deliberately infiltrated for "destabilization" purposes only. The interference is a function of our deviance from society. That is why I have keyed on the word *survival*. We have been trying to survive attacks from without. The purpose of these attacks is to keep the group from accomplishing its logistical steps so that it will (hopefully, in the minds of the attackers) never even reach the point of marketing a public platform.

One could easily pin this interference on the "religious community" in general, but that is not exactly the case. The greatest interference has been from "individual religionists," not from organized religious groups such as churches. When I say individual religionists, I have to modify that by saying individual religionists in social or economic power positions within the community. Twenty years ago the religious community as a whole did not perceive American Atheists as any threat whatsoever. Recently that has changed as the Pope and President Reagan have both now come to claim Atheists specifically as the origin of world evil. I don't know about you, but I am kind of proud of that. If we are getting noticed specifically now we must be doing something right.

Let me get back to the point of interference, and give you some specific examples of what I mean. American Atheists now has chapters in twenty-seven states. Each of those chapters has to be registered with the Secretary of State's office in each of those states in order to "do business" therein as a local committee of the national educational corporation. That registration process has not been an easy one. Every possible regulation has been used against us to keep American Atheists from legitimatizing its branches. A good example is one of the most recently established chapters in Connecticut. The State of Connecticut required a list of the Board of Directors and officers of the national office in its forms for local registration. Well, most states do; that was nothing new. Connecticut also required "street" addresses for those Board members and officers. Now two of the national Board members of American Atheists live on acreage they own. They only have a rural route or box address at best, not a "street" address. When the application for registration was submitted with a small town box address, Connecticut rejected it and said that it wanted *a plat of their acreage*. Now that is ridiculous to ask someone to provide a plat of their land for mailing address purposes. We are not currently registered in Connecticut due to the inordinate demands of an individual religionist in that state's offices.

When an organization forms and takes the option of incorporation and chooses the style of incorporation to be that of educational and non-stock, non-profit, the organization is then entitled to some classification of Federal tax exemption. When a religious group applies for a Federal exemption under the classification of religion its exemption is granted almost immediately. When American Atheists originally applied for exemption as an educational corporation, it took nine years of battle with the IRS in and out of its various administrative levels to gain the exemption. Additionally, a federal court suit finally had to be filed. Since the exemption was won, either the organization, Dr. Madalyn O'Hair (its founder), Richard O'Hair (her now-deceased husband), or I have been audited no less than seventeen times. Tell me the last time the IRS audited a church in your community? Never. The auditors got to know us so well at one point that they would bring their kids with them to play in the office while they went over our books.

American Atheists needed office space but could not afford traditional office space as such. It finally procured a small frame house out of which to operate. No sign was erected, just desks, a mimeograph and files, *etc.*, inside. The little house was immediately found to be in violation of Austin zoning ordinances, despite the fact that in Austin one may utilize one's home for any business activity as long as a sign is not erected in the yard, or put on the house. A special zoning trial was called for 11:30 P.M. — that's right, P.M.! —one night to "get the Atheists." In order to continue using that little frame house, Dr. O'Hair and her husband Richard had to declare it a church, the only entity free from any zoning restriction. Since Dr. O'Hair had been a long-time personal friend of Kirby Hensley, he sent her extraordinary documents to establish that the house was a Universal Life Church in order to get around the zoning laws being used to shut the office down. Since no sign had been erected, there was no violation — except if the business was Atheism.

The same sort of thing immediately happened when the office facilities were actually moved into an "office building." First, the fire inspections came. Well, that was OK. Fire inspections are a good thing, normally — but not three or four times as often as any other building in town. The fire inspector came once or twice a year to every other building on the block, but he came every month to the Atheist building with rule book in hand.

With the procurement of a regular office building came a regular mortgage on that building — and a mortgage meant getting insurance to cover the mortgage holder. That was easier said than done. We had a sign over the building saying "American Atheist Center." Not a single insurance company in the state would cover a building with a sign identifying it as "Atheist." The risk of our being bombed or burnt-out was too great, they said. That in itself is enough to show the need of having an organized group for Atheists in the first place. Finally, a composite policy of five companies — each covering a fifth of the needed amount — had to be put together to insure the building. One of those companies was Lloyd's of London. As you may imagine, that did wonders for the cost of that first policy. Now after years of operation with that sign intact and the building not burned down, the premium on the American Atheist Center policy has gone down every year.

An office needs telephones, and the Atheist Center was no exception. Here again, it was not easy. Installation was no problem, but when it came to billing there was the rub. The Center began to get monthly bills with calls made by other phone company customers billed to it. A lot of them were long distance charges that ran into a fair piece of money. This kept up for months until the hierarchy of the phone company traced it down to one employee in the billing department who was deliberately putting other customers' charges on the Atheist Center bill out of religious motivations alone. That employee was terminated and the problems stopped. That round was won pretty easily.

The demographics of American Atheists, like most groups, made it necessary to do virtually everything through the mails. When we first started, the return address legend of "Atheist" gave us problems you would not believe. We received "special handling" from the Post Office time and time again. For example, for some time we could not get a package delivered properly in Chicago with the word "Atheist" in the return address for any reason. Individual postal employees went out of their way to misroute and misfile and misdirect our mail-both outgoing and incoming. We found it necessary from the beginning to abide by all postal rules and regulations to the letter, with double the specificity of other postal customers. We are now to the point that we know the postal regulations better than most postal employees. We had to in order to survive. Through that effort, we have now gained the respect of the supervisory levels of the Post Office to such a degree that they will "go to bat" for us and enforce their "neutrality" guidelines for mail handling. Post Office supervisors are now policing workers to the extent that we have almost reached normalcy in handling of our mail. We still have the occasional item returned as "moved, left no address" when the person has been in the same house for twenty years and still is. It is nowhere near as common, however, as it used to be. When they know that everything that comes out of the Atheist Center is properly prepared, they cannot do otherwise but handle it with neutrality. We have handled and covered every "excuse" for the mishandling of our mail.

A cause group also necessarily has to have meetings of its membership. If you don't have your own meeting hall, you must seek public accommodations. We did — and found them closed to Atheists' meetings from the beginning. Hotels and motels did not care to "turn off" other customers by renting space to an Atheist group for meetings. We had to literally beg for space for the first three or four national conventions we tried to hold. We had to come up with exorbitant security bonds and we had to pay for security guards who were there not to protect us against religious nuts, but to "protect" the hotel from the Atheists. Rates were higher for us than for other cause groups. As in the case of the Post Office, however, as we had meeting after meeting and convention after convention without incident, we again gained the respect of hotel management. Now the hotels and motels fight tooth and nail with each other for our business in any given city. We have demonstrated that Atheists are good, normal people. We clean up after ourselves and comport ourselves with dignity and business like composure. We often leave the hotel managements shocked that we left the rented area cleaner and in better shape than we found it. We pay in advance or on time, which is even better than the majority of religious groups who rent meeting facilities (or so we are told by many managers).

An office also needs business equipment and business services. We had to establish accounts with suppliers, etc. For the first many years, American Atheists had to purchase all the products and services it needed with cash. We were not extended credit by anyone. Finally, after being good steady customers for years, one business at a time began to extend small amounts of credit under unreasonable conditions. We met those conditions and kept our credit in good standing and over a period of time we won their confidence, too — just like that of the Post Office and the hotels and the insurance companies and all the rest. Still, from time to time we run into bigoted persons. We recently tried to purchase some new video equipment from a local merchant in Austin. I had an appointment set up with a sales representative of the merchant on a Wednesday for the following Monday morning. The sales representative called me on Saturday and said that his boss, the business owner, had ordered him not to keep the appointment. His boss had said that he would not sell equipment to "that woman," referring to Dr. O'Hair. The sales person was so embarrassed that he could hardly speak. He said that he had never encountered this in many long years as a salesman in this field. He recommended his competition in town to me and offered his technical advice. These incidents are becoming very rare now, and I am glad.

When an organization sets up to do business, it needs to have money to operate. Money means (sooner or later) association with a bank. In the case of American Atheists, we have gone through some eight or nine banks now searching for one that would handle us just like any other customer. What could a bank do to an Atheist organization, you may ask. How about a bank clerk deliberately bouncing a check when more than enough funds were in the account to cover it? That has happened more than once to American Atheists. We have had Bible tracts show up in our deliberately inaccurate monthly statements. We have had bank employees write "God bless you" on our cancelled checks. We have been denied loans when we had adequate collateral and references. Our deposits have been mysteriously lost or credited to the wrong accounts. How did we overcome this? By now, you would say by winning their confidence like with the insurance companies, Post Office, hotels and merchants. No; sadly enough, that was not the case with the banks. In their case we simply finally amassed a large enough balance with them to make us a valued depositor. Only the attainment of a certain level of monetary investment did the trick in the case of the banks. They had to treat us right when we had enough money on deposit.

In all of the above examples American Atheists has over and over again expressed a willingness to work within the system with determination to be treated equally. We have not run from the system, and we are not freaks who are determined to overthrow the entire system that discriminates against us. We are instead reformers who feel that our continued tenacious participation within the system will serve to reform the system as a whole, thus making it better for all concerned. When one is confronted with a bigot blocking the path, it is not proper to get off the path and give way. The bigot must yield. If everyone placed in such a position would make the bigot yield, there would soon be far less of them around to block paths. Some organizations have retreated from society and gone into hiding, drugs, communes, *etc.* A far more logical and rational position is to stand your ground and make society accept you. This is what American Atheists has been all about.

In addition to surviving these attacks from individual religionists supported by the community, we have been assaulted on the legal front as well. Attorneys in our nation have been by and large scared to death of handling litigation for Atheist plaintiffs. They fear, for the most part, the loss of established clientele from the publicity surrounding association with an Atheist plaintiff. Over the years, as with some of the institutions already mentioned, attorneys who have handled American Atheists as a plaintiff have not lost their clientele. In fact, the publicity gained from an Atheist plaintiff has increased their "notoriety" and garnered them more business instead of less. Still, each new attorney that we approach to this day has the same trepidations and we still have a problem in this area.

Given the attorney situation, it became immediately necessary for Dr. O'Hair, President of American Atheists, to handle most of the litigation *pro se*. That is under her own name as an individual plaintiff, usually under the category of "a taxpayer." Legal ventures of this type, however, carry with them as a corollary attempts by the state defendants at "piercing the corporate veil." That means that the state tries to show that the educational corporation does not in fact exist but is merely the same as its representative individual litigant. Put more bluntly, they try to show that Dr. O'Hair is the organization and the organization is only one person — Dr. O'Hair. We have been able, however, to preserve the "corporation sole" status of American Atheists. It is important to maintain the identity of the group *as a group* rather than allowing the courts to isolate an individual so that they can dismiss litigation on the basis of the plaintiff being a "single kook." This has been a difficult task, but it has been accomplished.

Our ability to work within the legal structure has also been firmly established. We have shown the courts over and over again that we can defeat the arguments of state defendants (and we most often find ourselves up against state or federal entities in an attempt to coerce them to follow their own constitutional guidelines), with their own references, playing in their home court. We have thus again won respect as a legal adversary that cannot be dismissed as being kooky.

You may have gathered by now that respect is a very important goal for an unpopular cause organization. If you can win the respect of the persons who disagree with you, it is far easier to handle them and the harassment they generate.

Speaking of harassment in a legal context, American Atheists has survived at least a dozen major harassment suits of varying magnitudes. An example of a harassment suit is the case in which a religious attorney sued Dr. O'Hair for alienation of affection — his "affection for Jesus." He said that he should have damages because her speeches had placed doubt in his heart about this "Jesus." Although we have survived many such "suits," it is regrettable that a large portion of the energy and time and money of the organization has had to be expended in that effort. We could have used those funds and energies far more productively along the way in promoting the aims and purposes of the organization. The harassment suits accomplished their purpose, which was exactly to expend the energy and fund of an Atheist organization and keep it from going forward as rapidly as may have otherwise been possible. Even entities as large as nations have to "prove themselves" for the first many years of their existence. This nation had to do so after the initial revolution that separated it from England, and more recently, Israel has done so repeatedly since its formation after World War II. We have been able to get the job done, though. We keep coming back up after each swat like one of those roly-poly toys that bounce back upright after being punched. (Of course, that does not mean to say that we have not grown tired of being swatted.)

American Atheists has also had the United States government trying to put it out of business along the way. The organization was the subject of FBI and CIA Cointel operations for years. We had our suspicions all along, but they were not confirmed until the passage of the Freedom of Information Act. Through that act, we were able to obtain heavily censored copies of files kept by U.S. intelligence organizations on American Atheists. Censored as they were, they were enough to verify that the organization had been under surveillance for quite some time. I think that the most upsetting part of the surveillance was that our "crime" was being for complete-and-absolute separation of state and church. Yes, you are reading correctly. The government of the United States felt officially that being pro-separation of state and church was criminal activity for a citizen or a group of citizens. Speaking and writing and distributing information on that subject was viewed as detrimental to the security interests of the United States. Yet the principle of separation of state and church is a cornerstone of the Constitution. No matter how hard the surveillance agencies spied, we established beyond the shadow of a doubt that we were operating within the law at all times. Each and every form of protest venture in which we engaged was within normal channels set up and guaranteed by the Constitution to be maintained for dissent. When we could not be touched on a factual basis, the agencies fabricated "wrongdoing" and spread rumors to that effect in the media and elsewhere. That was, of course, the *modus operandi* of the entire Cointel operation.

This brings me to the topic of the media and its handling of American Atheists over the years. I can say unequivocally that the media in all its forms has slandered, maligned, abused, lied about, and misrepresented the position of both Atheist individuals and groups as a consistent policy for the last twenty years. I really can count on the fingers of one hand the times that we have been given a "fair shake" by any reporter or writer over the years. Atheists have had every trick in the book used against them to make them look bad personally or to misrepresent their positions on every relevant issue. We have demonstrated that we are capable of handling ourselves in every type of adversary situation. This comes with experience but it also comes from doing one's homework. We know our facts and we have demonstrated repeatedly that faiths are no match for facts. We have played the "rating game" with station after station and won. That means that we have shown them that the subject of Atheism can generate more controversy and hence more ratings for their station than about any other topic, short of perhaps politics or abortion. The fears of stations (similar to those of attorneys) of losing their advertisers over airing Atheist views have been allayed. Great progress has also been made in establishing the independence of "the organization" to represent its positions with a variety of competent spokespersons and not just a single "star." Dr. O'Hair has been unwillingly placed in a "star" role by the media over the years by their objection to accepting any alternate spokesperson for the cause. This "star system" predominant in the American media scene today is still a problem, but to a much lesser degree than it has been in the past. Many fine local and chapter spokespersons are now consistently speaking on behalf of the American Atheist organization in their areas.

I have been writing so far about only one of the two aspects of the the survival mode that American Atheists has been in for some twenty years now. That was survival with respect to attacks from without. The second aspect of survival is with respect to disagreements and attacks from within. We have had this survival problem as well. The first example of this goes back to what I said earlier about any organization needing to define and delimit its constituency and its objectives. American Atheists has had a problem with that definition process for some time now. At the first national convention of American Atheists, and to some extent again at the second one, the major part of the conference was spent in trying to define the word "Atheist." In three days of talks in two annual meetings in a row about one hundred or so delegates could not agree on what, "Atheism" was or was not. During the debate on Atheism, the problem of agnosticism came up also. I think now that American Atheists has been able to go beyond that stage now. We don't need to debate over agnosticism anymore or engage in countless hours of circular philosophical argumentation. Our basic premise is now firm and very simple. We have around us what is empirically verifiable through the scientific method at its present technical capacity. Anything that cannot be empirically verifiable, directly or indirectly, does not exist — period. Very simple. No matter how much one may wish it otherwise, we have only what does exist — what exhibits measurable properties. The concept of a god or gods does not fit into the existence set; therefore it is not. Plain and simple. No god. Godism in all its forms is simply individual or collective hallucination. There is nothing to argue about. All persons either fall into one of two camps: those who accept, on faith, that something exists outside of the set of empirically verifiable things; or those who accept on a rational and scientific basis the contents of the set of existing things. It is a total waste of human effort to try to debate over the possible existence of something which has no evidence to support even the possibility of it existing. It is simply ridiculous. If I say that little hobbits with hairy feet live in the woods, the burden of proof is on me in a scientific context to come up with a hobbit. If in a reasonable amount of time I cannot come up with one, or any tangible evidence for one, then hobbits simply don't exist. End of discussion. I do not have to "keep an open mind" about the possible existence of hobbits in order to remain "intellectually honest." The same goes for the concept of god as for the concept of a hobbit.

A group, any group, which wants to stand a chance of achieving a set of goals has to first get its basic principles down (which includes a definition) and develop a cadre system based on those principles. If you spend all your time questioning your basic position, how can you expect to get anything accomplished? The answer is that you can't expect to accomplish very much. In order to move forth systematically from a basic position, all the members of the group have to be educated as to what that basic position is. We have had a little problem with that educational process over the years, but we are progressing in our ability to turn out more and more printed (and other) information establishing and reinforcing the basics of American Atheism.

On the legal front we have faced internal dissent among members as to when and how and which issues should be litigated by the organization. We have overcome disagreement in this area by mounting a number of cases in various areas designed to "play the odds" of winning in a court structure. The religious community knows how to play this game very well. In the areas of creationism or tuition tax credits, they introduce legislation or litigate in a given state; if they lose there, they learn from the reasons why they lost and try again in another state. American Atheists has been trying as we can to do the same thing. We are, however, greatly limited by finances from doing exactly what the religious community can do in the legal area. For the financial reason alone, we often have to go with symbolic litigation when we cannot tackle an issue that would require large amounts of evidentiary research which is very costly. A suit concerning exemption of church property from taxation would require the gathering of millions of dollars of statistical evidence as to exactly what they do own and where. On the other hand, challenging the printing of money with the phrase "In God We Trust" on it is a very cheap suit to file and pursue, since the only evidence is a dollar bill and the cite of the law authorizing the phrase to be placed thereon.

American Atheists has also faced internal dissent on the issue of "democracy." The membership-at-large wishes to vote on what the organization's leadership does. In order to do so, however, they have to be informed on each issue so that they know enough about all the contingencies to vote. The national leadership, on the other hand, is privy on a daily basis to the information required to make decisions on each issue. The logistical concerns of getting that information to the rank and file membership are so great that the organization would do nothing but process and mail information and wait for any ballots. There would not be enough time or energy remaining to move on what the membership voted to do. The majority of the European "free-thought" groups have done this for some one hundred years or more now. They spend all their time stuck in arguments over procedure and voting and counting the ballots, and they have hence done little but stagnate. Most of them are now composed primarily of aged persons who have been talking over procedure and taking votes until they are now too feeble to actually do anything. When it comes to "cause" organizations, democracy kills. The individuals within the group who are, first, competent and, second, willing to assume a leadership role just simply have to take command and proceed while the others back them up with financial and moral support. American Atheists for many years was not even able to muster enough persons willing to participate in decision-making to fill all the slots for the required number of Board of Directors members. It is only a recent phenomenon that the Board of Directors now has a full roster.

Unfortunately, American Atheists has suffered some splintering over the issue of "democracy." It is curious, however, that each and every small group that has split off over the years over this issue has quickly come to the position of doing away with votes on a practical level in short order within their own little group. The proof of the pudding is in trying to operate on a day-to-day basis where decisions, some of which are very important, need to be made on a moment's notice. In such a setting polling the membership is not alone impractical, but downright dangerous. Also, when American Atheists has polled its rank and file or asked for a vote on a certain issue, the percentage return on that vote or poll has always been less than half.

American Atheists has competent national leadership and staff backed up by many competent local chapter representatives and officers. Over time, it has been demonstrated that a participatory democratic structure is not necessary to growth, maintenance, and success of the group. That does not mean that member input should be ignored; it is not. It is constantly taken into consideration and given paramount respect and weight in the decision-making process.

In conclusion then, American Atheists has over the past twenty years — to use a colloquial expression — been "getting its shit together." The organization has demonstrated the ability to survive both assaults from adversaries from without and to work out solutions to disputes from within. That process of getting organized has taken twenty years in the case of an Atheist group because of the fact that it represents a life view that is alien to that held by society as a whole for many generations. New ideas always require time to gain a foothold in society. It took more than twenty years for the general public to accept the automobile as a dependable means for transportation. I therefore really don't think that American Atheists has a thing to be ashamed of for laboring in a survival mode for twenty years to establish itself as a permanent fixture on the American scene. Our adversaries as well as society as a whole know now that Atheists are here to stay. We are viable members of the community. We are not to be outcasts. We must be dealt with in the same manner, with equality, as any other segment of society. We are not going to go away. Our presence has been firmly established. We have also established a physical base of operations and a permanent, dedicated constituency. American Atheists is now established as an entity above and beyond any single one of its members or leaders. It is a perpetual organization that will continue to represent the point of view of the Atheist segment of the population long after any present leadership no longer.

Given that the survival stage is now behind us, it is time now during the next twenty years for American Atheists to enter into a new era of activity. In this new era the thrust will be toward offensive, aggressive presentation of the aims and purposes of the group, rather than a primarily defensive posture as in the past. It is now time to move out on a more local level with strong national support and guidance. We have been accepted now in the community, but only as far as our mere existence. We must now reach the next plateau of being accepted when we take action on our own behalf, rather than merely existing.

The national leadership and staff of American Atheists have borne the brunt of the survival process for the first twenty years — and we have won. Now it is up to all of you individual Atheists out there to get into the act in phase two. All of you have to be ambassadors of reason in your communities. That is, after all, what Atheism is all about — reason and intelligence applied to life. We are over the beachhead and we have established a foothold. Atheists have now carved out their niche in society. We have not given up and Jim Jonesed it in some tropical jungle. The task has been realized and met.

Now that we are in, we have to do our best to make that which we are now an accepted part of a better society — better for us and better for the whole. Perhaps those with their noses in the air toward Atheism will now begin to realize that they have been keeping the "A" team out of the ball game for too long.

In recognition of our success, we have adopted a new motto for the organization, which was displayed on a banner over the speakers' platform at our Thirteenth National Annual Convention held in April of this year [1983] in San Francisco, California. The banner said "Unity Today, Power Tomorrow." We have the unity part down now, so on to the power.

Child Abuse And "God"

July 1983

The religious community in general over the past forty years has taken it upon itself to lobby the federal and state government for many categories of "exemptions." Some of these exemptions are from taxation of various kinds and some are from government regulations in different areas. The *American Atheist* journal has paid the most attention, as has the media, to the tax-related exemptions of various religious groups. These exemptions hurt those of us who must increase the amount that we must pay each year out of our hard-earned wages to the tax man. Their effect is one, however, that is easily overlooked. Another type of exemption is not so easily overlooked and is more directly harmful to a specific section of the population. I speak of religious exemptions in child abuse and neglect cases.

Most of you are probably unaware that almost every state in the Union has exemptions to their child abuse and neglect statutes for abuse perpetrated on religious grounds. The history of these statutes goes back to the federal government in the mid-1970s and one church in particular. In 1974, Congress wrote the "Child Abuse Prevention and Treatment Act." During that writing, the Christian Science church (which is headquartered in Boston) lobbied Congress vigorously to obtain the following language in Child Abuse Act.

> No parent or guardian who in good faith is providing to a child's treatment solely by spiritual means . . . shall for that reason alone be considered to have neglected the child.

The Christian Scientists did not stop at the inclusion of that wording. They then began to lobby the Department of Health, Education and Welfare (now called the Department of Health and Human Services). As a result of that lobbying, the HEW Department issued a ruling that states would be ineligible for federal child protection grants unless they had a religious exemption similar to the federal one cited above on their books. That ruling remained as federal HEW policy until January of this year. In January of 1983, the Department of Health and Human

Services, despite much objection from the Christian Scientists, notified the states that they no longer had to exempt religious groups from child abuse regulations to receive child protection grants.

The National Center on Child Abuse and Neglect of the federal government now says that forty-seven out of our fifty states wrote the required religious exemptions into their child abuse statues between 1974 and the end of 1982.

What will the states do now that the requirement has been lifted? Most likely, nothing. The director of the National Center on Child Abuse has been quoted by the media as saying "Most states will probably leave well enough alone."

You may now ask, "Well, so what? What trouble could such an exemption cause?" *Plenty* is the answer. Recently the *News-Sentinel* newspaper of Fort Wayne, Indiana, gave extensive coverage to the deaths caused by Indiana's compliance with the federal HEW ruling. Indiana law states:

> It is a defense that the accused person, in the legitimate practice of his religious belief, provided treatment by spiritual means through prayer, in lieu of medical care, to his dependent.

According to the Indiana paper, there have been fifty-two known deaths from lack of medical treatment among the followers of a particular sect called the Faith Assembly church, which is headquartered in that state. The deaths have occurred in Indiana and the five states of Missouri, Illinois, Kentucky, Ohio, Michigan; just recently, Pennsylvania was added as number six. Seven families accounted for eighteen of the fifty-two deaths. Only a few of the fifty-two who died were old enough to understand the teachings of the sect or make medical decisions for themselves.

Faith Assembly church was founded and is headed by the Rev. Hobart Freeman. He was born in Ewing, Kentucky, in 1920, a small town of perhaps 500. In 1952, he became "born again" when he went into the Southern Baptist ministry. In 1961, he earned a doctorate in theology and began to teach at an Indiana theological seminary. In 1963, he was fired for his radical departures from traditional Southern Baptist teaching. In 1966, he began forming his own congregation; they met in basements of private homes, adopting "babbing" in tongues type faith. In 1972, he hooked up with a reformed alcoholic with a criminal record who was running a drug and alcohol rehabilitation center in a barn. His congregation moved from basements to the barn and renamed it the

"Glory Barn." In the Glory Barn, Freeman began teaching shunning of medical treatment based on biblical verses. In his sermons in the Glory Barn he referred to Luke 9:23 and 24 (And he said to them all, if any man will come after me, let him deny himself, and take up his cross daily, and follow me. For whosoever will save his life shall lose it: but whosoever will lose his life for my sake, the same shall save it). He also referred to Luke 14:26 and 33 (*If any man come to me, and hate not his father, and mother, and wife, and children, and brethren, and sisters, yea, and his own life also, he cannot by my disciple. . . . So likewise, whosoever he be of you that forsaketh not all that he hath, he cannot be my disciple*). These references fell under the heading of "burning your bridges behind you," or leaving the modern world of science and medicine and caring for your life or the life of loved ones by faith alone.

That spirit of shunning the outside world was a constant theme of his sect's activity. Painted on the wall of the Glory Barn was the verse of 1 Corinthians 1:10 (*Now I beseech you, brethren, by the name of our Lord Jesus Christ, that ye all speak the same thing, and that there be no divisions among you; but that ye be perfectly joined together in the same mind and in the same judgment*), reminding his followers that diverse opinions were not welcome within the congregation. A very strict set of rules he called the "Faith Walk" outlined acceptable and unacceptable behavior for members. Those who broke the "Faith Walk" would be ridiculed before the rest, excommunicated, or sentenced to burn eternally in hell.

Another favorite verse of the congregation is Mark 11:24 (*Therefore I say unto you, What things soever ye desire, when ye pray, believe that ye receive them, and ye shall have them*). On the basis of the promise in that verse, parents in the Faith Assembly congregation looked on and prayed while their children died from lack of medical help.

The fifty-two confirmed dead included the following categories:

1) Twenty-eight babies whose mothers shunned doctors during pregnancy and delivery.
2) Seven children with untreated illnesses and injuries.
3) Ten adults who refused to submit to treatment for illness and injuries. An example is a man of thirty-seven who quit kidney dialysis treatment.
4) Seven mothers who died of complications from home deliveries.

Seven children died of untreated illnesses, and their cases are described as follows:

1) Age 16 months — male — died of chicken pox and pneumonia.
2) Age 15 months — male — died of *hemophilus influenza*, a type of meningitis usually not fatal if diagnosed and treated early.
3) Age 1 year — male — died of pneumonia untreated for a week. The parents prayed over the body for three hours after he stopped breathing before calling Rev. Freeman, NOT medical personnel.
4) Age 12 years — female — died of congenital heart disease. A local obstetrics-gynecology expert said, "That's a problem that can be corrected, but it takes open heart surgery, not prayer." Insertion of an artificial heart valve could have saved the girl's life.
5) Age 4 years — female — died of malignant rhabdomyosarcoma, a terminal cancer. A tumor near her right eye grew for two months, covering most of her face by the time of death. Her parents prayed while it grew. Her five year-old sister has the same type of cancer. She was taken into custody by welfare department officials and is now on chemotherapy. She now has a chance.
6) Age 15 months — male — died after authorities obtained custody of him after his sister died of untreated pneumonia. He had surgery to remove a large tumor from his abdomen. His lungs had filled with fluid as well.
7) Age 1 year — female died from blood poisoning and pneumonia contracted after receiving second- and third-degree burns over half her body. She had spilled an 18-ounce pot of scalding tea on herself at a restaurant. The parents refused medical aid, although the restaurant owner offered to pay for it.

None of the deaths listed above need have occurred. They took place out of blind stupidity and ignorance on the part of gullible parents who had been taken in by a fraud. Many of the media investigators of this particular sect and others of like mind have come to the conclusion that medical treatment is not a "considered" option for these persons. It simply never crosses the minds of victims or their guardians to call for medical help. They are taught divine healing from birth in such a closed social order that they simply don't even have a frame of reference to any other approach to illness. We can then see why the 1 Corinthians 1:10 verse was emblazoned on the wall of the Glory Barn.

Members of sects like the Faith Assembly reach the point very early in life of not being able to question what faith dictates under any circumstances. Rev. Freeman himself, for example, walks with a noticeable limp. He wears a lift on one shoe since one leg is shorter than the other due to a childhood bout with polio. One of a very few former Faith Assembly members said she had always wondered "If he's healed, why does he need a lift on his shoe?" That is why she is an ex-member. Current sect members don't wonder about the limp. They just have faith.

Members of the Faith Assembly are taught that when the hand of danger touches them they should chant over and over again "I plead the blood of Jesus." Members believe that this chant will protect them from dreaded outside influences such as reason or science. As they say the chant, they visualize a "shield of blood surrounding their heads and protecting them from spirits of ideas critical of Rev. Freeman."

No state legislator desires to tackle the "ugly" job of trying to repeal these federally-engendered religious statutory exemptions. They think more of retaining their seats in the legislature than they do of the lives of children who cannot protect themselves against the madness of their parents. Although the Fort Wayne *News-Sentinel* gave extensive coverage to the Faith Assembly sect's activities, only the *Pittsburgh Post-Gazette* and the *Detroit Free Press* picked up the story at all as papers with Assembly-related deaths in some of the counties they covered. Their articles were sketchy indeed compared to the *News-Sentinel* coverage. Outside of the seven affected states, we can only find evidence of the *Atlanta Constitution* picking up the story. A great number of persons in the U.S. don't even know that this sort of thing is going on in their nation and that their state (all but three) has religious exemption provisions in its child abuse laws.

It seems that some relief may be in sight, however. The state of Oklahoma just passed a new state law in April of this year that strips faith healers of immunity from child abuse statutes. It is ironic that Oklahoma, home of Oral Roberts and his 900-foot Jesus and new faith center (faith healing hospital) would be the state to take the lead in statutory reform on religious child abuse.

The largest part of the problem comes from the fact that in state after state, and the federal Congress as well, our "lawmakers" will only consider legislation with language "that wouldn't violate freedom OF religion," in the words of an Indiana legislator. Another Indiana legislator said, regarding the Faith Assembly sect," I know they are sincere. I was hoping they would make some changes on their own."

The Constitutional concept of freedom OF religion must embody the concept of freedom FROM religion if we are to avoid future casualties from religious ignorance. We seem to be entering a neo-Middle Age in this country where actions once condemned by society by virtue of the lessons of history are now being excused in the name of religion. Behavioral patterns based on reason are becoming suspect. The revival of the insanity defense in our courtrooms is a case in point.

Rev. Freeman of Indiana should have been held equally accountable along with the legal guardians for the murders of all fifty-two persons who died in six states. It is time that society made learned lunacy, as distinguished from biological mental disorders, an unacceptable excuse for criminal activity.

The Ace in Its Hole

August 1983

One of the themes that is repeated in the *American Atheist* by various authors is that Atheism and education have an irrevocable correlation. The further one goes in an educational process, whether formally structured or self-paced, the more likely it is that that person will be an Atheist. I think that about every sociological study that has ever been done on persons of fervent religiosity has found that such persons are below average in terms of educational achievement. Here at The American Atheist Center, however, we do get a lot of mail from persons who violently disagree with this. They say that the organization of American Atheists is elitist because it supports a stance of calling its members "smarter" than religionists in general. Most of the letters say "look how many intelligent and well-educated persons are also religious."

That may well be true, but that also says two things about these "well-educated" and "intelligent" religionists. First, they have taken to educational procedures and principles well, but they have not applied those procedures and principles to the area of religion. Second, they are hypocritical. How so? Well, if you do apply educational principles and procedures to religion, religion quickly does not make sense anymore. So, if you continue to be religious after applying educational principles to your religion and finding it nonsensical, you are a hypocrite. It is that simple. What are "educational principles and procedures"? That is simple, too. They are *all* based upon the scientific method. The scientific method is how we all assimilate information or "data" into our brains and make what we colloquially call "sense" out of it. That is, we accumulate data, compare parts of it to other parts looking for patterns and similarities, categorize it according to these patterns and similarities, formulate hypotheses from the categorized data, test these hypotheses, and therefrom draw conclusions. Now some is done over a long period of time — sometimes a very long period. Nonetheless, this scientific method is the universal educational procedure and principle.

If you look at religion the same way you look at any other

phenomenon during your process of education (which ends only when you do, at the time of death), you can only come to one conclusion about it —that it is *not* valid. It simply will "not compute." If you do come to a conclusion that religion is a valid proposition, you have simply not run the data on religion through the same process as the other data you take in. On the other hand, you may have run the data on religion through the same process and refused to admit the conclusion.

You can open any sacred book, the Bible or any one you choose, and just within a few paragraphs of reading you will run into something that "does not compute." It happens to *everyone*, but some admit it and some don't. The ones that don't are hypocrites.

Education is a central part of Atheism. In fact, it is a prerequisite. One may write to this journal and scream "elitism" or "fascism" or "dogmatism." That will not change the facts. Education is the number-one enemy of religion. It is unnatural to ignore or pretend to be immune to educational procedures or principles. Therefore, religionists seek to take over education. Education as a whole will not go away. Religion's only escape is to take education over and change its procedure from the scientific method to some nonanalytical form where one learns by rote.

Thousands of Christian schools are popping up around the country determined to do just that — create a new system of education by rote. A number of these new schools have adopted what they are calling an "accelerated Christian education" (A.C.E.) curriculum.

Let's have a look at this A.C.E. curriculum. It is based on the overall principle that a child *must* learn to see the world from god's point of view. A.C.E. says that a child is predestined to do so. All subjects are to be learned from god's viewpoint and the child must become convinced that he or she is doing it all for god — *not* for his or her own edification, but only to glorify and serve god. This is a very important point. All human activities, according to the Christian religion particularly, must be directed to serving god and not your own "selfish" interests. A comparison is made in A.C.E. literature between Christian and non-Christian schools in which it is said public schools teach:

— The world just evolved.
— Bible laws are out of date.
— Man is good.
— Do what you want to do.

as compared to Christian schools which teach:

— God created all things.
— God's word shows us how to live.

— Man is a sinner.
— Do only what is said to be right.

A.C.E. curriculums are also based on a number of biblical "truths." Of course, what else would it be based on? Some of these biblical "truths" are: Proverbs 1:7, "The fear of the Lord is the beginning of knowledge. . ."; Proverbs 19:27, "Cease, my son, to hear the instruction that causeth to err from the words of knowledge"; Colossians 2:8, "Beware lest any man spoil you through philosophy and *vain* deceit, after the tradition of men, after the rudiments of the world, and not after Christ"; the best is saved for last — 1 Corinthians 1:18, 19, "For the preaching for the cross is to them that perish foolishness; but unto us which are saved it is the power of God. For it is written, I will destroy the wisdom of the wise, and will bring to nothing the understanding of the prudent."

The A.C.E. curriculum is presented in P.A.C.E.'s self-paced, self-instructional individual packets of material. The teacher works with each student on an individual basis, mostly to answer questions about the material in the packets. The entire course of study "assumes the Bible is God's word and is *accurate*, but teaches every subject from the viewpoint of *eternal values*," according to A.C.E. literature. Presentations in every subject center around "what God would have us know to live rightly in his world." P.A.C.E.s quote scripture at every opportunity to reinforce the difference between what "God would have us know" as distinguished from what we may desire to know. All the P.A.C.E.s are keyed to glorify god and/or Jesus Christ.

A.C.E. curriculum recommends pastors as the best Christian school administrators because of their preknowledge of "the word of God." The A.C.E. program is also specifically designed to use in church facilities.

Each subject in the A.C.E. curriculum is divided into twelve P.A.C.E.s. What else? Twelve disciples and twelve P.A.C.E.s. A P.A.C.E. looks like a workbook, but it is a combination of text, learning activities, unit tests or checkups, a self-test, and a P.A.C.E. test. The self-test is one that the student takes and scores himself and studies to prepare for the P.A.C.E. test. The P.A.C.E. test is taken under supervision and scored by the teacher to provide the grade for the P.A.C.E. as a whole.

There are A.C.E. "coordinators" in Washington, California, Alaska, Colorado, Texas, Kansas, Tennessee, Georgia, Florida, Illinois, Virginia, Indiana, Ohio, Pennsylvania, New York, and Minnesota already —

and the idea is spreading fast. One of the A.C.E. national spokespersons says,

> The great revivals of history were a direct result of Christian education, and the depth and duration of the revival was in direct relation to the depth and duration of that Christian education . . . and all great revivals in history had in common . . . a rebirth of fundamentalism. . . . Fundamentalism is basically belief in the fundamental truths of the word of God. . . . Fundamentalism teaches that man is by nature sinful, that he is born a lost sinner. . . . No revival in history ever came as a result of liberalism or modernism.

This sort of distorted view of history is already a very real part of textbooks under consideration to become part of the *public* school curriculum here in the state of Texas. The staff of The American Atheist Center discovered this fact, much to their chagrin, during their investigations of world history textbooks up for adoption in Texas public schools during June of this year (while preparing for hearings of the state textbook commission).

All of the curriculum materials put out by the A.C.E. boys operate on two basic principles: 1) The basic fundamentals of the faith as expressed in traditional biblical orthodoxy; 2) The practice of being separated from the world, to influence the world, but not to be influenced by the world. A Christian is called to be separated from the world and to abstain from questionable practices.

There is a new Christian school opening in this country about every seven hours. I don't know about all of you, but that scares me. It scares me badly. The mission of these schools is made abundantly clear by all of their literature: "Nothing is doing more damage to America than American public schools." State government education is bankrupt economically, academically, spiritually; abolish it, and in one decade, private education under free enterprise will produce superior education for half the cost.

What is even more frightening is that more groups than just fundamentalists share this opinion of public education in America. Libertarians share this view as well as a number of "mainline" denominations.

We can only hope to continue the geometrical progression of our modern life-style by basing education on one thing, and this is the scientific method. Schools must teach students how to teach themselves and not just teach them to be living receptacles to be filled with religious directives. Organized religious groups know that a system of education that works the same way that our brains work will not produce followers, but doubters. With good scientific education, religion can only continue for so long, with an increasing number of alleged adherents becoming mere hypocrites. Religion must have true, convinced, unquestioning believers. The churches have limped along with congregations composed essentially of hypocrites for too long, and they are now beginning to realize that such an "army of the Lord" will not cut the mustard.

Unfortunately, we have a president and an entire administration now who back the disenfranchisement of universal public education. We also have teachers and administrators who are willing to go along with being disenfranchised. After all, from their point of view, it is better to be a Christian school teacher than to be no school teacher at all; isn't that right?

Another part of the problem is the individual Atheist or agnostic who approaches his or her position apologetically. All that most "freethinkers" can concentrate on is how to be the most apologetic and least offensive while attempting to stand up for education. In the meantime, on the other side of the fence, fundamentalists are not the least bit shy about their motives or what they desire to accomplish. They come out and say exactly what they plan to do to their children as well as to the children of the timid "freethinker" — and they proceed to do it.

What do we suggest to do about A.C.E.? I am glad you asked. I think we need to begin by informing parents about the goals of Christian education for their children. A great number of parents get in over their heads with Christian schools before they realize exactly what they are teaching. Some parents get involved with Christian schools for other than religious concerns — concerns like racism or misinformation as to what and how things are being taught in their public school.

We also need to monitor the public schools to make sure that they remain secular. In most subjects there is not too much "misinformation" to worry about, once the subject is free from religious propaganda or misinterpretation. Most facts — historical, scientific, mathematical — speak for themselves. In the review of the history textbooks here in Texas, we found that the vast majority of what was in each volume was good information. The religious bias was a small part of the overall material presented. There was no "secular humanism" or any "Atheism" included in the texts at all. Many parents are not aware of this and simply take the word of the fundamentalists that lack of religious propaganda constitutes the promotion of "secular humanism" and "Atheism."

We must teach our children at home to be objective and to apply the scientific method to everything they learn. Test it out; don't take someone else's word that something is true or not true. Christian schools are most certainly not going to tolerate that type of critical analytical approach to learning. Eclecticism is an essential part of a balanced learning approach and must be emphasized.

We must be prepared to come right out and say that the Bible and biblical teachings are absurd, without fear of offending someone's sensibilities. I could care less about offending some fundamentalist religionist. They need to be offended. A good hard slap in the face with reality is just what the doctor ordered for them.

The Christian educational scheme of learning by rote from a finite set of "God-given" imperatives is simply absurd and needs to be labelled as such and denigrated at every opportunity.

Atheism and education are inextricably intertwined and both are very simple. Rationalism is easy; it is natural. Religion is convoluted and is often very difficult to cope with since it does not follow the patterns by which the brain operates. I prefer to just do what comes naturally—to think, instead of just standing around like a sponge waiting to absorb a bunch of "bunk," as Thomas Edison put it.

Discount Purchase of Foreign Aid

September 1983

American Atheists, the organization, often gets a lot of criticism from both sides of the fence concerning politics. Some of its members say that it should form an Atheist political party or a political action committee, while others say that it should remain apolitical (as it was incorporated and as I.R.S. regulations dictate) even to the extent of not talking about "politics and religion" at all in the pages of, its monthly journal.

With the commentary often in the form of letters from both points of view, I would like to take this opportunity to look at one particular brand of religious political action to give you a view of what the opposition is doing. Once you have been shown what American Atheists would be up against, I think the argument can be easily settled as to why we do not and have not become directly involved politically for any candidate. The answer is that we are simply not in the league of the groups that make a specialty out of pushing Congress around on a variety of issues.

The particular religious group that is more active than any other politically is the Jews. No doubt a copy of this editorial will be in the Jewish Defense League files within a week of publication, but here goes anyway. Why pick out the Jews? They are the biggest and best at political action so they make the best example.

The Jewish community has some thirty-one separate political action committees on file with the Federal Election Commission. In the 1982 congressional elections, those thirty-one PACs raised and spent $1,676,016 helping to elect or defeat congressmen in districts all over the United States. They spent 58 percent or $972,089.28 of that money on U.S. Senate races with 74 percent of the $1.67 million being spent on incumbents overall. This kind of financial power now places them neck and neck with the other largest lobbies on Capitol Hill which are the the lobbies for the realtors, the auto workers, the doctors, and the milk producers.

The Jewish PACs are very well organized — which is perhaps one of the qualities that makes them the most successful. They are highly sophisticated as well, demonstrating on numerous occasions that they know how to do their homework when it comes to keeping track of congressmen's voting records and remarks in committee or on the floor. Part of their being well organized is that they have a hierarchical structure. At the top is what is called a "MEGA-PAC," known as just the "National Political Action Committee." In its first year of operation the MEGA-PAC raised one million dollars and spent $547,500 of it on 109 candidates with an average donation of $5,000 to any given one.

Most of the people who write about political action committees seem to agree that the major factor that gives the Jewish PACs so much clout is that their money goes into a very narrow range of issues, and they zero in on a small number of committees. Groups like the auto workers, for example, can be seen poking their noses in on the goings-on in half the committees on the Hill. They also do not concentrate on raising money in a particular district or state to give to a candidate running in that area. They bring in money from a wider national area to the local races. The rationale is that if there are enough local people, particularly Jews, to help a particular candidate, the PAC should look for other districts were there is lower Jewish visibility and fewer Jewish voters placing their funds in those areas. The result of this can be seen when one looks at various candidates and what they have received from Jewish PACs. The majority of the candidates receive the largest amount of the Jewish money from sources outside of their district or state.

What this does is subvert the whole meaning of our political system based on the principle of an elected official being responsive to his local constituency. If a candidate owes his election or reelection to money from those outside his home district or state, the idea of his being loyal or responsive to the needs of his home folk goes right out the window on the particular issues for which the PAC has bought and paid for his vote. This sort of thing goes on every day in this great "democracy" of ours, while the rank and file voter still flaunts his "one-man-one-vote" freedom at the polls. That single vote does not mean very much when in many (often crucial) areas the vote of the person you just elected is monetarily committed to one point of view.

The majority of the Jewish PACs are not up front with what they are doing, other than registering with the proper federal authorities. They register under names such as "The Committee for Eighteen," "Arizona Politically Interested Citizens Government Action Committee," "The Joint Action Committee for Political Affairs," "The National Bipartisan Political Action Committee," "Bay Area Citizens Political Action Committee," and "Washington Political Action Committee." Who would ever know that any of thse groups were Jewish PACs? The "Committee for Eighteen" uses eighteen because that number is a numerological symbol for the Hebrew word meaning "life." That is pretty obscure. The Roman Catholics do the same kind of thing when they buy up large corporate stock holdings under such titles as "Angel and Co." It is sometimes very difficult to find out from what source comes the money of a particular PAC.

The effectiveness of the Jewish PACs on Congress cannot be underestimated. In the fiscal year beginning in October of 1983, a record $2.6 billion in economic and military aid will be sent directly and indirectly to Israel by the United States. First of all, Israel is a theocracy. The government of the United States has no business financing a theocracy of any kind — Jewish or Moslem. It only does so for the same reason that the early Crusaders desired to capture Jerusalem. Israel is sitting smack-dab in the middle of what is considered to be the "holy land" where Moses and Jesus and all the rest of the Bible characters did their thing. The fact that none of these characters ever existed does not seem to deter our Christian congressmen one bit from their sacred "duty" of preserving the site of the little cradle of Jesus. Israel has nothing to offer us economically. They can only offer us a military platform from which we will have good bases for attacks on the U.S.S.R. or the on Arab oil fields. When we finally get fed up on paying OPEC's price and go in to take the oil by force, a well-equipped Israel will be a very valuable ally and base.

Israel already has the privilege of being the only foreign nation to which one can send donations and write it off on a U.S. tax return. One is also allowed to have dual citizenship between the U.S. and Israel. President Carter had an official liaison officer to the Jewish community in our nation. He was Mark Siegel, who now heads his own Jewish PAC since administrations have changed. I am sure that Reagan has one, too.

Working closely with the National PAC is the American Israel Public Affairs Committee (AIPAC) which is based in Washington, D.C. It helps to coordinate the activities of many of the thirty-one individual PACs. A lot of former White House staff people end up working for AIPAC when administrations change.

The National PAC itself is governed by a six-member board. They decide where and when the PAC's money is to be spent. The board consists of a chairman, naturally, who heads International Creative Management, Inc. (a large theatrical and literary talent agency) and five members. One of the other members is the chairman of the board of

Paramount Pictures. Considering these first two PAC board members, it is easy to see why, from the information that is available, many of the Jewish PACs get most of their donations from members of the entertainment industry. The other four PAC board members are a New York City developer, a New York City investment banker, the editor of *New Republic* magazine, and the lone woman, a New York City lawyer.

How about taking a look at some particular races from the 1982 campaigns? In the Springfield, Illinois congressional district, a Roman Catholic lawyer by the name of Richard J. Durbin defeated the incumbent representative, Paul Finley. Durbin was a Democrat and Finley was a Republican. Finley had been the ranking Republican on the House Committee on Foreign Affairs Subcommittee on Europe and the Middle East. This is one of the prime subcommittees that authorizes aid to Israel. He had become critical of Israel in recent years and had even advocated a more "evenhanded approach" toward Arab states and the rights of the P.L.O. Mr. Durbin (now representative Durbin) received $104,325 with all thirty-one Jewish PACs chipping in. His district is a good example of the strategy of the Jewish PACs that I was talking about earlier. His district has less than 2,000 Jewish voters. So, it was a good target for outside money from the PACs since the Jewish community locally could not generate enough impact to help to defeat a "foe of Israel" on a key House committee. Where did the Jewish money come from? The "Citizens Concerned for National Interest" in Highland Park, Illinois, a North Shore suburb of Chicago with a Jewish population, donated $5000 to Durbin's campaign. This Highland Park group gave twenty-nine candidates a total of $65,800. The "National Committee to Elect Dick Durbin" solicited Jewish leaders nationwide on his behalf. The "Citizens Organized Political Action Committee" of Los Angeles, California, gave Durbin $5,000 as a group, with $2,000 in addition coming from the husband of its founder directly. This Los Angeles group gave $137,000 to thirty candidates in the 1982 elections. Durbin and Finley both reported spending over $700,000 on a close race. The $104,325 Durbin received from the thirty-one PACs in total was about fourteen percent of the funds he expended. That is enough to buy a lot of his attention on the subject of aid to Israel on that House subcommittee on Europe and the Middle East.

Representative Clement Zablocki, a Democrat from Wisconsin, beat back the challenge of a state senator (who just happened to be Jewish) who had received $9,350 from thirteen Jewish PACs. Zablocki is the Chairman of the House Committee on Foreign Affairs, a very powerful post when aid to Israel is considered. It was Zablocki's closest race in thirty years.

Representative Dante Fascell, a Democrat from Florida, received a total of $43,250 from twenty-two Jewish PACs. He was successful in defending his seat against a former TV newsman in his district, which includes parts of Miami. Fascell is the second ranking member of the Democratic majority on the House Committee on Foreign Affairs under Chairman Zablocki.

Representative Clarence Long, a Democrat from Maryland, received $31,250 from eighteen Jewish PACs to help him in his race in the suburbs of Baltimore. He is now back in his chair as Chairman of the House Appropriations Subcommittee of Foreign Operations.

I have not talked much about the Senate so far, but they got their share of Jewish money as well. In fact, many of the Jewish PACs feel that the Senate is the best place to concentrate their funds in the coming elections of 1984. The Senate Committee on Appropriations, which is composed of twenty-nine members, had gifts from the Jewish PACs to six out of the twenty-nine members, totalling $232,039. That means about $38,000 per Senator. The Chairman of the Committee, Sen. George Mitchell, a Democrat from Maine, got $78,807 of that money — the lion's share. It came from twenty-eight different Jewish groups — all located outside of the state of Maine.

Going back to the House for some totals, the House Foreign Affairs Committee, which has thirty-seven members with Chairman Rep. Zablocki (who got $9,350 from Jewish PACs) at the helm, and the House Appropriations Committee Foreign Operations Subcommittee, which has twelve members with Rep. Clarence Long, an Ohio Democrat, as Chairman, together garnered $355,550.00 worth of Jewish PAC support for their members.

To see just how effective that money is, these same two committees of the House just added $100 million to President Reagan's original aid request for Israel. Being able to buy $100 million worth of aid for just $355,550 worth of campaign contributions is pretty good. That means that the Jewish PACs got about $281.25 worth of additional aid to Israel for every *dollar* they spent on campaign contributions to members of two select committees. This is a fine example of how targeting a narrow spectrum of issues and putting your money directly where it counts pays off.

American Atheists, with an annual gross income of only some half-million dollars cannot possibly compete in this kind of scenario. Most fund-raising groups, as a general rule, use up 85 to 90 percent of the funds they take in on operating costs. If you are raising money for a heart fund or an ecology group, you have to convince the persons you are soliciting that yours is a worthy cause. Sometimes that requires a great deal of reading material to be sent out or a lot of explanation over phone lines or through visual or audio aids. A lot of convincing takes a lot of money and narrows down the amount you can keep to apply directly to the "cause" considerably. Religious groups usually have much less of a problem convincing their constituencies to give. Richard Viguerie, who is one of the New Right's best fund-raisers, has developed his own "Viguerie technique" for pushing the right button on a religious nut to get him to give. You just mention communist-Atheists and pornography in your letters over and over again a significant number of times, and the checks come rolling in. It is like pulling the string on a Barbie doll. You just need to say the right thing to a born-again Christian and it sets him off and you get this week's grocery money in the mail. With many nonreligious groups, this is simply not so. This is particularly true with a group of self-determined, fiercely independent bunch of reasoned thinkers like Atheists. Atheists must be convinced sometimes from three or four different perspectives before they will donate to their "cause." The religionists usually use perhaps twenty to twenty-five percent of what they can raise for overhead. When you raise money emotionally and you have the trigger words down pat, it becomes easy. I suspect that the Jewish PACs are pretty much the same as the right-wing religionists. Mention the Holocaust on every third line and degrade a German or two along the way and you have it made. The Jewish groups also have the advantage of the nature of the Jewish religion itself, which stresses family unity. Jewish communities are usually a very close-knit bunch. That learned camaraderie can be played upon to raise funds by pitting the Jew against the world as an outcast.

The United States is a republic, to be precise, and not literally a democracy. We elect persons to office who we then invest with the power to exercise their judgment for us as they see fit. In a democracy we would literally exercise our judgment as individual citizens directly, by vote, on every issue. There are just too many of us to do that with any feasibility. The problem with the system arises when small groups of persons are able to manipulate the election of an agent known to be responsive to the small group's needs first, and the needs of the whole second. If you can get $281.25 worth of real return for every $1.00 invested in Congress, why play the stock market? As more groups realize this, our governmental system will soon become unworkable.

The solution to the problem of PACs in general is not to generate more PACs to fight the PACs that already exist. A "Star Wars" between PACs is hardly the answer. The root of the problem is that money — and not ability or integrity or the determination to be neutral — is the determining factor most often in who gets into which office. If funding was removed altogether from the political scene, then it could be a battleground of ideas instead of megabucks. That is what our "founding fathers" envisaged. They were all of the wealthy "planter" class, so money was not a problem when political ambition came along. They could wage a war of platforms and ideals and not need to solicit or worry about funding sources outside their own families or farms. They conceived of a government where men could fight ideological campaigns and let the public pick the best platform — not the man with the most name recognition on TV.

Too many politicians and too much time spent seeking to outspend the other guy have spoiled the soup. We don't have any ideological battles over real issues anymore. No one gives a shit about issues unless they are die-hard politicos.

If radio and TV time for politicians was free and equally distributed, and if legislative salaries were at a normal middle-class family income level, and never above that, the PACs would be useless. When that day comes, we may have to choose brains over a TV game-show smile. Things would be a lot simpler that way, and a whole bunch of actors like Ronald Reagan would be out of luck.

WAM-III and The U.S.S.R.

September 1983

During the months of June and July of this year [1983] Dr. Madalyn O'Hair, President of American Atheists, and I, as well as a list of others attended the third international World Atheist Meet and went on a short tour of the U.S.S.R. In the following pages I shall be giving you, the reader, my personal impressions of those two events. The impressions or comments that I make may differ from those of others who took part in the Meet or the tour of the U.S.S.R. I do not attempt at the outset to say that my description and analysis is the best. I simply present it as the way I saw it, firsthand, drawing on my experience with previous extensive world travel and organizational endeavors on behalf of Atheism domestically.

The first World Atheist Meet was held in India in September of 1968. The idea of World Atheist Meets was conceived by Dr. O'Hair. GORA of India (founder of the first Indian Atheist Centre) agreed. The second World Atheist Meet was held in India in December of 1980. These first two Meets were held in India chiefly in deference to the impoverished condition of the Indians and thus their inability to travel great distances to other nations unassisted. The third World Atheist Meet was held on June 24th, 25th, and 26th, of 1983 in Helsinki, Finland. Helsinki was chosen because the Union of Freethinkers of Finland is a generally well-organized and domestically strong organization. Their leadership took on the responsibility for the logistics of the Meet.

The participants in the Helsinki Meet came principally from eight countries. At the end of this article you will find a page of "World Atheist Meet III Resolutions" drafted at the conference; the leaders of the participating groups are listed at the bottom of those resolutions. In addition to that leadership, some rank and file members attended, of course. Most of the rank and file were from Finland and the United States, with the German contingent coming third in terms of numbers. Those attending from the United States were: Dr. Madalyn O'Hair, President of American Atheists; Jon G. Murray, Secretary of American Atheists; Robin Murray O'Hair, editor of the *American Atheist*; Shirley Nelson, member of the Board of Directors of American Atheists, and his wife, Virginia; Pam Thoren, curator of the American Atheist

Museum; Bruce Harvey, a member from Pennsylvania; Derek Nalls, a member from Texas; Leo and Alva Fried, members from California; Robert and Thelma Cook, members from Georgia; Steve Dahlby, a member from Florida; Minerva Massen, a Board member of American Atheists, and her husband, John Massen; Dan and Claudia Bravo, and their daughter Patricia, members from California; Toivo Helin, a member from Minnesota; Sarita Erwin, a member from California; and Jeffrey Vowles, President of G.A.L.A. (Gay Atheist League of America) from California.

The conference was held in a student hostel. The meeting space was adequate and functional but not fancy. The accommodations were passable by American standards, but not more.

The main problem of the conference was communication between the delegates, as may be anticipated at any international gathering. This was not so true in the first two meets where only Indians and persons from the U.S. or Australia were present, all of whom sharing English as a common language. American Atheists did indeed anticipate the problems of language and offered monetary assistance to the Finnish group to obtain translators. They declined the offer, and as a result the meeting was less productive than it could have been if everyone could have understood one another. A good example came at the time Dr. Victor Garadja, the delegate from the U.S.S.R., spoke. Two Finnish group members translated each sentence into Finnish and then into English. We therefore don't know how good was the version of what Dr. Garadja said that we English speakers received. Double translation like that is very difficult. In general, a great deal of time was spent repeating oneself or waiting for translators (being nonprofessionals) to catch up. The hiring of professional translators could have made the whole conference run much more smoothly.

The daily schedule planning of the Meet was poorly conceived and executed also. Lunch and dinner breaks each day took as long as three hours, with delegates finding places to eat, grappling with menus in a foreign tongue, and encountering the world's slowest table service (which we learned was somewhat customary in Finland). This cramped the actual meeting time into far less space than anticipated at the outset. One of the scheduled extracurricular activities was a visit to the national Finnish Summer Solstice bonfire celebration. The delegates were given the wrong time for the event, unfortunately, and arrived just as things were breaking up and the merrymakers were on their way home.

Travel to Helsinki was a hardship for many who attended since

Helsinki is so far north of central Europe and is across the Baltic Sea. Some of the European groups were not represented for that reason. I personally feel that the only viable site for all future Meets is a central European location such as Switzerland (perhaps Zurich, Bern or Geneva) or either Paris (France) or Frankfurt (Germany), which are rail and air hub cities for all of Europe. This does leave out the groups from Australia, New Zealand, India, and the U.S., but they are the ones most capable of affording travel (with India being sponsored most of the time by several of the other nations).

The purpose of a World Atheist Meet has to be, first, social. The members of the delegations from the various nations have to get to know each other well. With the intimacy achieved by repeat encounters of the same nations, the usual formalities can be set aside and more real business discussions held. In Helsinki, however, as in the first two Meets, too much time was taken up by delegates sitting and listening to speeches by the leaders of each country. This was most unproductive. It was in part, however, necessitated by the lack of translators and the size of the group. Except for the U.S. and the U.S.S.R., the topics of the speeches were essentially leaders bemoaning the fact that their country was a legal theocracy.

Let me reflect on this point of theocracies for a moment. Of the countries represented at the Meet, only the United States and the Soviet Union have any separation of state and church in their founding governmental documents. That fact quickly places the groups in most other countries in the position of not being able to do anything but be philosophical clubs. They have no legal basis from which to fight for their rights. France, Germany, Italy, Switzerland, Finland, England, and others have always had some form of "state church." They don't have any tradition of separation of state and church. That is true to some extent of the U.S.S.R., which had no separation of state and church prior to 1917. So the German, the Swiss, the British, and the Finnish leaders bemoaned the fact that they still must live in theocracies and called for their demise — when in actuality they can do little or nothing about it. One of the possible exceptions to this is India. India's problem is that it has an eighty-five percent illiteracy rate which has generated a plethora of superstitions. It matters little if the government of India is a legal theocracy or not. With that kind of illiteracy rate, the majority of the population is going to be saturated with primitive religions no matter what.

It was not until the last day of the Meet that I and others in the U.S. delegation suggested that the leaders from the various countries get together in a closed-door session to try to talk about common concerns. That was finally done after all the speeches. Out of that closed-door session came a list of "resolutions" to which I have already referred. Dr. O'Hair and I of the U.S. delegation did not like the idea of drafting "resolutions" at all. The freethought groups of Europe have been doing that for hundreds of years and have never accomplished one of the things they resolved to do. We did not desire for an Atheist Meet to do the same thing. We suggested that we come up with the things towards which we should pledge to return to our respective countries and *work* towards, with real emphasis on the word, *work*. We were outvoted in this area to the extent that what was produced for the press by the leaders' committee was a list of "resolves that we unite to work" statements. This was a satisfactory compromise for the time being. With the current trend in state/church litigation in this country, we may soon be following suit with the European groups (though not of our own volition). At present, at least, we still prefer to think in terms of working for something rather than being content to resolve to its general merit.

All concerned also quickly found out that we each did not have a good working conception of the problems of Atheists in each other's countries. We all had misconceptions and did not know enough about the day-to-day cultures in each other's lands to be able to come up with any solutions to common concerns in a one-morning round table discussion. We were such a diverse group that even the word "Atheist" had varying connotations in each language. That is why it appears only once in the resolutions list outside of the repeated title of the Meet. We did, however, come up with one absolutely common problem, and that was *apathy*. That one word can be translated into the question "How do we attract persons of like mind to our cause and how do we motivate them into action?" One of the unwritten actions we resolved to do was to increase the frequency of communication between groups and especially on the topic of apathy.

An overriding concern of the groups other than the U.S. was peace. That is why the two longest resolutions concern that topic, with resolution number one laying the predicate for resolution number two. As a delegate from the U.S., I sensed a definite reason for the Europeans to have a concern for peace beyond the obvious one of valuing life — as only one who does not believe in an afterlife can. They wished to be identified with the only public movement that is really, at least on the surface, licking the apathy problem among liberals in Europe. The peace movement there today is doing for "cause" groups now what the anti-Vietnam War movement did for "cause" groups in the U.S. in the sixties and early seventies. The European delegates were looking from some of the enthusiasm over keeping missiles out of their countries and peace in general to rub off onto their Atheist groups. This is not to downplay the sincerity of the delegates on the peace issue. They were all *most* sincere. I had a definite sense of their desiring to capture a little of the present charisma of the peace movement to use to bring their own constituencies to life. They were looking for something to rally the troops around, even if it is only collaterally Atheist and not directly confrontationalist on religion issues. We in the U.S. are not entirely innocent of this tendency either. We have a growing peace movement and an ecology movement and a tax protest movement as well in our country on whose waves we can hitch a little free ride. We can and do pick up members by generating publicity by bouncing off controversy generated by ecology, peace, and tax protest groups.

Money problems were also discussed by all the represented groups. Yet, despite all of the recitation of how poor they are, none have set up any kind of permanent sustaining trust fund as we have in the United States. We passed the idea on to them, and we must now wait to see if the seed takes root. The Finnish group was the worst in this category. They allowed their monetary position to influence their actions in this international outreach of hosting the Meet to the extent that they paid so much attention to the delegate from the Soviet Union that everyone else felt slighted. Why so much attention for the Soviet delegate? He represents to Finland a very powerful and (from their point of view) rich neighbor and a prime target for obtaining funding for their operation. The Soviet delegate spent most of his time huddled with a small group of Finnish rank and file members while ignoring everyone else. This was undiplomatic for the host group of an international group, to say the least. Financial negotiations with the Soviets should have been handled privately at another time and place.

The Finns also provided a very good example of the difficulties of groups from diverse cultures working closely together. In addition to deferring to the Soviet delegate, they deferred to a member of their group who was also a member of the Finnish Parliament and chairwoman of the Educational Committee. She spoke about a battle they had been having in Finland over religion in their public schools. Finland is dominated (and has been for some time) by the Lutheran church. The Lutherans placed released-time religion classes (that is the most appropriate U.S. analogy) for public-school students to be attended on a *voluntary* basis. At first it was outside of the school building, and then inside. The Finnish group then came along and through their representative introduced into the Education Committee a proposal to have optional classes in "humanistic ethics" also. The religionists in Parliament came back and said "O.K., let's have both kinds of classes for the children making it now *mandatory* to choose one or the other."

As outsiders, we of the U.S. delegation would never have consented to such a compromise. We would have demanded that all religion be out of the schools and that the schools remain neutral and secular. The Finns never even thought of that. They seemed very happy that they had won a great victory for the schoolchildren. Perhaps they had — from their point of view and considering the nature of the relationship between the state and the Lutheran church in Finland. Coming from a country with its foundations in the separation of state and church, we immediately took a varying point of view.

You can see then that each group being from diverse cultures had a different "mind set" on a subject of so basic a concern as religion in education. This signals to me that the best that a World Atheist Meet could do is establish a very, very loose coalition of national groups. All that we can agree on are principles such as those outlined in the resolutions at which we arrived. What constitutes an arrival at the achievement of a given resolution in a given country has to be judged by the group therein. Although we stood aghast at what the Finns had consented to, one realizes that in a theocratic state with no state/church separation legal precedent, they could do little else but try to get into the educational scene themselves as an equal to religion. They had no basis or precedent on which to stand to demand outright removal of religion from the school, at least not at this point. Perhaps after they have been in the schools for some time, they can make a point of their class being more academically advantageous to the student than a denominationally-slanted religion class and work that angle toward a better school law.

This school controversy in Finland also tells me that there is no need to have other than the leaders or their designated representatives at future world meets. If given nations are pretty well stuck with limited courses of action which they can follow, then a smaller round table type of meeting every two years would suffice. At a smaller meeting of leaders only (say in the range of a dozen or two), the parliamentarian formalities necessitated by a larger group can be bypassed in favor of more frank and to-the-point discussions. A smaller group would only require perhaps two good multilingual translators. Minutes of these "executive" sessions could be sent to the leadership of those countries unable to attend a given meeting.

This is not say "give up." Loose coalitions have been able in many cases to accomplish a lot internationally. The United Nations, for example, accomplishes much as a very loose coalition of nations with only "advisory" powers, at best. The key is to keep up regular communication among like-minded and similarly-purposed groups. That constant exchange of ideas, despite the hampering of distance and language, is of great long-term value.

World Atheist Meet III adjourned, problems and all, with each person who came leaving with just a little more knowledge of a fellow Atheist of another culture. The delegates returned to their respective countries knowing at least that they were joined with those of other lands, diverse as they were, by the common thread of being free from religion.

On Monday, July 27th, 1983, the day after World Atheist Meet III adjourned, a group of those who had been in attendance left for a tour of the U.S.S.R. which would return them to Helsinki on July 10th. The group consisted of fifteen persons: Dr. Madalyn O'Hair, Robin Murray O'Hair, Jon Murray, and Derek Nalls from Texas; Shirley and Virginia Nelson from Arkansas; Pam Thoren from Indiana, Bruce Harvey from Pennsylvania, Leo and Alva Fried from California; Robert and Thelma Cook from Georgia; Steve Dahlby from Florida; Lavanam from India; and Erkki Hartikainen from Finland. The itinerary consisted of four nights in Leningrad; three nights in Moscow in the Russian Republic of the U.S.S.R.; three nights in Kiev in the Ukrainian Republic; two nights in Minsk in the Byelorussian Republic; and one night in Tallinn in the Estonian Republic. The travel plan called for going from Helsinki to Leningrad by train, then flying on Aeroflot (the airline of the U.S.S.R.) between cities to Tallinn, and there catching a boat to Helsinki on July 10th to complete the circle. The first thing encountered was the "white nights," which means that it only got dark for a couple of hours out of each twenty-four, due to the latitudes of Finland and most of the U.S.S.R.

All of us on the tour were a little apprehensive about customs when going into the U.S.S.R. The Soviet customs inspectors came onto the train shortly after it crossed the border and went from compartment to compartment. When they came to the one occupied by Dr. O'Hair and myself, they found two Atheist books in my suitcase published by our affiliate, American Atheist Press. Both were authored by Dr. O'Hair. The customs agent looked at the books and looked at Dr. O'Hair and said in limited English, "You author?" holding up one of the books. She replied, “Yes, I am.” He said, “You no trust in god?” To which she replied, “No, I don’t. I am an Atheist. We are all Atheists.” At that point the customs agent was terribly puzzled. He had never encountered an American group that did not “trust in god,” obviously a phrase picked up from American paper money he had seen. Meanwhile, in another compartment another agent found some antireligious pamphlets in Lavanam’s (the Indian Representative) bag. Because they mentioned the name “Jesus” in the title, although in an overall derogatory sense, the agent thought that they were Christian literature. When a superior with more knowledge of English got involved, Lavanam was passed through with his literature.

We were met at the train station in Leningrad by an Intourist [official government tourist agency of the U.S.S.R.] guide. Her name was Olga, believe it or not. She was to be our overall guide, staying with us all the way to Tallinn. In addition to Olga, we would have a local guide in each city to narrate all of our local sightseeing tours. All of the guides were generally pleasant, but they all had a kind of underlying hostility at first toward Americans, and this surfaced from time to time. They also were all very defensive about their country in general. We managed as a group to overcome those initial feelings of the guides for Americans simply by explaining the nature of the group to them. It gave them something in common to be guiding fellow Atheists — an experience they assured us they had not had before with any American group. They all ended up on parting to say that they were honored to have drawn our group to guide.

In every city we mostly did sightseeing. We found out only late in the trip that one cannot just come to the U.S.S.R. for a meeting or business purpose as an ordinary citizen from another country. You must go through Intourist and come primarily for touristic purposes with meetings or any kind of “business” interspersed in between. That is, at least, what *every* guide told us. We saw many new things, as you can well imagine. One of the most unusual was in Leningrad when we stopped to see the remains of the 70,000-year old wooly mammoth that Soviet scientists had pulled out of the ice almost totally preserved, with flesh and hair still attached.

We did have some “business” meetings arranged with groups in three cities, however. In Leningrad we were taken on a tour of the main exhibit building of the Museum of the History of Religion and Atheism. Its collection was housed in more than one facility, but the main body of it was located, ironically enough in what used to be the Kazan cathedral. The museum consisted chiefly of the history of religion in the U.S.S.R.

The section on "Atheism" consisted of a limited number of busts and quotations by the ancient materialist philosophers, continuing on through the humanists and deists of the last part of the eighteenth century. Then there were exhibits of some of the documents concerned with making a constitutional separation of state and church after the Russian revolution of 1917. In addition, there was a good collection of icons from various periods prior to the revolution. At the time of the tour, we made arrangements to come back the next day for a meeting with Yakov Kozhurin, Director of the Museum, and his staff. We had a meeting the next day which lasted for about four hours. Two of the museum staff spoke English very well, so they were able to translate during the session. Dr. O'Hair, Lavanam, Robin Murray-O'Hair, Pam Thoren, and I attended the meeting while others went sightseeing on the bus.

In Moscow a meeting was arranged with Dr. Victor Garadja, Director of the Institute of Scientific Atheism. Also present at the meeting was the Assistant to the Editor of *Science and Religion*, the journal of the Institute. The delegates from our group were Dr. O'Hair and Lavanam only. I was stuck, unfortunately, with a problem of lost baggage at the arrival desk of the hotel and missed the meeting. The Institute of Scientific Atheism is the official government arm of the U.S.S.R. charged with propagating Atheism to the citizens of the country, chiefly the youth. Dr. Garadja occupies a place on the Presidium which makes him equivalent to a Cabinet member in the United States. The Moscow office of the Institute is the national office for a network of local Institutes of Scientific Atheism located in the capitals of each of the fifteen Republics that make up the U.S.S.R.

In Tallinn, a meeting was arranged with the Estonian Republic branch of the Institute of Scientific Atheism and was attended by all members of our tour.

A point needs to be made here which was driven home to us by each and every guide. In the Soviet Union they refer to their country by the name "Russia" only when referring to the period of time prior to October 25, 1917, which was the date of the revolution that overthrew the power of the czar. After 1917, they refer to their country as either the "Soviet Union" or the "U.S.S.R.," which is an abbreviated form of the "The Union of Soviet Socialist Republics." This may seem to be a fine semantic point to us, but to them it has great significance.

Those of us who attended each of these meetings did most of the talking, rather than the Soviets. An often wide-eyed audience listened to us intently. They were really interested in the United States and how we got along therein as Atheists. They were eager for information about politics in general, as well as politics and religion in the U.S. They had a lot of misconceptions about religion and government in the U.S. and we corrected them as best we could, often needing to draw some rather awkward analogies to get our point across.

One thing that was heard at all three meetings was an impassioned plea for peace. It was to the point of tears at times. Their message was loud and clear. "Why do you (meaning Americans in general) want to kill us for disagreeing with you?" "Please, leave us alone to go our own way. We do not desire to pour money into military projects, but we are afraid that if we do not, you will wipe us out." Does that sound familiar? We hear it every day here at home — only from the other side.

We were also hungry for information about the U.S.S.R., and particularly the state of Atheism and religion therein. We were told that religion is only a problem with the older generations of age fifty or better. The younger generations had an apathy toward religion and Atheism both, we were told. That was of concern to the groups with whom we met. They wished to have the new generations coming up to have an enthusiasm for the positive nature of Atheism. Instead, the young people are apathetic, and they fear that apathy may lead to some kind of return of religion from outside sources at some point in the distant future. To the best of our knowledge, this is already happening to their neighbor China with the Roman Catholic church, among others, being allowed entry by China's new administration.

In general, we gained only superficial information about religion and Atheism in the U.S.S.R. We were given, quite kindly by our hosts, numbers of books on the subject *in Russian*. We lost a lot of time to protocol on these first meetings. That happens unfortunately when ever you must say hello for the first time. Protocol meant something else in the Soviet Union, too — drinking vodka, a great deal of vodka.

The biggest barriers to our communication with the Soviets with whom we met were the language and international mail service. The Russian language, being in a different alphabet, is very hard for either side to translate from and to. Plus, there is the added complication of each republic of the Soviet Union having its own language in addition to the generic Russian. (That is correct, *their own language* — not just a dialect of Russian.)

In order to find out more, we are now in the position of needing reliable mail service between here and the U.S.S.R. We do not know at this point which nation is holding up the mails the most, but we suspect our own in view of the Cold War attitude of the present administration.

We also need to find a way to have material in Russian translated here at home. This is going to be both difficult and expensive.

Now I would like to give you some overall impressions of the Soviet Union from the cities visited. I will take them one group at a time.

1) My first impression was that the people of the Soviet Union are poor. Let me qualify that greatly. They are not the kind of "poor" that one would find in Mexico or India or in Appalachia. They appear on the street to be more like what we would call "lower middle-class" or "working-class." The cities (or at least the parts we saw) looked like the lower middle-class sections of Chicago or one of the boroughs in New York City — only significantly cleaner. We saw nothing like some of the ghetto sections of, say, Philadelphia or Newark. The people looked like they had enough to eat and were healthy. They were dressed in about Sears-quality clothing, as distinguished from Sacks Fifth Avenue or Neiman Marcus-quality clothing. The ones with whom we were able to communicate were friendly and seemed well educated, more well educated than a lower middle-class "Archie Bunker" type in the U.S. Many persons knew English or at least one other language besides Russian and their own Republic's language.

2) The rank and file citizens, at least, were obviously no threat to the security of the United States as some of the U.S. propaganda goes. They do not hate all Americans and do not live only for the chance to kill us while we sleep. In fact, the Soviets seemed to be more polite than people that Atheists are used to encountering here in the States. They were very conscious of social rules: holding doors for women, rising for women to leave the room, saying "please" and "thank you," *etc.* They obviously loved museums (especially art museums), plays, operas, ballets, concerts, and the circus. Every city we visited had its own *permanent* resident circus in its own building performing all year round. Our group attended one, and it was very well done.

3) Everyone with whom we talked was deeply concerned about peace. We were taken to war memorials in every city to understand why the Soviet people would have a deeper concern for peace than do most Americans. It was obvious that more persons died in just the battle to keep the Germans from taking Kiev than in all the U.S. losses in the whole of World War II. In all, 80 percent of the five largest cities of the Soviet Union during the 1940s were destroyed. Every family had a loved one (or two, or three, or four) lost. Americans have never had a foreign invader come to their own soil and kill that many people. In all, the Soviet Union lost some 20 million persons in World War II. The U.S. never even lost 1 million.

Consider this: Hitler launched his attack on the Soviet Union in June of 1941. In 1941, the Soviet government was only twenty-four years old. (It had been only twenty-four years since the October revolution of 1917.) Contrast that with the U.S. Our revolution was in 1776, and we did not actually become a nation ratifying our Constitution until 1789, some thirteen years later. If you add twenty-four years to that 1789, you get 1813, when we also were in the midst of a war defending our sovereignty against Britain. England did not inflict the kind of damage on us when we as a nation were only twenty-four years old and still getting our act together as Hitler did on a twenty-four-year-old Soviet nation.

Is it any wonder then that the Soviet people desire war never ever again? They know the taste of it as no American could — even our veterans. It is one thing to go over an ocean and fight knowing that your loved ones are safe at home. It is another to defend your very home and watch your family die around you as you fight. That is why they all referred to World War II as the "Great Patriotic War." For the Soviets, it was just that. They were fighting to save their very homes.

4) The public transportation in every city we visited was excellent. Buses, trolleys, boats, subways, and trains were everywhere. Every city gets a metro when it reaches one million population or more. All of these subways are as.clean as they can be.

5) Free education is guaranteed to all of these citizens. One goes to grade school, then middle school, then high school, and then takes a college entrance test like our SAT [Scholastic Aptitude Test]. If you score high enough, you may go to college free. During these years you are paid a stipend to stay in school. If not, you go on to vocational school. With either route you take, you are guaranteed a job when you graduate — usually a choice of two. Now I can see why the Soviet government does not like for a citizen of their country to take all that free education and defect with it without doing anything to repay the society that made it possible for him to get educated.

6) Free medical care is available to all. Two of the persons on our tour got very ill during the trip due to the cold and rainy weather we found in Leningrad for which we did not come prepared. They both had eye, ear, nose, and throat infections. One was treated and released, and the other spent two days in the hospital. It cost not dime one. Any foreign tourist to the U.S. who has to go into the hospital here would shell out thousands of dollars just for two days. The care was adequate and the doctors and nurses were friendly and responsive.

We talked to a nurse from another American tour in one hotel who said that she thought the Soviet hospitals were about like ours of the 1950s. They were adequate, but not up to our technical standards.

7) Everywhere we went we saw a sea of cranes. Construction on new housing and public transportation was going on at a furious rate. We found out that the Soviet Union is importing workers from other European countries because they are short-handed in the construction field particularly. The Soviet Union has 100 percent employment. That's right, 100 percent. We understand that they are still rebuilding from World War II.

8) We could not see any overt "censorship." We saw many bookstores and magazine and newspaper stands which looked like they had a variety of material available in a variety of languages on many topics. I cannot say any more than that, not being able to read Russian.

9) With the exception of a need to adhere to tour schedules because of buses waiting for us, on our free time we could come and go as we pleased — and we all did. We wandered up and down the streets investigating everything we could, and no one ever stopped us. We saw no police anywhere. We rode the public transportation, and people were very helpful when we became lost. They spoke some English. One woman even got off the bus with two of our tour people and took them on a little tour of her part of the city and showed them how to get back to the hotel after it was over.

10) We saw a good selection of produce. Meat and dairy products were in good supply, but we were astonished to see the entire animal in the meat stalls (head and all). *Basic* consumer goods were in the stores. I say basic because they did not have the massive selections of conspicuous consumption items like our stores do. I could not tell of anything in which they were lacking. I saw no lines for bread or butter. They seemed to have plenty, and it was very tasty as well. The food in general was very good.

11) Our accommodations were comfortable, but not "plush." The airplanes on which we flew were nice, clean, modern jets, just like our domestic carriers.

12) Probably the most shocking thing that we found out on the entire trip was that only 7 percent of the population are actually Communist Party members. The majority are not. One has to go through a one-year probation period to prove one is worthy before one can become a Party member. Their governing bodies are made up of ordinary workers who get a leave of absence from their jobs in factories, farms, and offices, to sit in the congress. Their remuneration is what they were being paid on their regular job. When their congress (or "Soviet," as they call it)

adjourns, the members simply go back to their jobs in their districts.

Overall, I found the people of the Soviet Union to be happy. They seemed to love their country and republic. They had a great sense of community pride. They were always concerned with what they could do to make life a little better for all concerned.

I look on the difference between the Soviet Union and the U.S. like this: We are like fish in a goldfish bowl. We think we have complete freedom, we can swim anyplace we like, we can have little baby fish, and so on. We are limited, however, by factors, most of which are economic. In a sense, we have different size bowls to swim in depending in which economic strata we belong. If we are rich, we have bigger bowls. To put it a different way, we can afford more freedom. If we are poor, we have smaller bowls. As long as we don't know too much about the other size bowls which are around or associate with the fish in them, we are happy in our own bowls. In the Soviet Union, they are all more or less in one size bowl. More or less money does not buy them any bigger bowls in which to swim. They cannot "get away" with more by having more money. Their still slim resources as well as their egalitarian philosophy prohibits it. That is the big difference. Still, each fish is happy in his own bowl because he really doesn't know that much about any other.

So why do we want to wipe each other out? We are all fish — all the same. Why not work to get everyone into the biggest bowl we can — all together?

Another thought has been bothering me since my return. What is the meaning of life? Now that is a rather large question. What I mean more specifically is this:

In the Soviet Union you would get up in the morning, do your personal hygiene, go to work or school, come home to some evening social life with family or friends, go to bed, and start all over in the morning. You would do that from the time you are very little until you are almost ready to die. The average person in our country and their country does the same thing every day. There is really no difference.

Every person in the world, in fact, has basic health, education, and welfare needs — and that is all. That is the meaning of life. The only problems we have beyond health, education, and welfare ones is what to do with the time left over that we don't spend taking care of those needs.

So why should two major systems of thought on the question of how best to take care of those needs that are the same for everyone be constantly at each other's throats? Why not get together and take the best of both points of view and make the job easier for everyone, and take more of that leisure time to add something to the meaning of life beyond a daily routine circle of events?

"Ah!" you say at this point. "This guy is a utopian nut and a com-symp."

Why not a utopia? Isn't that something better to shoot for than mutual self-destruction?

Of all the experiences of my Soviet tour, I came home with one thing firm in my mind. We must find some way to work with the people of the Soviet Union. We must help them as best we can, and in return they must help us with what they have learned as well. It can be done, and it must be done. It is the only rational approach.

WAM III RESOLUTIONS

1. This World Atheist Meet III (held in Helsinki, June 1983) DECLARES that Atheism is a positive way of life — an outlook based upon humans' ability and right to shape their own lives. Because equal rights for Atheism are necessary for a satisfactory and full human life, Atheists criticize state-supported religious privilege in many countries. Atheists therefore appeal to the United Nations for complete equality for Atheism.

2. This World Atheist Meet RESOLVES that we unite to work within our own organizations and our nations for an end to nuclear weapons build-up and against the threat of a nuclear exchange. The proliferation of missiles throughout the world, especially those to be placed in Western Europe this year, is an anti-life force and must be resisted so that a positive peace may be enforced. Peace in international relations is a precondition for human welfare generally, particularly in developing countries.

3. This World Atheist Meet RESOLVES that we unite to work within our own organizations and our nations for publicly-funded universal secular education.

4. This World Atheist Meet RESOLVES that we unite to work

within our own organizations and our nations for the total separation of church and state religion and government.

5. This World Atheist Meet RESOLVES that we unite to work within our own organizations and our nations for freedom of speech and expression and fair access to the media.

6. This World Atheist Meet RESOLVES that we unite to work within our own organizations and our nations against religious repression of human sexuality and in favor of women's rights.

7. This World Atheist Meet RESOLVES that we unite to work within our own organizations and our nations against special tax exemption for, and/or state-funding of, religions.

PARTICIPANTS

Erkki Hartikainen, Secretary General, presiding
Timo I. Vasama, President
Union of Freethinkers .... FINLAND

Barbara Smoker, President
National Secular Society .... ENGLAND

Brigitte Beeken
International League of
Non-Believers and Atheists .... GERMANY

Jon G. Murray, Director
Madalyn O'Hair, President
American Atheists .... U.S. of A.

Walter Baumgartner, Member of Presidium
Freethought Association of .... SWITZERLAND

Victor Garadja,
Dr. of Philosophy .... U.S.S.R.

Lavanam, Director
Atheist Centre of .... INDIA

Levi Fragell, Secretary
Humanist Ethical Association .... NORWAY

Jeffrey Vowles, President
Gay Atheist League of America .... U.S. of A.

Resolution Drafting Committee
World Atheist Meet III
Helsinki, Finland, June 1983

These resolutions were unanimously approved by the participating delegates and body.

To Hell with Ingersoll

October 1983

This year had been special for American Atheism since it marks the twentieth anniversary of the founding of the first openly-Atheistic organization in America. This anniversary year should go beyond a celebration of past achievements, however, and become a platform for launching ourselves into the next twenty years of growth. In order to do that, I think it is time to dump some of our old hang-ups as Atheists. One of these that has bothered this author for a long time is the reliance of Atheists on authority. Many Atheists constantly seek the "approval" of all kinds of "authority" figures, both contemporary and historical, for their position with regard to religion. Many of us have been reaching out to grab hold of famous persons to claim that they too are or were Atheists and to have that somehow add more validity to our own position. Perhaps this comes from our schooling where we are taught to play the "footnote" game. That is that we must cite a famous person from whom we derived a given idea that we put into a school paper to show that we have no original ideas and that we just got them from the "masters." This is a holdover from medieval scholasticism, where one had to show that any thought was derived from the Bible, the source of all "wisdom."

I think it is time now to stop playing the game of needing to quote classic philosophers on our behalf. We need no longer try to have some of the "authority" of famous people rub off on us. We, as Atheists, here and now in the twentieth century, are our own authorities on Atheism. There have only been Atheists, as we think of Atheism now, in the twentieth century. Those who have gone before were not Atheists. They only held beliefs that were precursors to Atheism — which has no belief system at all. Jefferson was not an Atheist. Franklin was not an Atheist. Ingersoll was not an Atheist. Lincoln was not an Atheist. Edison was not an Atheist. All of the heroes that we have clung onto and that the *American Atheist* journal has promoted over the years, were not Atheists. They were all precursors to those of us alive today who are Atheists.

The *American Atheist* was wrong in the past in presenting all of these "heroes" for you to worship. Most of you, dear readers, do worship them, for I have talked with many of you personally as I have travelled across the country.

What we need to do is to simply acknowledge what a given historical figure did, keeping that within the perspective of his or her times and knowledge limits, and make those past accomplishments part of our philosophical base to *move on from there*. Instead, what I see most Atheists doing is grabbing hold of those ideas propounded by great historical figures and fixating themselves at the level of those ideas, not going on to others. We must pick up all the new information and ideas that our increasing technology is bringing forth in abundance and use them to solve our modern-day problems. I have seen too many Atheists take the works of Ingersoll or Thomas Paine and keep them in the same manner as any Christian would keep his Bible, worshipping the words of that particular great "thinker." To hell with Paine. To hell with Ingersoll. I know more now as a citizen of the twentieth century than Ingersoll or Paine could have possibly known in a whole lifetime of accumulated learning. Why? Because I have access to thousands of times the information that they did. I learned more in junior high school than my mother learned in her four years of college. She in turn learned more in grade school by the fourth or fifth grade than her mother learned in school altogether.

If you look back over the history of mankind from the most primitive times, you find that religion has dominated almost every era. It was not until about the seventeenth century that the Renaissance finally started to break mankind out of abject stupidity. It was during that same era that the foundations of what would become Atheism in the twentieth century took root.

Deism sprang up in the last years of the seventeenth and the first half of the eighteenth century. It was defined, *at that time*, as a current of rationalistic *theological* thought. This is not to say that deism was not around earlier; it was. Its greatest period of growth and consolidation of thought came within the same half-century. The eleven most famous deist writers from England were born within twenty-five years of one another. England was not the only country with deistic thought, but it was the country where the events of the times provided the best breeding ground for deistic thought.

The word "deism" or "deist" appeared for the first time in the middle of the sixteenth century in France. It first appeared in connection with those who thought that the first cause of the universe was a personal god who was distinct from the world he created and apart from it and its concerns. The term "rationalist" and the German term *freidenker* (or freethinker) were considered synonymous to "deist." At the same time, led by Spinoza and others, the "naturalists" were emerging by the latter part of the eighteenth century. The deists of the time grouped themselves more with the rationalists and freethinkers as "excluding the belief in providence or in the immanence of God" to separate themselves from the naturalists and Atheists.

There were a number of factors in seventeenth-century England that made it a good place for deviance from established orthodoxy to be on the rise. In addition to the obvious fact that England during the sixteenth century had been the country with a monarch who had the balls to tell the pope where to go, many things helped nurture deistic thought:

a) The Copernican model of the solar system with the planets revolving around the sun, which was in direct contradiction to the established Mosaic hexaemeron (or six days of creation from Genesis 1), was becoming increasingly popular.
b) Cartesian physics had led to Newton's law of motion and the mechanical explanation of the world in distinction to the biblical explanation.
c) Many academicians in England were growing weary of Protestant scholasticism and were seeking new ideas and explanations.
d) Religious wars had been the mainstay of English foreign policy for many years and still were in the seventeenth century. This turned a great number of the peace-loving intellectuals off.
e) A multiplicity of new religious sects were springing up in England about this time and there was failure after failure in attempts for any substantial reconciliation between them. This provoked distrust among many bystanders of the common basis on which all of the sects were founded.
f) The latitudinarians were becoming more influential in the Anglican church. These were the churchmen who favored the Episcopal form of ritual and government (remember all governments at this time were theocracies until the American Revolution broke that tradition), but denied that it had a divine origin or authority. The idea of the divine right of kings was being questioned within the church for the first time.
g) Many churchmen were willing to extend tolerance on actions or beliefs not specifically prohibited in the scriptures for the first

time. This included going beyond just toleration or ignoring of Protestant ritual into allowing the questioning of a systematic divinity system which spoke of layers of angels and military lines of authority from god through the pope down to the clergy.
h) Arminianism was on the rise. This was the teaching of Jacob Arminius, a Dutch theologian (1560-1609), who proposed that Christ died for all men, and not only for the elect — as was the common theological position of the time, particularly among the Dutch sects.
i) Numerous scholarly writings were coming out on theological and philosophical topics by virtue of a new toleration of the concept of a "free press" in England.
j) The English Revolution (1688-89) had been successful in expelling James II, and men who had been involved in the active political and theological controversies surrounding that revolution could now turn to reading, speculation, and theory.

All of these factors and many more too numerous to mention here made England an ideal place for deistic thinking to come of age. Just what did the deists think? They were as divided on that as many religionists are today between thousands of denominations. Let's take a look at just some of the various things that deists thought during the period of its emergence.

a) Lord Herbert of Cherbury (1583-1648) became known among his peers as the "Father of Deism." He outlined five articles of what he termed his new "theology." They were that there is *one* supreme god; that he is to be worshipped; that worship should consist of virtue and piety; that we must repent of our sins and cease from them immediately; and that there are rewards and punishments here and in the hereafter.
b) Some writers focused in on various themes, but among the most popular were:
1. An historico-critical examination of the Old and New Testaments.
2. Pointing out that the Jews were indebted to older religions for their theological ideas.
3. Emphasizing the absurdity of accepting biblical miracles as actual historical events.
4. Criticizing what was called "accommodation" by church leaders of "the truth" to meet the views and secure the favor

of "ignorant" (as they put it) contemporaries —meaning, of course, the nobility.

5. Putting together evidence, *from biblical sources*, to invalidate the resurrection of Christ.

c) Many of the deistic writers said that ethics should be founded on the nature and cultivable capacity in men to appreciate worth in men and actions. They associated the apprehension of morality with the apprehension of beauty. This made morality wholly independent of scripture for them.

d) Some of the deists insisted that religion was "the crown of virtue" and that it was "inseparable from a high and holy enthusiasm for the divine plan of the universe."

e) Some said that the root of religion was in feeling, not in accurate beliefs or meritorious works.

f) Some pointed out that Christianity was not mysterious to be interpreted by the clergy. "Though we cannot know the real essence of God, yet our beliefs about God must be thoroughly consistent with reason." This was very much the same thing as the agnosticism that was to come from Huxley in the mid-nineteenth century.

g) Some tried to counter the idea of sin by saying that all sin could be compacted into one category by saying that all sin equaled just lying.

h) Still others tried to show that Christianity is not just doctrine but a life. That is, it was not just the reception of a system of truths or facts, but a pious effort to live in accordance with god's will or *natural law*. This was done to try to say that true Christianity was really just a rewritten version of natural laws.

Overall, most of the energy of the deists was spent in attacking specific Christian positions, rather than seeking to form a foundation on which to build the edifice of a "natural religion," as they called it. They all came to the same conclusion despite differences; religion, *though not identified with morality*, had its most important outcome in a faithful following of the eternal laws of morality which they regarded as the will of a god.

The deists were, by their own admission, generally willing to go along with the quietistic accommodation to the established forms of faith of their day until "better times came along." There are many persons to this day who are modern-day deists for the same reason.

Beyond deism some moved to pantheism, which was the notion that the material universe and man are only manifestations of god, and god is the reality that transcends all matter. Others moved to Unitarianism, which was only a rejection of the trinitarian concept of god as three persons at once. It was just another Protestant denomination and still is. Most of our "founding fathers" in this country allowed their deism to fade into Unitarianism and talked about "one god" being nature.

The investigations of the Renaissance and the birth of modern science fueled questioning minds who moved toward Protestantism, then deism, then to pantheism or Unitarianism, then to humanism and agnosticism, and finally by the twentieth century to Atheism. All along the way, the increased availability of information and the increased ability to communicate has made each generation more certain of the valuelessness of religion.

With the benefit of twentieth-century science we no longer need any of the evolutionary stages that have brought us to where we are today. We don't need to go back any more than a bird needs go back to being a reptile. There are those among us now who have not managed to evolve. They are stuck at the early stages of deism, rationalism, freethinking, naturalism, pantheism, Unitarianism, humanism, and agnosticism. The information available now has made all of those forms of thought obsolete. They are no longer relevant to human life as they may have been at a time when answers did not abound as they do today. We should abandon them all as obsolete, as dinosaurs, if you will. They have outlived their usefulness in a historical sense.

We must proceed now from a new Atheistic base for our culture for the next three hundred years. That is what is most important. We cannot change what happened during the last three hundred years.

If you desire to have an Atheist hero, look in the mirror. There is your Atheist hero. Those who came before did the best they could with the tools they had, but that is not good enough by our standards today. If you prefer humanism or Unitarianism or agnosticism or freethought today, it only means that you still have a seventeenth- or eighteenth-century mind in a twentieth-century world.

Every one of the precursor positions to Atheism was system of thought based on the assumption that something of some undefined spiritual quality and quantity either does exist or might exist outside of the "known" world. We know now that that sort of thinking is pure "bunk." Science, the same thing that started the deists to merely wonder, has now made it possible for us over 200 years later to stand firm as Atheists with no "feelings," as they said in the seventeenth century, of some kind of eternal power being "out there" someplace.

Reply to A Small Town Atheist

November 1983

Some months ago the American Atheist organization which publishes the *American Atheist* sent out a survey to former members and former subscribers. The purpose of the mailing was to ascertain the reasons why a given individual failed to renew his membership in the organization or his subscription to this journal. Many replies were received, some positive and some negative. The majority of the negative replies were for economic reasons. The individual simply was now out of work and could not afford any "memberships" or "subscriptions" and had let them lapse to a number of publications. Of the positive responses one was received from a small town location here in Texas that was, in a single reply, a good example of the thinking of many Atheists generally. In my wide travels both inside and outside this country, it has been my pleasure to meet a number of Atheists of many varieties. The particular reply letter of which I speak was so "typical" of most of what I have heard from individuals across the country that I felt it was of value to reproduce it here in its entirety and to comment upon each of its points one by one. What follows is the exact and entire text of this reply with only the identity of the respondent omitted:

Mr. Jon Murray, President
American Atheist Organization
P.O. Box 2117
Austin, TX 78768-2117

Dear Sir:

I greatly admire the courage and convictions of you and Dr. O'Hair. I have thoroughly enjoyed and been tremendously influenced by your fine magazine and literature.

However, I decided not to renew my membership when it expired nearly a year ago for two reasons. I shall attempt to explain since it occurred to me that others may sometime feel the same.

1. Religion — or the lack of it — is just not an important part of my life. Nor do I see it as a threat to my way of life as the authors of *Holy Terror* do. I've come to believe that it's not that big a deal with *most* people. Even those who attend church regularly. In fact, to a great many, church is a SOCIAL OUTLET — their *only* form of community contact and involvement. Many business people are motivated strictly to make contacts. I'm convinced it's their *only* incentive to attend. What better place than a large prosperous congregation to find insurance clients; sell your wares or services; and find support for your candidacy!? When a person moves to a new community, what better place to meet the people of a clannish town or neighborhood (as most are), and be immediately accepted? I've lived in this town two years now and I'm as much an obscure stranger and outsider as the day I arrived. The praying and worship is a minor and most often a secondary part of church. A great many take it with a grain of salt. I believe that most would never admit it, but they don't have any clear, strong, well-thought-out belief system. Other than a few irrational fanatics, the only time most give religion serious thought in a busy life is when they are old, sick and preoccupied with *dying*. Otherwise, most simply do not have the time or inclination. My wife is typical. She was born and raised a Catholic. When we met she had little knowledge of the Bible and was totally indifferent on the subject of religion.

2. Being a non-participating member of your organization just isn't fulfilling enough!! I eagerly read with great interest your magazine and ordered your booklets. I believed with all my heart what you had to say. I got excited and motivated. For what?? Let's face it, I am *powerless* to act. My need to be an activist is frustrated and so, I lose interest. I then put things in proper perspective and face reality. There is no local outlet — no nearby chapter in which to get involved, attend meetings, interchange ideas, *etc.* I alone can't organize a group. I don't know anyone — don't have the finances, experience, influence or know-how. I don't have the confidence that I can articulate well enough to proselyte, persuade and motivate others. Yet I feel a great need within to be an *activist*. So, I turn to what is available — community affairs, civic organizations, and politics. For example, I expect to put forth an enthusiastic, whole-hearted effort in support of the Democratic candidate for John Tower's senate seat. I will be involved, if only as a precinct worker.

There is a limit to what every individual can be genuinely interested in. Everyone must make a choice as to what will occupy his or her limited attention, time and energy. You have dedicated yourselves to a cause. You have made it your life's work. It is the cause you perceive to be the one most vital. I admire you very much, wish you well, and will continue to support your organization in what has to be a small, insignificant way.

It's easy for you to be vocal on the subject, but I question the wisdom of the Atheist layman to be outspoken in his or her convictions. Who, but those of you making Atheism a *career* can afford to alienate employers, employees, clients, customers, neighbors and associates??? We laymen have to live everyday among those who may not be strong believers themselves, but are nonetheless intolerant of strong sentiments against religion. Contrary to what you would have us believe, the fact is, most people, religious or not, tend to *distrust* one who readily professes to have no belief system at all. To me, it's a personal thing best kept to myself and those few I know share my feelings. Here and now, that few comprises a very tiny minority! I can't afford to lose *any* friends over something as *unimportant as god*.

Here are two suggestions I humbly submit that may help your members feel more involved in your important movement:

I wish you would consider offering a seminar to be held in Austin on HOW TO ORGANIZE A LOCAL CHAPTER. Offer instructions on how to become an *active*, involved member of the American Atheist movement. I feel sure there are many, such as I, who would pay to attend such a conference. Second, every magazine I read regularly from *Time* to *Mother Jones* has a "LETTERS to the EDITOR" or "FORUM" section, in which your readers can comment and express their opinion on your various articles. It seems to me that it would give you valuable feedback to encourage comments from fellow Atheists, freethinkers, and even theists now and then. Often your readers may agree with your basic premise but take exception to a point. I can even imagine an enlightened, intelligent challenge from a liberal-thinking christian — perhaps even a minister — would be of profound interest. Of course, I don't mean to suggest publishing irrational right-wing fundamentalist hate letters, but only good sound logical decent. To me this would be healthy involvement.

I don't like to think that all your articles are from a small intellectual elite staff who sits somewhere in an "ivory tower"

> cranking out atheist ideology. That is much too similar to catholic monks cloistered far from the *real* world in their lofty monasteries, meditating and writing church dogma that the masses MUST believe and obey.

The author of this letter numbers his first two points. I shall refer to those numbers in my thoughts here.

1) I would have to agree that, as an Atheist, religion is not an important part of *my* life. Taken from a personal perspective, religion is irrelevant to "life" in general for me. I am a second generation Atheist and that makes me unique even among Atheists. Religion to me is nothing but a set of rules for operating within a fantasy system, much like the rules to a Monopoly game. The game is not "real." It is just a game. The rules, *within* the context of the game, are very important, though. Without them, there would not be a game at all. Religious dogma to me is like that — just the rules to a game. Outside of the game, in real life, the rules are meaningless and irrelevant. I am not so naive as to discount the relevance of religion to persons who spend part of their time mentally in reality and part of it richly outside of reality. Don't take me wrong; we all get involved in fantasy on a daily basis. When I pick up a novel and read it, I get involved in the story line and the characters, *etc.* I am then involved in a small fantasy. I can, however, close the book at any time and by that simple act of putting it down on the table, I withdraw from the small fantasy it has provided, and I become totally involved in the real world again. A religious person cannot do that with the Bible, for example. Some of the fantasy spills over into their everyday lives.

I do see this as a "threat to my way of life" only in the instances when the part of the religious fantasy that spills over into real life influences the day-to-day action of an individual, particularly in his or her relations with others. A good example is President Reagan. He cannot separate the fantasy concepts of "good vs. evil" scenario gained from a novel, the Bible. That does affect me in that it increases the chances of my becoming a casualty of war, nuclear or conventional. He is a "threat to my way of life." The public official who decides that alcohol cannot be sold on a particular day of the week or that stores in general cannot be open on a certain day of the week, again based on the fantasy stories in a novel, affects me. The censor who dictates what should be available for me to read is a "threat to my way of life." The problem lies in the fact that these "threats" are mostly covert and not overt. If a storm trooper came into your house and arrested you for not going to church, you would see religion as a threat. The fact that you cannot buy certain things on Sunday or that you don't find any criticism of religion allowed in the media is much less immediately threatening. Those things are minor inconveniences *now*, but an accumulation of them over a period of years can easily lead to those storm troopers at some time down the line. It is hard for the average person to put all of the little things together into an overall picture. When you do, however, you see that we live in a society that systematically discriminates against the person who does not allow fantasy to mix with reality. The threat is that over a period of time persons such as myself who keep fantasy and reality in their separate spheres will be bred out of the culture. By sticking to my separation of reality and fantasy I am helping to preserve an endangered species — me.

The author of the letter next says essentially that religionists are hypocritical. They go to church for social reasons and really don't pay much attention to the dogma. I think we have some common fallacies here to deal with. In the first place going to a church "worship service" is about like going to a movie. You go in, either by yourself or with your family unit, sit quietly and listen to a presentation, get up and go home. Very little socializing is done before or after *in the church*. You will socialize after church at a brunch, for example, but that socialization period has nothing whatsoever to do with the content of the sermon you just sat through or its purpose. The socializing is something that you are very capable of doing *on your own* with no reference to the church dogma. The only thing that the dogma does is to mentally condition the religionists, like Pavlov's dogs, to congregate in the same spot at the same time each week when the bell rings. The very same people from the very same neighborhood could get together for a meal or recreation, *etc.*, every week at the same time and same place on their own very easily. The church is only relevant to such get-togethers in that it emotionally and psychologically motivates persons to gather together rather than taking the chance of letting them do so on their own initiative. It would be better and far healthier if they did so on their own.

Week after week the message in every church is the same. You are worthless, impotent, and need to be outer-directed by a "force" of some kind or you will surely run screaming up and down the street with murder in your heart. Every churchgoer receives this subliminal message along with the message that he must return for more of the same next week, same time, same place, every Sunday. You must return to that "holy" spot to meet a mate, to make your business work, to solve your family problems, to make your kids pay attention to you. Of course, persons return to the church to "make contacts," because they are conditioned into thinking that they are incapable of making those contacts in any other context.

Where else can you make contacts? You can make them in school (at any level), at your place of employment, and in your neighborhood. That is about it. So, the churches see to it that your school, your employment, and the stores in your neighborhood are closed on one day of the week so that you only have one option open for social contact — "the church."

It is not an *even trade* to take indoctrination in return for a social outlet. Alternative social outlets to school and employment can be set up by citizens on their own without the emotional and psychological ills of religion as a tradeoff. Just as a dog is perfectly capable of eating when it is hungry instead of when the ringing of a bell tells it to be hungry, we are capable of socializing on our own when and how we please without waiting for a church bell to toll to tell us when to socialize.

Now, I must admit that this kind of thinking makes me an "obscure stranger and outsider" here in Austin, Texas, just as the letter writer sees himself in his town. The fact that I am an outsider does not bother me in the least. I have made up my mind that the tradeoff price that I must pay to be an "insider" is too high. It is sometimes not pleasant being an outsider all the time, but in the long run it is much healthier.

I also used to think that churches were social places and the persons therein could not possibly believe all that baloney. I have disabused myself of that kind of thinking over the years, though. One cannot get dressed up to the point of being uncomfortable, go into a darkened place, sit for hours and get picked on, abused, and downgraded, and then go home and look forward to doing it all again next week unless he or she is psychologically hooked on that kind of abuse. It has to be like a drug addict who will endure the pain of the needle and the other side effects for that moment of being "high." I cannot see enduring all of the abuse just to get a chance to "mingle" before and after. Why not just get together and mingle without the self-abuse?

A final aspect about the perceived "social" role of church attendance jealousy on the part of the Atheists. The writer is envious of the churchgoer who has a place to congregate on Sundays even for a hoped-for, if not a real, meeting with others in the community. It is normal to be jealous when you see others having what you perceive to be a social outlet and "good times" that you would like to have and find yourself left out. That jealousy is nothing to be ashamed of. It is natural. I know probably better than anyone that we Atheists need a meeting place in every community where we can congregate. That is where the similarity would end, however. I envisage a meeting place where persons could get together and have a *learning* experience. A lecture or film or seminar where they could ask questions afterwards and discuss the topic of the week with persons knowledgeable thereon. A place where people were forced to meet, please. That is, families and couples were forced to split up and not sit together. Instead of rank and file pews, how about round tables where persons would have to sit with strangers and face each other and exchange ideas?

A desire on the part of Atheists for this kind of thing is why many of them end up in such institutions as the Unitarian church. The problem with that setting is that it is still too rank and file and retains too much of the church atmosphere. Unitarian churches have the form of a church without the substance. They try very hard to mimic traditional church form with a change of content. I think that it is far better to abandon the content and the form altogether. The form of traditional churches is set up to work hand in hand with the dogmatic message content being delivered. The hard pews, the rank and file, the genuflection, all have the purpose of reinforcing the message.

2) This brings us to part #2 of the letter. I have to start out here, too, in agreement with the writer when he says "Being a non-participating member of your organization just isn't fulfilling enough!" Even in my position as a national spokesperson for Atheism I feel like I am not participating enough on a daily basis. It is very difficult, indeed, to truly "participate" in anything. How much does one person on the mailing list of an ecology group or a peace group or an economic-reform or social-reform or even a political group really "participate." They don't. They sit at home and get a newsletter or a magazine or other publication mailed to them each month reporting on what the full-time salaried persons in the particular movement have done or are planning to do, with a plea for funds. At most, a member can once a *year* attend a convention or a demonstration or a local lecture by one of the national leaders who *happens* to be in their area. In a political movement you can do precinct work perhaps for one or two months out of the year at most. Once the election is over, that's it. You really don't get an opportunity to get politically "stirred up" for another two or four years in most cases.

Considering the way in which our social and governmental and economic systems are set up today, to "participate" in anything means to spend money. It is money more than your time that makes you a "doer" instead of an "onlooker." This is true in two ways. If you have plenty of money that frees you from the need to work; you have all the time in the world to participate in anything you like. If you have plenty of money you can donate to a number of "causes" and feel fulfilled in that you are helping them reach their goals with your money. In many cases, you can buy a great deal of the say-so of which goals are laid out to be attained if you are a large enough donor to a small organization.

It is very difficult, indeed, for any organization to provide some activities for its members while at the same time trying to conduct an educational, often also a legal or quasi-legal, campaign among the persons who do not already side with them on a particular issue, or among those of social or political clout who can help the organization persuade others. The problem with every cause organization is, no matter what the cause, that you must ignore your own membership to a certain extent to concentrate your efforts toward a change in society at large. Every group is organized with one ultimate goal in mind — to change the thinking and/or behavior of society at large. While a small group of persons labors in a mercenary relationship for those who already share their views among the general public, they tend to lose sight of those backers. It is very much like a football game. If you are a fan, you yell and scream and you may put in money to help buy the uniforms and equipment and pay the coach; but when the players actually get onto the field, they don't pay any attention to the cheering at all. A player is worried about finding a running opportunity or about how hard he is going to be hit by another player, and the crowd is vague background noise at best. All cause groups work in the same way. At the pep rally beforehand, the leaders (or the team) acknowledge the supporters and talk with them and take their encouragement and ideas. When the game starts, however, they are very much preoccupied with making the next first down and cannot be bothered with the supporters until the post-game party. Those are simply the realities of the way the game is played. Members of cause groups just have to be content with helping financially or through moral support and not being able to play in the game.

Of course, you feel "powerless." You feel powerless because the logistics of cause groups necessarily limits your involvement to a sideline support role. Only so many persons can actually be trained and get out on the field and play at one time. Logistically speaking, it is only practical to have local chapters or groups of cause organizations primarily in big cities. In a big city there are more members and more things going on relative to the particular cause. More things to comment on, more things to protest, more things to march about. That is why cities like Washington, D.C. are teeming with cause groups. All of the persons they hope to influence are there, and all of the meaningful places to march or hold similar protests are there. State capitals are also very popular places.

The finances of any given group and the amount of exposure they are given by the media limits the number of their persons who have any experience or know-how enough to be active. How many of you Atheists out there reading the *American Atheist* have ever been on TV or radio in your life, for any reason? Very damn few. The media will only acknowledge and come to a handful of persons from each cause because there are so many causes. So, only a very limited number of persons get the opportunity to have media experience and get the training to be activists. Should they take that training and use it to try to train many rank and file members to do the same, when the media will only acknowledge a couple of them? No, that would be a waste of time. The few who have the experience must use it to further the ends of the cause as a whole. In the long run it is desirable for the continuance and survival of the cause to train others to be activists. In the short run, however, it hurts the group. Cause organizations are all stuck in the short run mode of operation because of money problems and because social and political situations in the twentieth century now change very rapidly. It is hard to plan for anything but the short run in a cause group. Twenty years from now, the situation socially and politically may make American Atheists, for example, obsolete as a cause group.

This columnist is involved in many other political and social organizations in addition to American Atheists. My involvement is, however, a sideline supportive-type involvement. I get their newsletters and I send them a donation from time to time and I buy one of their books and read it with interest — just as the letter writer does with American Atheists and then says "For what??" I think the best answer to that in both cases, the letter writer and mine, is that it makes us feel good. That is not a cop-out answer. It gives me satisfaction to know that I am in some small way helping the furtherance of a point of view that I feel is correct on a particular subject. It *does* upset me that I cannot do more. I know that realistically I must do what I can do and stop at that. Every time I watch the evening news I get infuriated over a dozen topic areas and want to jump into activism on behalf of all of them. Then I get up the next morning and I forget all about those cause célébres until I get home again in the evening and something on the news or in a paper or in a book rekindles my interest. I am sure that the vast majority of

Atheists and non-Atheists alike do the same thing. My doctor, at the time of an annual physical, said something to me that I will never forget and that is appropriate here. I have a lot of gastrointestinal trouble brought on by too many hours at work and too much stress. After examining me, he said "It is OK to be *concerned* about many things, from a health viewpoint, but not OK to be *worried* about them." All that American Atheists asks with this journal and its other publications is that Atheists become concerned about various issues. We don't ask you to be worried about them to the point where you will drop your concern altogether if you can't get into a real good fight over them on a personal level.

I have to agree with the writer about the wisdom of having Atheist laymen be outspoken on their convictions. This is to be encouraged on a one-to-one level among co-workers or peers, but not on a public media level. If one is to speak out on any topic on a public level, especially with the media, they had damn well better know of what they speak. I have to strongly disagree about extrapolating from not making a fool of oneself on TV or radio to going back or remaining in the closet with an Atheist position. Sure, religionists distrust you if you "readily profess to have no belief system at all." They are envious of you as well. They wish that they could operate without a dependency system and be a freethinker like you. If you stand by your convictions, they will respect you for that in the long run even though they disagree with you. You will not lose or alienate clients, employers, employees, customers, *etc.* You will gain their respect. I have been personal witness to hundreds of examples of that around the country. I know a small town restaurant owner who thought that if everyone in the little town knew he was an Atheist, it would be all over for his business. Well, one day it came out loud and clear. His business has never suffered. The people in the small town respect him for his views and still trade at his restaurant. Of course, there are the few bigots who refuse to come to eat at his place; but they are so few, they are hurting themselves by depriving themselves of his products. As far as neighbors and associates and peers go, do you really want a "friend" that cannot respect your right to your opinion? I don't desire to have friends like that. They are not friends worth having. Anyone can afford to lose plenty of "friends" because new ones are readily obtainable. What is most important: having friends or being honest with yourself? Any friend who makes their continued friendship with you conditional on agreement with their point of view on a given subject or on complete avoidance of that subject at all is not a friend worth having. I can talk with any of my friends on any subject whether we agree or not. It is far better to have a smaller set of friends like that than to have a large set of inflexible ones.

The idea of seminars on "How to organize a local chapter" is a good one. For some time now I have felt that organizing without such training sessions is foolish. American Atheists has organized without such seminars, however, simply because of many letters (such as the one being commented on here) which pressed for immediate chapter formation. American Atheist leadership allowed the outcry for local activity to override the better judgment of the leadership and went ahead with local chapter programs without sufficient training or material being available from the national headquarters. American Atheists now finds itself in trouble in many local areas because of that decision. Organization on a local level should not have been attempted until the national organization was strong enough to provide the required level of support and training for those locals. It cannot do that to this day after twenty years as a national group. There are simply not enough funds and not enough national persons with the required experience to teach the seminars to make it practical. The only practical way it could be done at this point is to have seminars set up at a single national location and require those interested to travel and house themselves at their own expense, just like going to college, to attend.

As far as letters to the editor are concerned, the *American Atheist* has reactivated that option in its pages. I do agree that it needs to be expanded and that more letters of disagreement need to be published than currently are being chosen. I have taken it upon myself as a columnist and editor to see to it that this becomes the case in future issues of the journal. I would invite not only letters to the editor but full columns by persons of differing opinions who wish to comment on what any of the "regulars" have to say. As for letters from "liberal thinking Christians," I think that they have plenty of journals of their own in which to voice their opinions that greatly outnumber the single Atheist journal in print. We should not be made to devote precious column inches to religionists, liberal or not, who can submit and have their views printed almost any place. Atheists have a very limited forum indeed where their views can be published uncensored.

I really don't think of myself or other columnists of this journal, past or present, as being "somewhere in an 'ivory tower' cranking out Atheist ideology." I hope that I don't come on as having lost all touch with the average activist or would-be activist Atheist. I think, on the contrary, that I know all of you pretty well, perhaps better than some of you know yourselves. We shall always strive in the *American Atheist* to bring you, the reader, a variety of Atheist news and thought reflecting and analyzing the "real" world. We don't ask our readers to believe anything. We ask them to read, analyze, question, and be concerned with those of us who write for this journal.

In summary I would like to thank the author of the letter reproduced here for a well-written and thoughtful piece. I have attempted to be honest and straightforward and not patronizing or placating with my responses. The fact that I have left the letter writer in the same position as when he started is because he has asked for things that I cannot give him at this time. I only hope that he and all of you readers understand why you must be content with a supportive role, for the most part, in any cause organization. If I could make it possible for you all to be activists overnight I would — and so would the church. Even the church has the same problem. There are leaders and there are supporters, and only so many cooks can stir the broth at once. I think the moral of all of this (if there is one) is that we must all do what we can with the means that are available to us and not try to knock ourselves out trying to do it all. I would like everyone reading this editorial to go away with at least one message: Do not become discouraged or disgruntled when you support a cause, any cause, and the leadership thereof does not stroke you personally in return or call you off the bench to carry the ball. Be content with their success in the overall fight and take some inner pride in the fact that, small as it may seem, you helped. That is so important, and the persons on the front lines have a very special place in their hearts for each and every one of you who help (again, in any cause). They have not forgotten you. Without you who would they be playing the game for?

'Tis The Season to Be Rational

December 1983

That time of year is here again. The time of "season's greetings," cold weather in the northern hemisphere, and a renewal of the "commercial" spirit at least in the capitalist countries. It is also a very special time for the religious zanies of the world. The celebration of the birth of their mythical savior is the central holiday (or "holy day," literally) of the Christian religions. I like to refer to it as the Christian "heat" season. They get about as worked up about the birth of their alleged Christ as a bitch in heat.

It is especially important at this time of year for us, as Atheists, to know what the importance of the season really is and why we should celebrate — if indeed we even feel like celebrating at all. Personally, I feel that celebrations are personal things and should be conducted for reasons of importance to an individual: a birthday, an anniversary of some type, finding a better job, getting a raise. One can celebrate many events large and small throughout the year and his or her life. Historically, however, it is important to know that humankind, as an animal species, has been celebrating some natural occurrences for as long as humans have been distinguishable as a separate species. In fact, all animal life to some degree has a conscious awareness of a set of common events from which all life on earth cannot escape. This set of common events is the seasons. In both hemispheres the patterns of the movement of the earth, the sun, and the moon affect the lives of all animals every day of the year. When it is rainy, dark, cold, and windy outside you tend to feel a little depressed or gloomy — just like the weather. If it is a nice, bright, sunny, comfortable day, you feel more invigorated. You cannot help it. It is hard to feel gloomy on a bright, pleasant, sunny day.

The seasonal changes that affect all life transcend all boundaries of culture, geographical location, language, skin color, physical stature, *etc.* All animals have the effect of such change upon them both physically and emotionally in common. You can deny this effect until you are blue in the face, but it will not go away. Your sexuality especially is cyclical. A woman can jump up and down and scream and say "no" as many times as she likes, but she has heat periods just like a dog, a cow, a bear, or any other mammal.

The chief goal of the Christian religion since its inception has been to deny any association between man and the other animals or natural life cycles. The church, each and every denomination, has always said, "you are not an animal; you are a creation of god; you are different; you are special; you are apart from nature." This is the biggest lie ever to be swallowed by anyone. Yet it has been swallowed by the majority of the populations of most of the world's nations for thousands of years. This is the most stomach-turning part of religion to me, and it should be so to every other Atheist. I will not have anyone tell me that I have to deny my own species in order to be a "whole" or "saved" person. That is really *sick*.

So, as Atheists, we need to know that what is important about this time of year, and what has been important anthropologically is that the days (in the northern hemisphere) begin to grow longer again from the winter solstice day forward. In primitive times the weather was of much greater concern than today. When you are sitting bare-assed in a cave and it starts to get cold, it is of some immediate concern. In those times, the weather turning cold was a major event in one's daily existence. Light and humans' ability to handle fire were "big magic" in an effort to beat back both cold and darkness. When the winter season comes, cold and darkness go together. It is dark more of the time when it is cold. It is light more of the time when it is warm. Naturally our ancestors would celebrate the return of longer days and warmer temperatures after they had been through the struggle of trying to keep from freezing to death over a period of months. The "evergreens," or conifers, and the mistletoe and other parasites stayed green when everything else turned brown and *died* (as far as the primitives could tell) during the winter months. These plants were then something special. They looked like all of the other plants would look in the spring (that is, green), only they kept looking that way all year round. They were a source of much mystery. When you go out and buy an evergreen tree and stick it in your living room when it is cold outside and everything else turns brown, you are doing it because your ancestors did it to remind them that if they stuck out the cold, in a couple of months everything would look again like this funny tree that did not die. The only thing is that now people put up a tree and connect it with the birth of a mythical Christ. It has nothing whatsoever to do with that.

Actually, no one needs to celebrate the change of the seasons at all. You can get along quite well without ever celebrating anything. That would be a rather dismal existence, however. It is nice to be able to celebrate something at regular periods of time. The change of the seasons provides that catalyst for four big parties a year. All cultures have taken advantage of this to celebrate; that is, until the Christians came along to muck it all up with their J.C.

The ancient Druids held mistletoe to be sacred, but they did not kiss under it. The Romans kissed under it and used it in their Saturnalia celebrations. After the Roman times, the old mistletoe customs did not re-emerge until the Tudor period in England. That is where we, here in the modern U.S., get it.

Santa Claus, who as we all know lives in shopping centers and not at the North Pole, came from tales of Saint Nicholas. Nicholas was an early Christian bishop in Asia Minor, known locally for his generosity to children. The Dutch sailors of the period carried home tales of Nicholas, and December 6 was set aside in Holland as a day for children to receive presents. The Dutch called Nicholas *Sinter Klaas*. It was not until 1809 in America that Washington Irving portrayed "Sinter Klaas" as a fat and jolly man in a red suit as we know the character "Santa Claus" (in our anglicized spelling) today.

Part of the celebration of the change of seasons from winter to spring was the sharing of food. No more hoarding was as the crops would come back again (or the wild foods to pick) when the days got longer and the nights shorter and it became warm again. Sharing the light and warmth of the fire was also a big part of the celebration. "Chestnuts roasting on the open fire" and "yule logs" are not terms out of a song writer's imagination alone. The "yule log" was a large block of wood that traditionally formed the back log of the fireplace during the Christmas holiday. It was also known as "yule block" or the "yule clog." "Yule" is from the Icelandic *jol* and Middle English *yole*. The source of the word "yule" appears to have been in the proper meaning of noise, clamor, yuling or yelling, the season being one of rejoicing at the turning of the solstice, especially in the Scandinavian countries blocked into ice and cold. For some time two months of the year were known as the Yule months, those immediately before and immediately after the solstice.

The idea of the birth of a "savior" on the winter solstice day is a damn clever association. The sun took away darkness and cold, or "evil" in the minds of the primitives. In order for the budding Christian establishment in the early days of the church to get the masses to buy their Christ story, they made the association of the *son* of god coming to conquer the sin (darkness) of evil. If you cannot get people to give up their winter celebrations, you merely pervert them to your own ends and change the terminology a little. Even prior to Christianity, many cultures placed the birth of their "saviors" around the winter solstice. This was the time of year when the tribe or camp was "saved" from winter, and so it was logical to have any "savior" figure born on the same day. The Chinese had a "redeemer" born in the winter of 3467 B.C. In Persia, the god Mithras was born in winter, and he was the "god of light," appropriately enough. In Greece, the god Hercules was born in winter, and he was known for his strength and for performing twelve labors (we have twelve months). The Romans celebrated their "Saturnalia" for their sun god "Sol," beginning December 17th and running one week to December 24th. (The first month on the Roman calendar was March, so that December was the 10th month, *decem* meaning ten). The Mayans and the natives of Nicaragua, Peru, and Guatemala had their "sun god," Quetzalcoatl, born in winter. The Druids of Britain and Ireland had their god born on December 25th.

In fact, all of the following persons or characters were said to have been born of a virgin, had a baptism, had a communion supper, were worshipped in caves, and had a son or were the son to take away the sins of the world: Zeus, Buddha, Krishna, Plato, Genghis Khan, Tamerlane, Zoroaster, Julius Caesar, and Aton (the Egyptian sun god). They were all also supposed to have been born on or around December 25th. In fact, it was said that Aton was born in a manger.

Most people don't know that it was Amenophis IV (Akhenaton I) pharaoh of Egypt from 1379 to 1362 B.C., who was the first to have the concept of "one god" and that god was the *sun* god, Ra. Prior to that time, cultures all thought in terms of many gods, from the early polytheistic beliefs to the elaborate pantheons of the Greeks and Romans. After the "one god" idea was established and latched on to by the early Christians, a struggle immediately began to place the birth and baptism of Jesus concurrent with the winter solstice celebration days already being observed.

The early Christian church in Alexandria, Egypt commemorated the baptism of Jesus on January 6th as early as around A.D. 200 That was the same date as the rites for the sun god, Aton (as the sun god was called by that time, some 1500 years after Amenophis IV), at the time of the winter solstice on the Egyptian calendar. January 6th on the calendar of the Eastern Mediterranean church was known as "Epiphany." From the Greek *epiphaneia* which meant "manifestation" or "appearance," the Epiphany celebration commemorated the birth of Jesus, the adoration of the Magi, his baptism, and his subsequent *manifestation* and ministry. The Roman emperor Aurelian in A.D. 274

decreed that the birthday of the "unconquered sun" be celebrated on December 25th by the Julian calendar. (That calendar had been established by Julius Caesar in 46 B.C., with 12 months of 30 or 31 days, except February with 28 days, and 29 days on every fourth year.) Before A.D. 336 the church at Rome had established the birth of Jesus on December 25th also. The evidence used for establishing the birth of Jesus on December 25th rather than January 6th was from a "chronograph" or an almanac used by early Christians that had an entry in it reading "Christ born in Bethlehem of Judea" for December 25th. The entrees in these chronographs date from as early as A.D. 336. They were discovered around 1850 by a German scholar and historian by the name of Mommsen. The birth of Jesus was not made to occur officially on December 25th until Pope Julius I established that date during his reign of fifteen years (A.D. 337-352).

It had been a general Roman custom to celebrate the birthdays of outstanding persons, though not always in coincidence with their actual date of birth. For example, the birth of Plato was celebrated on the feast day of Apollo (May 29th on the Julian calendar). Meanwhile, in the East around A.D. 381, Gregory of Nazianus spoke in an Epiphany sermon of *recently past* "Christmas." Then in A.D. 386 a December 20th sermon on the martyr Philogonius by John Chrysostom spoke of *upcoming* Christmas festivals with a reference to the visit of the Magi being celebrated concurrently. These sermons took place in Antioch, which was in what is now central Turkey. Some five days later in another sermon, Chrysostom said that December 25th had been a festival known among the Antiochians for less than ten years, though longer in the West. Then, on January 6th, A.D. 387, Chrysostom in another sermon said that the name "Epiphany" ought *not* to be applied to the birth of Christ because Christ became "manifest" to others and began his ministry *after* his baptism, which did not occur until twelve days (there is that magic number twelve, for twelve months of the year, again) after his birth.

Thus, the separation of the Epiphany celebration from the Christmas celebration began and by A.D. 432 had spread over much of Egypt. Opposition to the separation of the two celebration dates remained in Jerusalem until the sixth century. The present-day Armenian Apostolic Churches still, as a last holdout, celebrate Jesus birth and baptism both on the same day, January 6th. Most of the Eastern Orthodox churches of the Slavic countries observe Christmas (the mass of Christ's birth) on January 7th and the Epiphany twelve days later on January 19th. They use the old Julian calendar, which is thirteen days *behind* our

Western Gregorian calendar. (The Gregorian calendar is named after Pope Gregory XIII.) When the Julian calendar was introduced, another important natural celebration day, the Vernal Equinox, fell on the 25th, of March. By that time of the reformation of the calendar by Gregory in 1582, the equinox fell on March 11th, due to inherent errors in the way the Julian calendar had been calculated. In order to restore the equinox to March 25th, which the Christian fathers had designated as its rightful date at the council of Nicaca in A.D. 325, Gregory ordered that ten days be suppressed in the calendar. Thus, the Julian error was reduced to three days in every 400 years. Gregory then ordered the intercalations for correction to be omitted on all the centenary years except those which are multiples of 400. Thus the "leap" year was born. Thus, every year which is evenly divisable by four (except the centenary years) are "leap" years. Centenary years are only leap years when divisable by four after omitting the two zeros (*i.e.*, 1600 was a leap year. The years 1700, 1800, and 1900 were not, but the year 2000 will be.)

The celebration of December 25th as the birthday of Christ did not really become popular, however, until around A.D. 1100 That was also with a very interesting exception. The Puritans issued a ban on Christmas in the English Parliament in 1647. In 1659 the Puritans of the new Massachusetts Bay Colony made Christmas illegal as well. It carried a *fine* of five shillings. One could not read common prayer, dance, play cards, play musical instruments or eat mince pie or plum pudding (English favorites of the period) on Christmas day. In addition, because they were associated with the early pagan feasts, they denounced holly and ivy as well. The Pilgrims in Plymouth colony also denounced Christmas.

We find ourselves now, in the twentieth century, going through many rituals that the true intent thereof has long since been forgotten or perverted to other ends. The only thread of truth that remains is that our primitive ancestors celebrated the changes of the seasons in general because their lives were so closely tied to those seasonal weather changes. With our modern technology we have escaped some of those ties, and we can now operate our homes and businesses all year round without holing up in a cave for winter. We are still glad, however, when spring comes again. Winter is the harshest of all the seasons. The early colonists found that if they could get through the winter, they could make it through the rest of the year.

It was obvious, too, that the Christian church itself has no idea when its own "savior" was born, if indeed one was born at all. It is beyond me why we have all allowed a simple seasonal festival to be so perverted and twisted so as to become the cornerstone of a mythical pyramid built over hundreds of years. I will have a conifer in my house this year, as last, but I will do so for a far different reason than most. I will continue to remind myself that I am an animal and part of the animal kingdom and the rest of nature. I will not take this seasonal holiday to remind myself that I am some sort of "special creation" on earth only here to serve some demented mystical being drifting around the universe someplace.

I have no intention, now or ever, of spending most of my life trying to deny what I am, trying to deny that I am part of the animal species here on earth, the only home I know. It is really sick, I repeat again, to pervert even nature in an effort to establish and maintain a human control system. This season will be a reminder to me of the need to combat this sickness — not to join in it.

The *American Atheist* Magazine

This is where it will happen; in this journal, the new intellectuals, American Atheists, will hammer out the philosophy of living and the moral/ethical values of our nation — for now and for the future.

This is *the* journal of Atheist news and thought! It is dedicated in spirit and content to Atheist activism — *doing* something about the drive organized religion is making to turn the United States into a theocracy, rather than debating the issue with philosophical detachment. Its purpose is educational: to inform Atheists about the doings of Atheist activists in the U.S.A. and all the world, and to provide the knowledge which *proves* the Atheist position that Atheism is the only viable life-style, both intellectual and social, in a civilization that has advanced to the point where robot probes explore the planets and the awesome secrets of DNA are being unlocked.

This magazine contains cartoons for which the editors are constantly reprimanded, "blasphemous" articles concerned with the most holy of holies, exposes of religious monetary shenanigans, private peeks into the marriage of politicians lusting for power and churches out for tax dollars, historical articles on great American Atheists, investigations into religious frauds, poetry, book reviews, an exciting "Letters to the Editor" section, and regularly-featured columnists offering opinions on nearly everything.

Though a subscription to the *American Atheist* is free to members of American Atheist, it is also available to non-members on a yearly subscription basis.

☐ Subscription, $25
☐ Foreign subscription, $35
☐ Sustaining subscription, $50 (tax-deductable)
☐ Sample copy, $2

Last name: ____________________ First name: ____________________
Address: ____
City/State/Zip: ____

☐ I am enclosing a check or money order for $ _____ payable to American Atheists.
☐ Please charge my credit card for $ ...... ☐ Visa or ☐ Mastercard

Return to:
American Atheists
P.O. Box 2117
Austin, TX 78768-2117

"AIMS AND PURPOSES"

(as recorded in documents of incorporation)

AMERICAN ATHEISTS ARE ORGANIZED:

1. to stimulate and promote freedom of thought and inquiry concerning religious beliefs, creeds, dogmas, tenets, rituals and practices;
2. to collect and disseminate information, data and literature on all religions and promote a more thorough understanding of them, their origins and histories;
3. to advocate, labor for, and promote in all lawful ways, the complete and absolute separation of state and church;
4. to advocate, labor for, and promote in all lawful ways the establishment and maintenance of a thoroughly secular system of education available to all;
5. to encourage the development and public acceptance of a humane ethical system, stressing the mutual sympathy, understanding and interdependence of all people and the corresponding responsibility of each individual in relation to society;
6. to develop and propagate a social philosophy in which man is the central figure who alone must be the source of strength, progress and ideals for the well-being and happiness of humanity;
7. to promote the study of the arts and sciences and of all problems affecting the maintenance, perpetuation and enrichment of human (and other) life;
8. to engage in such social, educational, legal, and cultural activity as will be useful and beneficial to members of American Atheists and to society as a whole.

Atheism is the *Weltanschauung* (comprehensive conception of the world and of total human life value systems) of persons who are *free* from theism —*i.e.*, free *from* religion. It is predicated on ancient Greek Materialism.

American Atheism may be defined as the mental attitude which unreservedly accepts the supremacy of reason and aims at establishing a life style and ethical outlook verifiable by experience and the scientific method, independent of all arbitrary assumptions of authority or creeds.

Materialism declares that the cosmos is devoid of imminent conscious purpose; that it is governed by its own inherent, immutable and impersonal laws; that there is no supernatural interference in human life; that man — finding his resources within himself — can and must create his own destiny. Materialism restores to man his dignity and his intellectual integrity. It teaches that we must prize our life on earth and strive always to improve it. It holds that man is capable of creating a social system based on reason and justice. Materialism's "faith" is in man and man's ability to transform the world culture by his own efforts. This is a commitment which is in every essence life-asserting. It considers the struggle for progress as a moral obligation and impossible without noble ideas that inspire man to struggle and bold creative works. Materialism holds that humankind's potential for good and for an outreach to more fulfilling cultural development is, for all practical purposes, unlimited.

American Atheists is a non-political, non-profit, educational organization. Another of its functions is as a "watchdog" to challenge any attempted breach of what Thomas Jefferson called "the wall of separation between state and church," upon which principle our nation was founded.

Membership is open only to those who are in accord with the "Aims and Purposes" above indicated and who are Atheist Materialists. Membership in the national organization is a prerequisite for membership in state, county, city or local chapters.

Membership Application For American Atheists

Last name: ______________________ First name: ____________

Companion's name (if family or couple membership)

Last name: ______________________ First name: ____________

Address ____

City/State/Zip____

This is to certify that I/we am/are in agreement with the "Aims and Purposes"* and the "Definitions"* of American Atheists. I/we consider myself/ourselves to be Materialist or Non-theist (*i.e.*, A-theist) and I/we have, therefore, a particular interest in the separation of state and church and American Atheists' efforts on behalf of that principle.

I/we usually identify myself/ourselves for public purposes as (check one):

☐ Atheist	☐ Objectivist	☐ Agnostic
☐ Freethinker	☐ Ethical Culturalist	☐ Realist
☐ Humanist	☐ Unitarian	☐ I/we evade any reply to a query
☐ Rationalist	☐ Secularist	☐ Other: ________

I/we am/are, however, an Atheist(s) and I/we hereby make application for membership in American Atheists. Both dues and contributions are to a tax-exempt organization and I/we may claim these amounts as tax deductions on my/our income tax return(s). *(This application must be dated and signed by the applicant(s) to be accepted.)*

Signature _______________________________ Date__________

Signature _______________________________ Date__________

Membership in American Atheists includes a subscription to the monthly journal *American Atheist* and the monthly "Insider's Newsletter" as well as all the other rights and privileges of membership. Please indicate your choice of membership dues:

☐ Life, $500	☐ Individual, $40/year
☐ Couple Life, $750 (Please give both names above.)	☐ Age 65 or over, $20/year (Photocopy of ID required.)
☐ Sustaining, $100/year	☐ Unemployed, $20/year
☐ Couple/Family, $50/year (Please give all names above.)	☐ Student, $12/year (Photocopy of ID required.)

Upon your acceptance into membership you will receive a handsome gold embossed membership card, a membership certificate personally signed by Dr. Madalyn O'Hair, founder of American Atheists, our special monthly "Insider's Newsletter" to keep you informed of the activities of American Atheists, and a subscription to *American Atheist*. Life members receive a specially embossed pen and pencil set; sustaining members receive a commemorative pen. Your name will be sent to the chapter in your local area if there currently is one, and you will be contacted so you may become a part of the many local activities. Memberships and subscriptions are non-refundable.

☐ I/we am/are enclosing a check or money order for $__________payable to: American Atheists

☐ Please charge my/our charge card for $__________. ☐ Visa or ☐ Mastercard

Credit card number ______________________________

Expiration date: __________ Bank number/Code letters __________

Signature ______________________________________

Return to: American Atheists, P.O. Box 2117, Austin, TX 78768-2117